The New British Drama

The New British Drama

Oleg Kerensky

Fourteen Playwrights
since
Osborne and Pinter

HAMISH HAMILTON
London

First published in Great Britain, 1977
by Hamish Hamilton Ltd.
90 Great Russell Street
London WC1 3PT

ISBN 0 241 89628 2

For my father, who took me to my first serious plays, and in memory of my mother, who was my regular and devoted companion at the theatre for so many years.

Printed in Great Britain by
Ebenezer Baylis and Son Ltd.
The Trinity Press, Worcester, and London

Contents

Contents

List of Illustrations

Preface

The theatre has taken over from the novel and from journalism as the most tempting medium for young British writers with something to say. In recent years new British plays have increasingly come to dominate Broadway and the serious theatres of Europe. These are surprising facts, not yet generally realized or fully explained. Nor is the full extent of the revolution in the British theatre during the last twenty years yet widely understood. Most people know about John Osborne and the 'angry young man', the 'kitchen sink' drama of Arnold Wesker, the black comedies of Joe Orton, and the non-realist verbal games of Harold Pinter. Books have been written about all this, and to some extent it is now 'old hat'. But it is impossible to exaggerate the influence these writers have had on their successors, and on the whole future of the theatre. Some of them developed new styles and techniques; all of them expanded and transformed the areas of life which could be treated in the theatre, and made it seem much more directly relevant to present-day lives and problems. They laid the foundations of the new British drama.

In particular, virtually all young dramatists today acknowledge the crucial influence of Osborne and Pinter in liberating the theatre from old rules and in introducing new styles of language. This influence is not limited to Britain, but has affected the whole English-speaking theatre. David Mamet, the young American playwright who was acclaimed both on and off Broadway in 1977, told me that he did not see how any American dramatist today could escape the influence of British playwrights, especially Pinter and Storey. Osborne's influence may have been less significant in the United States, where writers like Tennessee Williams and Arthur Miller had already brought the realistic language of the bars and the streets into the theatre. In Britain, stage language before Osborne was middle-class and genteel, or if it was working-class it was heavily bowdlerized. It was Pinter who showed how language could be used non-realistically, even obscurely, to heighten dramatic effects, a technique which has been widely adopted, with differing degrees of success, ever since.

There are now so many interesting and provocative writers working in the British theatre that it is difficult to keep track of them all. Even specialist critics often find difficulty in remembering which plays are written by Howard Brenton and which by Howard Barker, and what exactly is the difference between them. Many regular theatregoers get confused between several other new writers and often ask for more detailed information about them. This book is an attempt to sort out some of the most important, to explain who they are and what makes them 'tick'. Originally I had hoped to make it a comprehensive guide to all the interesting playwrights of the past decade. This would have involved covering at least thirty writers, and would have made the book impossibly long. I therefore decided to limit myself to those who have achieved a measure of established success and who have not yet been spoilt or made barren by it. (The 'wastage' among playwrights is enormous.) I have excluded those who have already been fully and sympathetically discussed in print, those who no longer seem to be writing interesting plays, and—more reluctantly—those who are now making their names in 'underground' and regional theatres but have not yet confirmed their success with major productions in London. I have also excluded those, however good their work and however much I enjoy it, who are in the traditional mainstream rather than contributing to the 'new drama'. In the last resort the choice must be personal and arbitrary. At one end of the time scale, I am sorry to have left out Peter Terson, whose *Zigger Zagger* for the National Youth Theatre is almost a classic, using songs and music-hall techniques to paint a powerful picture of the discontent and empty lives of youthful urban football fans, and who followed it with several other plays combining profound understanding of adolescent rootlessness with an original form of theatricality. In recent years, however, he has been less prolific and less inventive. At the other end, I almost included Nigel Baldwin, Richard Crane, and Barrie Keefe who have had interesting plays produced in various small theatres and who may get major opportunities in the very near future. There was also a temptation to discuss Heathcote Williams and Snoo Wilson, much more surrealist writers whose plays have aroused considerable interest on the 'fringe' but who seem unlikely to join the mainstream.

I make no apology for using London as the touchstone of success. Despite the importance of British regional theatres in recent years, and the exciting work done in club basements and attics, the accolade of success is still a major London production. This may be in the commercial 'West End' or, more likely nowadays, in one of the subsidized theatres. The majority of the plays discussed in this book were produced by the National Theatre, either in its old home at the Old Vic or in its impressive new complex on the South Bank, by the Royal Shakespeare Company at the Aldwych, or by the English Stage Company in the Royal Court or its even more intimate Theatre Upstairs. Only three of the plays, two by Howard Brenton and one by Simon Gray, have not yet had London productions. In general, a playwright has not 'arrived' until he has reached London; in most cases he reaches the United States, Scandinavia and West Germany soon after.

The lists of plays for each writer are, I hope, complete. They include all their full-length stage works, with dates of first production, first London production, and the first major American productions. They do not normally include one-act plays written for lunch-time or late-night performances, television plays or film scripts. There are exceptions, however, when television plays have been transformed into stage ones, or one-acters into full-scale evening productions. Not all the plays listed are discussed in detail, but the most important and successful ones are.

The biographical facts given have been checked with the writers concerned. In addition I have interviewed them about their lives and work. My method was to talk with them quite informally, making only brief notes which I wrote up shortly afterwards. A tape-recorder would have been too formal and intimidating. When in doubt, or when specifically requested, I sent my transcribed notes to the playwright for comments and corrections. The results are not verbatim texts of our conversations but edited versions, presenting the salient points. I realize of course that writers are not always the best judges or exponents of their own work, and that any interview is necessarily selective and arbitrary. Tom Stoppard feels this very strongly, and was most reluctant to be interviewed, though he eventually agreed. Edward Bond and David Storey refused, partly for similar reasons. They believe that a writer's work should speak for itself and that interviews can seriously misrepresent it. Bond has taken to amplifying his views in lengthy introductions to the published versions of his plays. My experience is that some playwrights are extremely good at explaining their methods and motives, I also believe that even the most unsatisfactory interview gives some clue to the mind and personality of the playwright and is more helpful than no interview at all.

The interviews in this book are used to supplement my own accounts of the plays, and my comments on them. In some cases the playwrights shed light on obscurities in their plays. I have tried to indicate the principal strengths and weaknesses of the plays, and to reflect the general climate of opinion about them, indicating my own opinion when it differs. I have also speculated about the reasons for the recent renaissance of British theatre and about the prospects for the future. Naturally the playwrights are in no way responsible for the opinions expressed about them, nor for my synopses of their plays.

These synopses are partly based on my recollections of the plays in the theatre; I saw almost all of them when they were first produced and have seen several of them again in various revivals. But memory is notoriously fallible, and I have refreshed it with the published texts or with the writers' typescripts. The direct quotations from the plays are of course taken from the published texts; the lengthier ones are included by permission of the playwrights and their publishers, for which I am duly grateful. A full list of the plays and their publishers is provided in the bibliography.

I am particularly grateful to all the playwrights for their courtesy and help. Meeting many of them for the first time, I was amazed by their willingness to sacrifice their time to hold extended conversations with me. Some were interviewed more than once, or had repeated telephone conversations with me, and several took the trouble to revise and amplify my transcripts. Howard Barker, Howard Brenton, Trevor Griffiths, Stephen Poliakoff, David Storey and Ted Whitehead lent me typescripts of plays which were unpublished or out of print. Margaret Ramsay and her staff, Joanna Marston at Rosica Colin, and Clive Goodwin, who between them represent so many of the playwrights, were helpful in putting me in touch and providing information. Jo Rogers, then my agent in New York, encouraged me with her enthusiasm when I first had the idea for this book and her successors, Henriette Neatrour and Arthur Martin, bolstered my confidence when it flagged along the way. I am also indebted, as ever, to Roger Machell for his encouragement, helpful advice and careful editing, to Hilary Rubinstein, my British agent, for prodding me into action and making it worthwhile, and to Patricia Entract for once again collecting and helping to select the pictures. Steve Kline did some most helpful research on New York productions. I hope all these people will think their efforts have been rewarded; any faults or mistakes that remain after their help are entirely my own.

Introduction: Background to revolution

The new British drama is easy to recognize, but hard to define. Before Osborne, Wesker and Pinter, the most provocative and original plays in London came from New York and Paris; now they are nearly all British. Conversely, New York is dominated by British plays, and Paris has quite a number of them. Twenty-five years ago, Arthur Miller and Tennessee Williams, Jean Anouilh and Jean-Paul Sartre, were the writers arousing most interest among serious British theatregoers. There were of course good new British plays; writers like J. B. Priestley and Terence Rattigan even dealt with contemporary Britain, but in terms which seemed slightly outmoded. Theirs was still a middle-class Britain, debating liberal values and philosophical concepts, or concerned about traditional family and domestic problems. It was a Britain which still believed in logic and polite discussion. Plays were written in well-bred drawing-room language and they respected hallowed social taboos on open discussion of sex, religion and the establishment. The basic assumptions of our society remained unquestioned.

The plays were also written in conventional theatrical styles, requiring realistic sets and embodying well-organized plots with carefully planned beginnings, developments and conclusions. It was the era of the 'well-made play', staged in a theatre with footlights, a proscenium arch and a front curtain, before an audience familiar with those conventions and prepared to make the effort of concentration and the suspension of disbelief to appreciate what was put in front of it.

All that has changed. Audiences today are still largely middle-class but they are now more accustomed to watching drama on television than in the theatre. New audiences start watching the box in their infancy, long before they could possibly go to a theatre. The theatre therefore has to offer them something different, more theatrical. It also has to make them feel at home, and break down the barriers which used to some

extent to separate the stage from the audience. Arriving in even
the most conventional West End theatre today, the audience is
likely to find the curtain already up, the set visible and the
actors already disporting themselves and miming some kind
of action around it. The set is likely to be non-representational:
a scaffolding construction, a backcloth with slides projected on
it, or a few screens with suggestions of place and mood created
by lighting. Speedy changes of place and time are thus facili-
tated; writers no longer feel obliged to divide their plays into
formal acts or to restrict themselves to a maximum of three sets.
The action can zoom from place to place, backwards and for-
wards in time. The actors may speak directly to the audience,
explaining or commenting on the action, and the play may be
interrupted or enhanced by song and dance, jollying the audience along in the style of the defunct music-hall. Excitement
and entertainment is often more important than a continuous
plot development; dramatic visual effects or witty dialogue
take preference over logical argument; and 'well-made play'
becomes a term of abuse. The audience is constantly and explicitly reminded that it is in a theatre, while the play is made
as accessible as possible. In many modern theatres, it is even
made more accessible physically, by having the spectators on
three sides of the stage, or all around it. The audience thus
becomes very conscious of itself. Fellow spectators are often
clearly visible on the other side of the stage, a disconcerting
experience for older theatregoers accustomed to traditional
buildings in which the aim was to accept the stage picture as
an illusion and forget about being in a theatre. The new Royal
Exchange Theatre in Manchester is a scaffolding 'theatre in
the round', almost like a circus ring, within the precincts of a
stately Victorian edifice. The new National Theatre in London
is a complex of three auditoria, one of the largest of which (the
Olivier) has a thrust stage with the audience sitting well round
to the sides. The Chichester Festival Theatre brings the audience even further round the sides of the stage. More conventional modern theatres, like the Shaw and the Mermaid in
London, still dispense altogether with proscenium arch, footlights and front curtain. 'Fringe' studio theatres in basements,
attics and the back rooms of pubs have mushroomed all over

the country and have often provided the new plays with their first homes.

These new buildings and techniques are not totally new in concept, nor are they specifically British. Some of them mark a return to the styles and techniques of Elizabethan theatre, with its greater intimacy between stage and audience. Most of the new fashions in stage design and theatrical production come from Continental and American pioneers. Even the fairly realistic plays of Tennessee Williams and Arthur Miller often had non-realistic sets, enhanced by subtle lighting plots. Studio and 'underground' theatres originated off-Broadway; two of the leading London clubs of this kind, the Open Space and the Ambiance, were founded and run by Americans, Charles Marowitz and Ed Berman. British theatre was heavily influenced by Brecht's Berliner Ensemble, by Jean-Louis Barrault's use of mime and spectacle, by American 'method' acting, originally inspired by Stanislavsky, and by many others. The Irish-born Samuel Beckett and the Romanian-born Eugène Ionesco, both writing in French, accustomed British audiences to the non-realistic use of language, which was later adopted by N. F. Simpson, Harold Pinter and Tom Stoppard among others.

But it was the content of the new plays, not their style, which first marked the specifically British aspect of the new drama. Osborne's *Look Back In Anger*, rightly accepted by everyone as the start of the revolution in British drama, was written in conventional form, with a realistic set and with a continuous, logical, easy-to-follow plot. Its novelty was in the outspokenness of its language, its open criticism of establishment values, and its articulate, thoughtful working-class hero. Peter Shaffer's *Five Finger Exercise* was even conventional in language, though it hinted at the forbidden subject of homosexuality. Both these writers adopted much more radical techniques in their later works.

The content of British plays has got more iconoclastic and revolutionary since those early days. No other western country has reflected a social revolution and a sense of doom so strongly in its theatre. Perhaps no other western country has experienced such a dramatic and complete social revolution in the past twenty years, and perhaps no other has such a sense of doom. Long before talk about Britain's economic collapse and imminent bankruptcy became commonplace, British playwrights were reflecting moral collapse and bankruptcy. Some of them were predicting the total collapse of the political and economic system, with varying degrees of glee or anguish.

During the same period, American playwrights were concerned, naturally enough, with very different problems. The Vietnam war and the oppression of minorities, especially black and gay minorities, were obsessive themes. Some American writers, notably Edward Albee, were also concerned with personal relationships, but they were not questioning the whole basis of social and family life to the extent British writers have done. Most American writers and intellectuals, like American trade unionists, accept the general basis of their society, while wanting to improve it. The revolutionary aspect of British theatre in recent years has been that many of the best writers have not accepted the basis of our society at all. They do not want to improve, but to destroy, though they are not nearly as interested in sketching a replacement as they are in picking holes. Even writers who want to preserve rather than destroy, who support evolution rather than revolution, have consciously or unconsciously formed part of a theatre of protest. Despite the differences in styles and attitudes between them, they are all protesting—against the society we have, against the inadequate way it is being changed, or against the direction in which it is changing.

One irony of the situation is that the protest has been made much easier by the very establishment which is under attack. Few of the new playwrights would have been able to make a living by airing their views in newspaper articles or books, or dressing them up in novels. The harsh economic times we live in make those outlets increasingly impractical and unprofitable. But the theatre is heavily subsidized, by the Arts Council, by regional authorities, and by private companies. Virtually every play discussed in this book was staged with support from the Arts Council; many of the playwrights benefited from the scheme organized by Thames Television for playwrights in residence at key theatres. George Devine would not have been able to start the English Stage Company at the Royal Court, which has been the cradle of so many of our new writers, without Arts Council support. Neither the Royal Court, nor the National Theatre and the Royal Shakespeare Company, nor regional theatres like the Bristol Old Vic and the Nottingham Playhouse, nor the small 'fringe' theatres, could exist without it. Few of the new plays discussed in this book have been commercial successes.

The protest has also been made easier, and perhaps even made possible, by the abolition of the Lord Chamberlain's powers of theatre censorship in 1967. Before that time, the actual language spoken by people in real life, especially by people without middle-class inhibitions, could not be spoken on the stage. Everyday 'four-letter' swear words were banned. Whole areas of discussion were also forbidden. Homosexuality could not be discussed and no real sexuality of any kind could be depicted. Nudity was totally taboo. Blasphemy, including jokes about church ceremonies as well as about God, was forbidden; there is still a common law against it, as there is against obscenity, but this does not seem to affect the theatre. Other things on the Lord Chamberlain's embargo list were representations of living people, including politicians, and jokes and criticisms about the Royal Family. For a time, after the abolition of censorship, it seemed as if every play contained constant swearing and as if homosexuality and nudity were obligatory. Frequently these things were used merely for shock value, or for commercial motives. Too often writers, producers and even critics seemed to think that obscenity and extreme sexual permissiveness in themselves constituted interesting, 'highbrow' theatre. However this new freedom did enable writers to tackle the subjects which really concerned them, and which have increasingly concerned the British people as a whole, in a natural and realistic way. Traditional rules of sexual morality and conventions of marriage and family life have been questioned and overthrown, a questioning reflected and encouraged by our dramatists. They have also mocked and abused leading figures of the political, social and religious establishment. They have luxuriated in their freedom.

The breakdown of what Shaw used to call 'middle-class

morality' reflects one of the biggest changes in British social life since the Second World War—the destruction of class barriers and the dramatic increase in social mobility. The expensive fee-paying 'public schools' are no longer essential for entry to the 'good' universities, and those universities are no longer essential for top jobs. The Education Act of 1944 resulted in bright working-class children being streamed off into superior schools, learning new life styles and forming new ambitions. Some of them went to drama schools and became actors, providing the new writers with exactly the interpreters they needed for their plays. Previously, acting too had been a middle-class stronghold.

This new social mobility has created its own problems of adjustment; many of the writers who have emerged from working-class backgrounds into middle-class or intellectual milieux have felt alienation from their families, and guilt at feeling it. They are very conscious that better opportunities and greater social mobility do not mean the end of the British class system, and this makes them angry. Their skill as dramatists is in expressing their anger in entertaining and theatrical terms.

Part 1

Two 'Outsiders'

TWO HIGHLY PRAISED dramatists, David Storey and Edward Bond, are in many ways typical of the new British drama. Storey has written repeatedly, out of his own experience, about the rifts in families and the moral dilemmas set up by the class conflict. Bond is obsessed with the alleged violence and exploitation of our society. Neither of them is very specific in his protests; Storey's plays are fairly conventional and descriptive, Bond's are mostly historical or pseudo-historical. Temperamentally they seem to find it difficult to write plays making direct statements of their views about our society; yet they both think their views should be evident from their plays.

There was a slight temptation to leave both of them out of this book, not just because they were unwilling to be interviewed. Bond has already been much discussed in print, and he himself suggested that I would do better to make room for some other writer who does not get discussed often enough. Storey, superficially at any rate, is more conventional than the other writers with whom I am concerned. But it so happens that I do not agree with a lot of what has been written about them. I am therefore discussing them both in these preliminary chapters.

One: David Storey

Born: Wakefield, Yorkshire, England, 1933.

Father: a mineworker.

Education: Queen Elizabeth Grammar School, Wakefield, Yorks. Wakefield Art School. Slade School of Fine Art, London.

Played professionally for Leeds Rugby Club 1952–56.

Plays:

The Restoration of Arnold Middleton (Edinburgh 1966; London 1967; New York 1972). *In Celebration* (London 1969; New York 1974. *The Contractor* (London 1969, New Haven, Conn. 1970; New York 1975). *Home* (London 1970; New York 1970). *The Changing Room* (London 1971; New Haven, Conn. 1972; New York 1973). *Cromwell* (London 1973; *The Farm* (London 1973; Washington, D.C. 1974). *Life Class* (London 1974; New York 1975). *Mother's Day* (London 1976).

Evening Standard Drama Awards, 1967, 1970. Variety Club Award 1971. NY Drama Critics Circle Awards 1971, 1973.

Novels include *This Sporting Life* (1960), *Radcliffe* (1963), *Saville* (1976).

STOREY WAS ALREADY an acclaimed novelist when his first play was produced, and *This Sporting Life* had been made into a successful film for which he wrote the screenplay. This, like most of his plays, was directed by Lindsay Anderson. *The Restoration of Arnold Middleton* was actually written about the same time as *This Sporting Life*; it was an immediate critical success when staged at the Royal Court and was transferred to the West End.

Arnold, a discontented but popular and evidently talented schoolteacher, is henpecked by his wife and mother-in-law and at one point physically assaulted by them. He feels he has not fulfilled his early promise, collects old armour, identifies himself with Robin Hood, and yearns for a wider dimension in his life. In many ways his discontent recalls Osborne's Jimmy Porter in *Look Back in Anger* or Wesker's Beatie in *Roots*. At the beginning of the play, however, Arnold is apparently reconciled to his lot, and is even egged on by Joan, his wife, to show some rage or indignation. It is Joan who tells her mother to leave their house; Arnold is willing to acquiesce in her continued presence. By the end of the play, Arnold has stopped attending his school and is on the borders of lunacy, pretending that his mother-in-law does not exist, behaving rudely and outrageously to his colleagues who come to help him, and brandishing a sword as an 'instrument of honour, which the world is a feebler place without!'

Some of *Arnold Middleton* is very funny, for example another teacher's description of Arnold's bizarre behaviour at the school assembly, and the drunken party at Arnold's home attended by two colleagues and a girl pupil who has a crush on him, at which he first shows signs of insanity and threatens a colleague with a loaded rifle. He is a fascinating and theatrical character who is never fully explained and whose future is left uncertain. He goes off into quasi-poetic flights of fancy and tells apparently irrelevant but amusing anecdotes, contrasting with the extremely naturalistic dialogue of the rest of the play. In most of his later plays, Storey concentrated on realism and naturalism, rather than fantasy, until he shocked and dismayed most of the critics and some of his audience by returning to fantasy with a vengeance with *Mother's Day*. All his plays were first staged at the Royal Court, and most of them transferred to the West End; nearly all were also staged in New York.

The programme for *Arnold Middleton* included a quotation from D. H. Lawrence, but *In Celebration* might almost have been written by Lawrence. It marks the beginning of Storey's ultra-naturalistic style, taken still further in *The Contractor* and *The Changing Room*, and the beginning of his collaboration at the Royal Court with Lindsay Anderson, who staged his plays with a wealth of realistic detail. *In Celebration* shows the three grown-up sons of a Yorkshire miner returning home for their parents' fortieth wedding anniversary. Their father took trouble to make sure they were educated and had a better life than his; their mother, forever tidying the house and remembering what she learnt at school about 'human hygiene', feels she married beneath her. Andrew, the eldest son, has given up a career as a solicitor to take up painting; by the end of the play it transpires that he has a grudge against his mother for farming him out to a neighbour when his youngest brother Steven was born and resents her smug 'religiosity'.

He is sarcastic about his middle brother Colin's success and even makes jokes about his unmarried state, suggesting that he might be gay. He is critical of everything and has a grudge against society in general. He threatens to blow up the domestic celebration by saying what he really thinks of it all, and does tell his father a few home truths in the middle of the night after their dinner party in a posh hotel. But his father is too drunk and sleepy to take it in and Andrew leaves in the morning without confronting his mother. The role provided Alan Bates with the first of those partly-charming, intellectual and rude characters which he was to play again in *Life Class* and in Simon Gray's *Butley* and *Otherwise Engaged*. Colin, the middle brother has accepted society's values, and is making big money in industrial relations, using his gifts as a diplomatist to soothe workers and prevent strikes. Steven, suffering from *angst* and failing to write a book, stays ominously silent most of the time and cries in bed at night.

All the family, and two inquisitive but friendly neighbours, are very convincingly drawn, and the dialogue is natural and true. Hidden conflicts and deeper sorrows are mostly hinted rather than made explicit. It is a play in the main tradition of family drama, except that Andrew's outbursts smack of the 'angry young man' and the conflict between the working-class parents and their well-educated middle-class sons is particularly typical of Britain after the Second World War and the Education Act. The father will not retire a year early, though it would be good for his health, because he feels a certain pride in finishing fifty years in the mines. Andrew and Colin simply don't understand this feeling, and regard it as absurd. (This conflict of generations and of class attitudes recurs in plays by Trevor Griffiths and Howard Brenton.) Steven realizes that his father's work actually has significance for him, 'while the work he's educated us to do . . . is nothing . . . at the best, a pastime, at the worst a sort of soulless stirring of the pot.' The play got an enthusiastic response from many critics and theatregoers with similar backgrounds and similar problems who found it extremely moving. But in theatrical terms, it was less original and less interesting than *Arnold Middleton*.

With *The Contractor*, Storey gave up anything like a plot and concentrated on setting a realistic scene and presenting a group of convincing characters. His stage instructions describe these characters in novelist's detail. Ewbank, the contractor, is 'a solid, well-built man, broad rather than tall, stocky. He's wearing a suit, which is plain, workmanlike and chunky; someone probably who doesn't take easily to wearing clothes, reflecting, perhaps, the feeling of a man who has never found his proper station in life. The jacket of his coat is open as if it's been put on in a rush.' While other modern playwrights abandon plots in favour of a series of theatrical 'happenings' or dramatic outbursts, Storey's bent in this and several other plays is for the merest suggestion of human conflict and for activity which is only indirectly related to it. Ewbank, a self-made boss of a tent manufacturing and hiring firm, is having one of his marquees put up in his own garden for his daughter's wedding reception. The characters are his family and his workmen; the action is entirely concerned with the marquee. In the first two acts it is put up, in full view of the audience, and this has its own visual fascination. I well remember, however, that at the preview, when there had not yet been any press reviews to reveal the nature of the play, members of the audience were asking each other after the second act whether anything would happen in the third. When I suggested that the marquee would be taken down again, I scarcely took myself seriously, but that is exactly and entirely what happened.

During the course of the play there are occasional hints of drama. One of the workmen is a well-meaning simpleton who is unmercifully ragged, and at one point reduced to tears, by the others; another has been in prison for embezzlement, and tries to sack a man who harps on the subject. Ewbank's son Paul does not get on with his more earthy father, and there is

quite a touching little scene when he exchanges half confidences
with his mother and tells her he will be off after the wedding.
But none of these hints are ever developed. The play depends
for its success on creating the feeling that we have actually
watched the men at work, and on the rough and sometimes
crude humour with which they lace their badinage. The dialogue is very realistic, laced with dialect phrases. working-class
colloquialisms, and typical schoolboyish jokes about sex and
smelly feet. Sometimes there are even quite witty *doubles
entendres*, as when one of the workmen quips, 'She was only a
tentmaker's daughter, But she knew how to pull on a guy.' But
the play is probably intended as something more than a mere
slice of working life and is certainly regarded as much more by
many critics. It observes the social and personal gaps between
self-made, rough father and university-educated son, and the
way the father, despite being the boss, finds it easier to get on
with the working men than with his own son. It shows how
success in business can fail to produce, or can even damage,
domestic and personal happiness. *The Contractor* may also be
seen as a lament for the decline of craftsmanship and the disappearance of personal pride in work, with the contrast between past and present underlined by Ewbank's father, who
wanders around clutching a bit of rope he once made by hand.
There are hints that the building and destruction of the marquee may be an allegory of all the things we attempt to build
in our lives. When Ewbank surveys the mess after the party,
and talks to one of his men, he seems unduly depressed.

Ewbank: You pay a price for everything, Kay. Best not to
look, then you never know whether you've got it, or you've
gone without . . . (*Calling off*) Put it straight, for Christ's sake.
All that lot'll bloody well fall off. (*To Kay*) There's one thing,
though . . .
Kay: Aye?
Ewbank: Ah, well . . . (*Uncertain for a moment. Then*) I came out
here you know, this morning . . . saw it all . . . Damn near
broke my bloody heart . . . You saw it. God. What a bloody
mess . . . Seen nowt like it. I haven't.
Kay: S'all made to be used.

Ewbank: Aye. You're right. Doesn't bear much reckoning. Best get on with it while you can.

But these thoughts are never developed, and the play's rather obvious social themes are only gently touched upon. There is no feeling that Storey has discovered anything very original about our society, nor that he has anything very profound, if indeed he has anything at all, to say about it.

The content of *The Changing Room* is even more elusive. Its three acts show, respectively, a Rugby League team preparing for a match, nursing their injuries and being given instructions by their coach at half-time, and recuperating and preparing to leave after it. One of them is badly injured in the face and taken to hospital; his main concerns before he leaves are that someone should take care of the 'do it yourself' kit he has just bought and that his wife should be informed. The chairman and accountant of the club spend part of the time in the changing room drinking, rather than watching the match; Harry, the attendant, is obsessed by the Communist threat— he believes that even the cold weather is being sent over by the Soviet Union as a secret weapon, and threatens the players that everything they say and do is being written down and reported to Moscow. There is a lot of badinage and horsing around between the players, and they are shown stripping and dressing, being massaged and greased, and constantly going to take showers and to the toilet. After seeing the play, the audience feels it has actually been in a run-down, rather squalid changing room in the north of England during a match. Storey has obviously drawn upon his own experience as a professional player to depict the scene, and the physical activity in the changing room has a certain fascination for spectators most of whom have obviously never experienced the real thing. Nevertheless, the play leaves a feeling of emptiness, of lacking any sense of purpose.

The same is true of *Cromwell*. Ostensibly it is a realistic historical piece, though it is never precisely stated when or where the action is taking place, apart from the clue provided by the title. A group of wandering working men, on their way to enlist in the royalist army meet up with a mother and daughter and a simpleton son, akin to the one in *The Contractor* whose farm has just been pillaged by the republican forces. They are wheeling a coffin on a cart, looking for a Roman Catholic priest, and the daughter says the coffin contains the body of her grandfather who died on the farm. When they are stopped and searched by republican troops, it turns out to contain a soldier with his throat cut. They are all arrested, the mother is tortured and goes mad, one of the men escapes, the others cheerfully change sides. Later they all meet up again, and the men reunite to form a farming community outside the war area. Once again they are raided, and one of them is killed. The dialogue is in archaic poetic style, slightly stilted.

Joan: The battle's gone . . . the soldiers went away . . . the fields are burnt . . . the house is down.
Logan: New principles, I can see, must be fashioned now.
O'Halloran: The war has gone . . .
Logan: And left its principal behind.
O'Halloran: I can see the fellars now . . .
Logan: And where's the men with all the stripes?
O'Halloran: Proctor was the name.
Logan: Fell on the field . . . or deserted, sir.
O'Halloran: Which is all the same when the fighting's done.
Logan: When the fighting's o'er, and the battle won.

The play has a mystical ending. Proctor wants to 'find a place for moral argument' and finally takes Joan on a mysterious boat ride.

Proctor: Boatman, do we cross the stream?
Boatman: Aye.
Proctor: The land behind is dark.
Joan: The one in front is darker still.
Proctor: Boatman, do you know these shores?
Boatman: The stream is all I know . . . its shoals, its rocks, its crevices, . . . its gleams . . . the pattern of its light at dawn and dusk . . . the rushing of its waves . . . its stillness when it floods or lies, dwindling, in a summer heat . . . I know the river, and the manner of the boat; that's all.

They leave the lesser mortals behind on the far shore, and

travel on into darkness from which there is no return. When they land on the far shore, they peer into the dark and in the play's final line, Proctor asks, 'Do you see the light?'

The early part of *Cromwell* recalls Brecht's *Mother Courage*, while the final scenes are more like a poetic drama of the thirties or the libretto of a Michael Tippett opera. It made remarkably little impact in the theatre.

The Farm is a return to the Lawrentian manner of *In Celebration*, with the addition of the father-son conflict hinted at in *The Contractor*. The family in this play consists of Slatter, a successful but rough and frequently drunk farmer, who has had a heart attack, his more genteel wife who is having evening classes in psychiatry and sociology, their three daughters, two unmarried and one divorced, and Arthur, their 21-year-old son who returns home like the prodigal, announcing that he is going to settle down and get married. Arthur wants to be a poet, is idolized by his mother and despised by his father. His proposed bride, who never appears in the play, is over 40, an ex-actress and divorced, with two children almost as old as Arthur. The news throws the family into a state of excitement. Slatter pours out a torrent of abuse and has a further heart attack. He recovers and they all put on their best clothes to receive the bride. Arthur turns up alone, having decided not to bring her to meet them. He tells his father that neither his character nor his manner have changed—if anything, they have got worse. He leaves home without even saying good-bye to his father, who cheerfully and informally receives Albert, his daughter Brenda's working-class boy-friend, at breakfast.

That is all. Once again Storey shows how a self-educated father finds it easier to get on with the workers than with his own more polished son. Once again the members of a family are convincingly depicted with the tensions between them indicated more strongly than in the earlier plays. They are very similar to those in Shaffer's much earlier *Five Finger Exercise* and are indeed a familiar theme of literature and drama. But Storey does not throw any new light upon them, nor is his ultra-realistic dialogue particularly witty or exciting.

Life Class is a detailed and apparently realistic study of an art school, though many people found the behaviour of the students and teachers incredible. Smutty jokes and fooling around in class suggest small boys rather than mature students; these don't seem very devoted to their subject. The teachers are little better. Storey himself went to an art school, and presumably knows what they are like. The play's main interest is provided by its central character, the disillusioned teacher Allott, played in the original production by Alan Bates. Allott was once a good artist, but now prefers to write limericks and slogans on the walls. His troubles are exacerbated by his wife's decision to divorce him. He makes a student pose and solemnly draws him for a long time; afterwards the student discovers there is no drawing, only some limericks on a pad. The theatrical climax is provided when Allott offers to strip and act as a model himself. Instead, some of the male students strip, and one of them pretends to rape the nude model, fooling the class and shocking the girl students. Allott sits by allowing the 'rape' to happen; actually it is only simulated as a jest. Allott loses both his job and his wife.

A group of students and teachers is amusingly depicted, and various teaching methods are contrasted, but the total effect is not as convincing a slice of 'real life' as *The Changing Room*. It may not have been intended as such. On the other hand, there is not enough plot or characterization for the play to stand on its own feet, apart from its realism.

Storey has been type-cast as a naturalistic writer, though in fact all his plays contain elements of fantasy and deliberate theatricality. *Home* and *Mother's Day* abandoned realism more or less completely and *Home*, produced between *The Contractor* and *The Changing Room*, has no plot. Instead of a realistic slice of life, we have a Pinteresque series of dialogues. Nothing is certain. The setting is evidently some form of mental home, perhaps the convalescent wing; the five characters are inmates. Harry and Jack, the principal characters, tell various tales to each other and to two women patients about their past lives and their families. They confuse the names of the other patients and sometimes we wonder if they know who they are themselves. Jack, at any rate, is aware that very little communication is taking place between them and the other people. Their

inconsequential exchanges include a lot of muddled nostalgia for
their schooldays and the days when Britain was 'great'. They
both have an air of faded gentility which contrasts with the more
robust and earthy humour of the two women. Alfred, the fifth
patient, is hardly more than an occasional presence, wandering
on and off with pieces of furniture in a simple-minded way.
The play starts and finishes with Harry and Jack chatting
alone; in the end they agree that God must be disappointed
with his world, and won't make the same mistake again. They
both start to cry.

Sir John Gielgud and Sir Ralph Richardson, who created
these roles at the Royal Court, invested them with immense
depth of feeling, suggesting the characters' hidden sorrows and
tragedies, which are never made explicit or even vaguely
explained. These actors made the play poetic and moving as
well as amusing, as they did later for Pinter's *No Man's Land*.

Mother's Day was the first of Storey's plays to get a really bad
reception from the critics. It was widely dismissed as sub-
Orton, vulgar and unfunny; it was even condemned by J. W.
Lambert in the *Sunday Times* as fit only for the waste-paper
basket. Storey himself denied that it was so different from his
other plays, claiming that a constant theme runs through all his
work. Like several of his plays, it deals with an awkward family
reunion, but this time the treatment is more like black comedy
or farce, less like a 'slice of life'. The audience at the preview
I attended, before any reviews had appeared, enjoyed the play
hugely. Personally I found it more amusing and more theatrical
than many of Storey's highly praised earlier efforts. If it had
been a hitherto undiscovered piece by Orton, it would probably have been hailed as another of his comic masterpieces.

Storey's programme note said: 'If you live in the enemy's
camp long enough you begin to resent the deprivations made
upon him by his attackers.' The play shows an eccentric,
amoral family, the Johnsons, and the way Judith, their apparently innocent and respectable lodger, speedily accepts their
self-centred behaviour, sexual promiscuity and disregard for
moral laws and conventions. The household is dominated by
Mrs Johnson, endlessly boasting of her titled family background (the de Johns, who invented the water closet, hence the

slang title 'the John'), hiding the tea caddy from her family and locking their things in her bedroom, while locking her husband out. Mr Johnson also claims ancestral fame—descent from Dr Johnson, the lexicographer—and suggests that the marriage of Johnson and de John may be incestuous. Their sons Gordon and Harold have Oedipal tendencies—Gordon seduces every girl in sight, idolizes his mother, and is idolized by her as a paragon of virtue; Harold, who is in the Royal Air Forces because he likes playing with model gliders and thinks he is defending the Queen, plans to murder his father. Their daughter Lily is another of Storey's simpletons who spends most of her time hiding in the cupboard. The other characters include Farrer, Judith's 'husband' who is already married and lives off the seduction of heiresses, her parents who come to rescue her and get tricked into paying the Johnsons a huge reward, and Peters, a private detective who becomes convinced that he is a criminal lunatic being sought by a doctor and the police, and disguises himself in 'drag', pretending to be Judith's mother.

The plot is ingeniously worked out and the dialogue is very funny. It is outrageously brazen in its reference to Gordon's sexual activities, and this shocked even some of the tolerant reviewers and audiences of 1976. When Harold announces that he is going to marry his sister Lily, his mother's contented response is, 'You don't have to leave home to fuck your sister.'

Lily is not quite as mad as she seems; she is often the one to draw attention to what is really happening. But every remark she makes is automatically greeted by her mother with the explosive retort, 'Liar!' Her very madness is casually dismissed.

Mrs Johnson: That child would be a raving lunatic if I didn't watch her.
Mr Johnson: She is a raving lunatic.
Mrs Johnson: There; you see. All my care for nothing.

The humour in *Mother's Day* comes from matter-of-fact statements of what is normally unmentionable contrasted with conversations of bored conventionality. When Judith's 'husband' arrives to join her, he finds her locked in a bedroom with

2

Gordon. In the morning, Gordon comes down to breakfast and is totally cool.

Gordon: I've just been fucking your wife upstairs. I fucked her everywhere I could. I fucked her up the front, then I fucked her up the back, then I fucked her in the throat, then I fucked her between the breasts, then I fucked her between her thighs. She's resting now. It's been quite a night.

Mrs Johnson: Gordon always was active as a child.

Gordon: Not too late for breakfast, Ma?

Farrer: I say . . . is this true? Your son's been with my wife?

Mrs J: Gordon has a room of his own in town . . .

Gordon: In Clarendon Street.

Mrs J: In Clarendon Street. It's one of the older parts of town.

Gordon: Georgian.

Mrs J: Georgian. Immediately beneath the walls of our Cathedral. You can see its spire from the station when you arrive.

Farrer: Is Judy up there?

Gordon: I shouldn't disturb her. Needs time to recover. My mother—God bless her—is a little eccentric. I wouldn't believe everything she says.

Mrs J: Gordon's always had a disposition, Mr Farrer, to use his imagination; he has a notebook in which he keeps his secret thoughts. He was reading it to us as a matter of fact last night, entertaining your wife, my husband, Mr Johnson, and myself.

Gordon: Fucking's my main interest. I'll fuck anything. I draw a line at men. I've tried them in my time, but a woman is better than any man. I'm a great believer in female supremacy. The female is the superior of men in all departments: better cunts, bigger breasts, more to get into, more to get hold of.

Mrs J: Gordon has a great appetite for life. He's been like it since a child.

Gordon: Anything for breakfast? After all that fucking I'm feeling parched.

Mrs J: Call Lily from her cupboard. She'll get it for you, dear.

Gordon: I'll fuck her too if I'm not too tired.

Mrs J: He's also—you may have noticed—a sense of humour. I'm very proud of my youngest child (*kisses him*).

Gordon (*to Farrer*): Give her five minutes, then go on up (*goes*).

Mrs J: His father's side; a disposition to ideas and spectacular statements. It's all there in his antecedents. Coming as he does, from two such parents, his antecedents, are very strong.

Farrer: Look here, I better go up. You don't mind if I bang on the door and rouse her?

Mrs J: Not in the least. Treat this house as you would your home.

By the end of the play, even Judith's respectable bourgeois mother has accepted the prevailing standards, and is happily ensconced in the bedroom with Farrer and Gordon. There is a hilarious farcical scene when Peters is knocked out; he is trying to regain his memory, but is duped by the Johnson family into thinking he has killed Mr Johnson, who is not in fact dead though Gordon intended to kill him. Peters is desperately trying to count the numbers from one to ten, and Mrs Johnson rounds on Lily.

Mrs J: Lily get into your cupboard. I want you to hear no more of this.

Lily: I haven't done anything, Mother.

Mrs J: You let this dangerous criminal into the house. What else have you been doing with him?

Lily: Nothing, Mother.

Mrs J: He's even killed your father.

Mr J: I'm not dead.

Mrs J: Liar! That's where she gets her lying from.

Peters: Four . . . four. What comes after four?

Farrer: There must be some simple solution to this.

Gordon: There is: kill him (Mr Johnson); send for the police; put the poker in his hand (Peters); all four of us are witness.

Lily: I don't want to see my father dead.

Mrs J: Are you going to stop your own brother, Lily?

Lily: No, Mother.

Mrs J: In that case we can go ahead.

Mr J: I don't want to be dead. I want to go on living.

Mrs J: You've lived long enough.

Mr J: I've only lived as long as you.

Mrs J: That's been my tragedy. (To Peters) Mr Johnson seduced me when I was only sixteen. During the course of which he averted his eyes; that's the kind of man he is.

Mr J: It was the custom in those days; as opposed to nowadays when you can look as much as you like. One never interfered with a woman's private parts, except in the course of illness, and then, of course, not always then.

Mrs J: We shall assume those words were never spoken.

Peters: Is this man dead or isn't he? I spread-eagled his head on the pillow. Blood, brains, bones—everywhere. I can see it vividly—I shall never forget it as long as I live.

Mr J: I shall go upstairs in that case, and wait for your decision.

In *The Times*, Storey said the play should be 'vulgar in the fine sense of the word; it needs to be played with vulgar energy and directness, much in the manner of *The Changing Room*.' He wrote the play at the same time as *Life Class* 'and like all my better plays it was completed very quickly. They almost compose themselves. The first sentence flashes into my mind one morning and I work on without revision. *The Changing Room* was finished in two days. When I try to improve, I end up with a mess.'

Storey regards playwriting as a light relaxation from the much harder work of writing novels, which take him years to complete. In an interview with John Walker in the *Observer* magazine he elaborated on the way his plays just happen, without being planned. He originally intended *Mother's Day* to be a 'Dostoevskian masterpiece involving a real bastard who was going to kill somebody. To my amazement the characters turned out to be a family of maniacs, completely potty. They are a family who intrinsically invert every decent value. But I think they're genuinely a microcosm of English domestic life with their delusions, illusions and fantasies, and their inveterate capacity to live in the past. English urban life is sexually rapacious, and the play embodies that. Everybody involved in it is screwing everybody else, which is a reflection of the world we live in.'

Storey's writing springs from a dislike of his working-class background, in which he felt 'a total spiritual outcast', and from the dichotomy between that boyhood and the new artistic life he found in London. In the BBC series of talks, *Writers on Themselves*, broadcast in 1963 he described how he spent the unhappiest two years of his life trying to combine the two worlds, being an art student in London and going to the north of England to play professional rugby football at weekends. He explained how the north embodies the masculine virtues— toughness and physical work—and how it seemed to him more closely bound up with our society than the feminine, intuitive and even precious values of the south. Northern working people, he said, distrust isolated and solitary men; they think physical work good, while mental work is evil. They believe men should be absorbed in society and they condemn the solitary artist. Storey himself shared some of these beliefs; one reason he switched from painting to writing was to become less isolated. As a drowning man starts to swim, so he began to write, producing his first novels as 'acts of despair'. Even today he is not fully reconciled to British life, and says that if it were not for his children he would probably live in New York—because it has 'a provincial city's vulgarity and vitality'.

Storey's 'realistic' plays were so skilful in concealing their revolutionary content, their comment on our society, that most people failed to appreciate that they contained any. Hence the shock of *Mother's Day*.

Two: Edward Bond

Born: London, England, 1934.
Education: State schools till age 14; National Service in Army.
Married: 1971.
Plays:
The Pope's Wedding (London—Sunday night 'production without décor', 1961). *Saved* (London, 1965; New York, 1970).
Early Morning (London, 1968). *Narrow Road to the Deep North* (Coventry, England, 1968; London, 1969; New York—1969).
Lear (London, 1970; Yale Repertory Theater 1973). *The Sea* (London, 1973; Chicago, 1974; New York—1975). *Bingo* (London, 1973; Cleveland, Ohio, 1975; Yale Repertory Theater, 1976, where it won the off-Broadway 'Obie' award).
The Fool (London, 1975; Washington, D.C., 1976). *We Come to the River* (libretto for Hans Werner Henze's opera—Royal Opera House, Covent Garden, 1976). *A-A America!* London, 1976).

EDWARD BOND is the most controversial of the modern British playwrights. His work has been highly praised by serious critics like Martin Esslin and Simon Trussler, whose monograph on Bond in the British Council's series *Writers and their Work* is a most sympathetic study. Critics who do not like Bond's work tend to be apologetic or defensive, though recently they have been more openly hostile. The British theatre-going public has on the whole shown its lack of enthusiasm; none of Bond's plays has yet had a commercial success or been transferred to the West End. His apologists always claim that he is more popular on the Continent, especially in Germany; his plays have been frequently produced there but there is some doubt whether they are much more popular with German audiences than with British.

Bond is a severe critic of the society in which we live and his plays are intended to express his criticisms. The lengthy

introductions to the printed texts of some of his plays, com-
parable to Shaw's prefaces, explain his objections to our
society's values and organization. Yet he does not suggest anything very constructive in its place, and his plays are strangely
distanced from present-day life. They are mostly placed in
historical or exotic settings, and are more noticeable for their
extremes of violence than for their direct relevance to present-
day social and economic problems.

He first became famous, or notorious, with *Saved*, in which a
baby in a pram is tortured and stoned to death by a group of
louts. This play is his only specific study of modern Britain. It
is concerned with unmotivated and badly educated people who
have nothing to occupy themselves with except mindless
violence and sex. In Len, the chief character, it contains something like a Russian 'holy fool', who reappears in various forms
in Bond's later works. Bond describes Len as 'naturally good',
but 'not wholly good or easily good'. At the beginning of the
play he is picked up by Pam, a sexy girl who lives with her
parents and entertains her boy-friends under their noses. Len
has an affair with Pam for a time; she switches her attentions
to Fred, by whom she has the baby, but Len remains in the
house as a lodger. When Pam leaves the baby with Fred and
his mates, they start idly teasing and baiting it; carried away
by excitement and a sense of daring, they strip it, cover its
face in its own excrement, squeeze and punch it, and finally
throw stones at it. Len watches from a distance but neither
participates nor attempts to stop the others. Later, he visits
Fred in prison and looks after Pam. Pam's mother flirts with
him at one point, and this is seen by Harry, Pam's father. Len
plans to leave the household, but Harry makes peace with
him and Len stays, at least for the time being, Fred comes out
of prison and goes off with his old mates. Len's staying in the
house is what Bond calls an optimistic ending. 'If the spectator
thinks this is pessimistic, that is because he has not learned to
clutch at straws. Clutching at straws is the only realistic thing
to do.'

Despite the controversy over the killing of the baby, which
many people found objectionable, the violence in *Saved* is
credible and the characters are recognizable members of our

society. The play truly reflects the emptiness and futility of many lives. In his later plays, however, Bond's violence often seems gratuitous and incredible, despite his attempts to justify it. These plays become more and more directly concerned with capitalist exploitation of working people, and are set in earlier times when oppression and cruelty were greater and more evident. We are apparently expected to think that things have not improved.

Early Morning is a surrealistic fantasy play, which achieved notoriety because it portrayed Queen Victoria as a Lesbian having an affair with Florence Nightingale, and heaven as a place where cannibalism is the normal way of life. It was the last play banned by the Lord Chamberlain before his powers as a theatrical censor were abolished. Originally it had only two club performances. It is notable for being bizarre and repulsive, rather than for conveying any clear message or for having any great entertainment value. The behaviour of its characters has so little basis in reality or logic that the result is often boring.

Narrow Road to The Deep North is, by contrast, extremely restrained. It tells a Japanese legend in terms partly of oriental theatre and partly of Brechtian alienation techniques. There *is* violence in it—a naked body is hacked to pieces and nailed to a board, upside down, a massacre is depicted by a pile of bodies on the stage, and the play ends with ritual hara-kiri— but this is incidental to a parable about despotism. A cruel eastern despot is overthrown by Georgina, a benevolent Christian one. In a long Shavian speech she explains how her form of despotism differs and how she uses Christian morality as an oppressive force.

Georgina: . . . instead of atrocity, I use morality. I persuade people—in their hearts—that they are sin, and that they have evil thoughts, and that they're greedy and violent and destructive, and—more than anything else—that their bodies must be hidden, and that sex is nasty and corrupting and must be secret. When they believe all that they do what they're told. They don't judge you—they feel guilty themselves and accept that you have the right to judge them.

That's how *I* run the city; the missions and churches and bishops and magistrates and politicians and papers will tell people they are sin and must be kept in order. If sin didn't exist, it would be necessary to invent it. I learned all this from my Scottish nanny. She taught our Prime Minister, the Queen, the Leader of the Opposition, and everyone else who matters. They all learned politics across her knee.

The opposite point of view, that people may actually *need* discipline and government, is not put, so the argument loses its force; this one-sidedness is a characteristic weakness of Bond's work.

Lear is an extraordinary modern reworking of Shakespeare's tragedy, in a vaguely modern setting with violence running amok. Lear is strapped in a chair and placed in a frame before being blinded with a complicated pseudo-surgical machine which the 'doctor' describes in gory detail. Before that he is made to watch a mock medical autopsy on one of his daughters, who has been shot from behind. Cordelia is raped. The other daughters, Fontenelle and Bodice, are sadists—Bodice knits (shades of the French Revolution) while Fontenelle urges on soldiers who are torturing a prisoner.

Fontenelle: Use the boot! Jump on him! Jump on his head!
Soldier: Lay off, lady, lay off! 'Oo's killin' 'im, me or you?
Bodice (*knits*): One plain, two purl, one plain.
Fontanelle: Throw him up and drop him. I want to hear him drop.
Soldier: That's a bit 'eavy, yer need proper gear to drop 'em——
Fontenelle: Do something! Don't let him get away with it. O Christ, why did I cut his tongue out? I want to hear him scream!
Soldier: Look at 'is eyes, Miss. Thass boney-fidey sufferin'.
Fontenelle: O yes, tears and blood. I wish my father was here. I wish he could see him. Look at his hands! Look at them going! What's he praying or clutching? Smash his hands! Kill his hands! Kill his feet! Jump on it—all of it! He can't hit us now! Look at his hands like boiling crabs!

Kill it! Kill all of it! Kill him inside! Make him dead!
Father! Father! I want to sit on his lungs!
Bodice (*knits*): Plain, purl, plain. She was just the same at
school.
Fontenelle: I've always wanted to sit on a man's lungs. Let
me. Give me his lungs.

Among the other scenes of *grand guignol* in *Lear* is the killing
of Cordelia's husband, who becomes a ghost, befriends Lear,
and then is killed again by angry pigs! The pig squeals are
heard off stage, and the 'ghost' comes stumbling on covered in
blood.

The play contains some discussion of government and some
situations which may seem directly relevant to the modern
world. For example, Lear builds a wall to keep out his enemies
and to protect his people from outside 'contamination'. His
daughters plan to marry noblemen from beyond the wall, and
deny that there is any real enemy. This might be an analogy
with western attempts to guard against Communist infiltration,
and with those in our midst who deny that there is any such
danger. Or the wall might more obviously be seen as a
reference to the Berlin wall. But Bond is not attacking
Communists.

In his preface, he says: 'I write about violence as naturally
as Jane Austen wrote about manners. Violence shapes and
obsesses our society, and if we do not stop being violent we
have no future. People who do not want writers to write about
violence want to stop them writing about us and our time. It
would be immoral not to write about violence.'

It is at least equally arguable that our society is less violent,
more caring and more civilised than any previous one. Bond's
obsession with violence and his skill in presenting it with
detailed relish, recall the popular newspapers which give
details of pornography and sex crimes while preaching that
these things are disgusting. It seems as if he is exploiting an
audience's fascination with violence and sadism, while ostensibly condemning it. Bond of course denies this, saying he only
uses violence to help us understand what is happening around
us.

He first assumes that we are violent and aggressive and then proceeds to explain *why* our society makes us like this. His preface to *Lear* puts the argument in detail. 'It does not matter how much a man doing routine work in, say, a factory or office is paid . . . Because he is behaving in a way for which he is not designed, he is alienated from his natural self, and this will have physical and emotional consequences for him. He becomes nervous and tense and he begins to look for threats everywhere. This makes him belligerent and provocative; he becomes a threat to other people, and so his situation rapidly deteriorates.' This is obviously true of some people; it is equally obviously untrue of the vast majority.

Bond thinks otherwise. He argues that we spend our lives making things we don't really need, and are then subjected to commercial pressures to buy them. This is so unnatural that it makes us tense and aggressive. 'Tension and aggression are even becoming the markings of our species. Many people's faces are set in patterns of alarm, coldness or threat; and they move jerkily and awkwardly, not with the simplicity of free animals. These expressions are signs of moral disease, but we are taught to admire them.'

The Sea, although more closely related to modern British life than any of his other plays except *Saved*, is set in the very class-conscious Britain of 1907. It is Bond's funniest play, including among its characters Mrs Rafi, a grand lady of the manor who imperiously conducts bizarre amateur dramatics and organizes a funeral on the edge of the cliffs, with a piano perilously perched there, and a local draper who believes that the town is threatened by beings from outer space who are gradually replacing human brains with 'artificial material brought here in airships'. *The Sea* is a slight work, notable more for its comedy than for its social comment, which is in any case obsolete.

Bingo is a fictional treatment of Shakespeare's life in Strat-ford-on-Avon after his retirement. He has given up writing because he cannot solve his moral problems and is living off unjustly collected rents, tortured by guilt. Finally he commits suicide. In his introduction, Bond says that this flatters Shake-speare: 'If he didn't end in the way shown in the play, then he was a reactionary blimp or some other fool. The only more charitable account is that he was unaware or senile.' Bond also goes into further discussion of aggression, both the aggression of the weak, trying to secure their rights from the strong, and the aggression of the strong against the weak. This leads him into a simplistic account of the reasons for the American bombing of Vietnam. An American could only be persuaded to drop bombs on peasants in a jungle, he says, as a result of years of 'false education and lies, indignity, shabby power, economic insecurity'. 'He drops bombs because he believes that if the peasant ever rowed a canoe across the Pacific and drove an ox cart over America till he came to his garden, he'd steal his vegetables and rape his grandmother—history proves it.'

Bond's solution to his own exaggerated statements about our society is that we must learn to live justly, in the way for which we were evolved. He claims that capitalism and technology prevent this. In his preface to *Lear* he admits, however, that 'I have not answered many of the questions I have raised.' He does not admit that he makes it easier to avoid answering them, to avoid the questions themselves being questioned, by distancing his plays from us. In his introduction to *Bingo*, he is more explicit about the solution—we must have complete and total democracy. 'Most working people no longer believe there are other people who know better than they do how they should live and work.' Bond does not discuss whether they are right to believe this. He does not give any serious consideration to what is nowadays called the 'elitist' view that there *are* leaders among men, people who *do* know better, and that it is the belief that everyone knows equally well which may itself be responsible for many of our troubles. Yet, despite his populist views, it is often the ordinary people in Bond's plays who behave the worst. This is especially noticeable in *The Fool*, where only the rich behave with courtesy and consideration.

The play is about the nineteenth-century farm labourer and poet John Clare. It is also about the struggle of the working people on the land against landlords and exploitation. The people are in revolt—the local village clergyman is stripped and robbed on the stage. And they are reduced to the status of animals—when Clare visits London with his rich patrons, boxers being forced to fight in a cruel and vicious way are shown in the background. In the end we see Clare in the madhouse, run by a well-meaning but toadying doctor, his treatment paid for by his benevolent landlord. Of course Bond cannot resist showing one of the other patients being pushed across the stage in a straitjacket.

Clare does not emerge till half way through the play, and we are not told how he came to be a writer or to find his rich patrons. His madness is explained by the sudden failure of his books and by his wife's fury with his poverty and her jealousy of his work and of the 'Mary' he constantly writes about. The domestic scenes are convincing and moving, but seem quite unrelated to the social upheavals which dominate the first act.

Bond's libretto for Hans Werner Henze's opera, *We Come To The River* is overtly political and anti-militaristic. The central character is a victorious general who believes that he is going blind (from a wound in the knee!). He becomes disillusioned with war and with his emperor's regime as he loses his sight. As in *Lear*, blindness becomes an allegory for 'true' vision. The Emperor puts the General in a mental hospital and, when he does not actually go blind, sends two hired assassins, modelled on the murderers in Shakespeare's *Richard III*, to do the job for him. The obvious parallel with the use of mental hospitals for political dissidents in the Soviet Union is not drawn; instead the opera is meant to be taken as an indictment of capitalist society. The contrast between the privileged officer class, with their expensive whores, and the suffering of the common soldiers and their families, recalls Brecht and also *Wozzeck* but it has little to do with Britain in the second half of the twentieth century. The action takes place in a nameless country at an indefinite time and is extraordinarily irrelevant to our present social and economic problems. In so far as the oppression of political dissidents and the assassination plots have relevance to the modern world it is to communist and fascist dictatorships rather than to the English-speaking countries in whose language the libretto is written.

Bond's two lunch-time plays for the Ambiance Club's American bicentennial season, grouped together under the title, *A-A-America!* are equally irrelevant to present-day America. Both are set in the deep south. In the first, *Grandma Faust*, something called 'Nigger Foot Pie Day' is being celebrated. A caricatured Uncle Sam is fishing without any success and is told by Grandma (a man in drag who represents the devil) to get her a simple man's soul. Sam fights with a negro for his soul, represented by a doll, and cheats by concealing a cosh in the doll and beating the negro with it. However the negro escapes from the ring by a ruse, grabs the 'soul', and goes fishing in his turn, catching a shoal of silver fish. In *The Swing*, which lasts an hour and a half and is virtually a full-length one-act play, there is a very realistic public lynching on the stage of a theatre, with the audience encouraged to buy the dearer seats, so as to have the right to more shots at the negro on the stage. Both plays refer to an earlier age of racial tension in the South, and are very wide of the target as comments on the racial problem in the United States today. Even *The Stone*, a short lunch-time play for the *Gay Sweatshop* group, is a very abstract *Pilgrim's Progress* parable about a man conned into carrying a heavy stone on a long journey and has no direct relevance to the problems of homosexuals in our society.

There is obviously no reason why plays should deal with the problems of society, but there is something irritating about a playwright who claims to be doing that but in fact seems to be living with the problems of the past. There is also something annoying about a writer who constantly attacks society for its abuses, and blames all the wickednesses of man on the social institutions around him, without offering any practical or concrete remedies. And there is something distasteful about a writer who claims to be revolted by violence but whose plays contain scenes of sickening cruelty and sadism. All this might be forgiven if the plays were more entertaining and theatrical. Certainly they contain some imaginative quasi-poetic dialogue; certainly the sadistic scenes *are* theatrical. But Bond's plots are either absurd or so rudimentary, and many of the characters so two-dimensional, that interest flags and the audience is bored. In so far as Bond is making a comment on the inequalities and injustices of our society, the same comment is made more pointedly, more relevantly and more acceptably, by other writers.

Part 2

Domestic Bliss?

ALL DRAMATISTS MUST naturally be concerned with personal relationships; several of the modern British ones concentrate on the conflicts and sufferings involved in family life. Peter Shaffer, Peter Nichols, Ted Whitehead and Christopher Hampton treat them in very different ways and blend them with wider social, political, religious and philosophical themes. But they are all protesting, in one way or another, about our inhumanity to each other in our homes, and in Whitehead's case about the inhumanity of the conventions which keep us there.

Three: Peter Shaffer

Born: In Liverpool, England, 1926. (Twin brother of Anthony
Shaffer, author of *Sleuth*, etc.)
Father runs a property company.
Education: St Paul's School, London, and Trinity College,
Cambridge. Did compulsory national service as a 'Bevin
Boy' (conscription by ballot into coal-mines instead of the
armed services), then briefly worked for his father's firm.
Thought of going into publishing but 'I was more interested
in reading than in competitive business'. Worked in New
York Public Library, in a Doubleday Bookshop, New
York, and in Boosey and Hawkes, the London music
publishers. Left Boosey and Hawkes in 1955 'to try to
write, with £5 a week support from my father'. 1956–57,
literary critic of *Truth*, 1961–62, music critic of *Time and
Tide*.
Plays:
Five Finger Exercise (London 1958, New York 1959). *The Private
Ear* and *The Public Eye* (London 1962, New York 1963). *Merry
Rooster's Panto* (London 1963). Sketch in *The Establishment* (New
York 1963). *The Royal Hunt of the Sun* (Chichester and London
1964, New York 1965). *Black Comedy* (Chichester 1965, London
1966, New York 1967). *A Warning Game* (New York 1967).
White Lies (New York 1967, rewritten and retitled *The White
Liars* London 1968; further rewritten as *White Liars* (London
1976). *It's About Cinderella* (London 1969). *The Battle of Shrivings*
(London 1970, rewritten as *Shrivings* York (England) 1975).
Equus (London 1973, New York 1974). *Evening Standard* Award
1958, New York Drama Critics' Circle Awards 1960, 1975.

SHAFFER'S FIRST STAGE PLAY was produced two years after
John Osborne's *Look Back in Anger*, with which it has some
similarities. Both are family dramas, in seemingly conventional
style; both express the discontents and uncertainties of a new

generation and both seemed particularly relevant to their time. Osborne's, with its tirades against society, its working-class 'angry young man', and its rough colloquial language was the more revolutionary. It was produced at the Royal Court, while *Five Finger Exercise* was staged at the Comedy, a West End house which had recently been functioning as a club to circumvent censorship and make possible the London productions of three American plays—*Tea and Sympathy*, *A View from the Bridge*, and *Cat on a Hot Tin Roof*. Shaffer's play was not actually a club production, but it was presented under the same management —New Watergate Presentations (in association with Tennents). Like the American plays, it dealt, sympathetically but indirectly by present-day standards, with homosexuality. In fact its references to the subject are so indirect that it was possible for a management reviving the play for a regional tour in 1975 to claim that it is not about homosexuality at all. Even in 1958, *Five Finger Exercise* did not seem shocking, and it was made even more 'respectable' by lavish West End treatment—a cast headed by Adrianne Allen and Roland Culver, both associated with traditional Shaftesbury Avenue comedies, and directed by John Gielgud. Three outstandingly talented younger players— Juliet Mills, Brian Bedford and Michael Bryant—completed the original cast; when this team was eventually replaced, the management took the unusual step of bringing in a new director, Peter Wood, so that the new cast was not just a carbon copy of the original. *Five Finger Exercise* ran at the Comedy for a total of 610 performances, a very long run for a serious drama.

Unlike many of the new playwrights of that time, Shaffer has continued to develop and progress, exploring new theatrical forms and tackling a wide range of styles and subjects. But already in *Five Finger Exercise*, his three most notable characteristics were clearly apparent:—sympathetic understanding of all his characters, not just the immediately appealing ones, lifelike and yet theatrical dialogue, and the ability to plan and plot a truly 'well-made' play.

The characters and plot of *Five Finger Exercise* are superficially reminiscent of those in Turgenev's *A Month in the Country* which Shaffer had not seen or read at the time. In both plays the drama springs from the cathartic effect on a family of

an attractive young tutor. Louise Harrington, dissatisfied with
her husband and full of affectations, turns for sympathy and
companionship to Walter Langer much as Natalia Petrovna
turns to Beliaev. But Shaffer is mainly concerned with Clive,
Louise's 19-year-old son, his rebellion against his father and
his tentative awareness of a homosexual feeling for Walter.

Stanley Harrington, Clive's father, is a successful self-made
furniture dealer. He is sarcastic about his wife Louise's preten-
sions, her gentility, her attempts at cultural interests and her
extravagance. He also sneers at Clive's literary and cultural
interests, and 'arty-tarty' friends. Louise, in return, is crushing
about his background.

Clive is to some extent a pawn between them, criticized by
his father and fussed over by his mother, and needed as an ally
by both of them. It appears that we are being asked to side
with him against his impossible parents. The play is partly
autobiographical and Clive is to some extent Shaffer himself.
But Shaffer has always been objective enough to see other
people's points of view. Walter, the perceptive tutor, reproves
Clive for making fun of his father.

Walter: I think if you forgive me . . .
Clive: Well?
Walter: You have a duty to your father.
Clive: Duty? What a very German thing to say . . . Oh, that's
terrible of me, isn't it? Forgive me, I'm not quite sober.
Walter: I did not mean duty like that. I meant that it seems
to me . . . Clever children have a duty—to protect their
parents who are not so clever.

Nor are we allowed to take sides unfairly with either Stanley
or Louise. Their daughter Pamela grasps the 'chicken or the
egg' situation about which of them is the most to blame.

Pamela: I know mother's frightful to him about culture, and
uses music and things to keep him out—which is terrible. But
isn't that just because *he* made her keep out of things when
they were first married? You know he wouldn't even let her
go to concerts and theatres although she was dying to, and
once he threw a picture she'd bought into the dustbin, one of

those modern things, all squiggles and blobs . . . But then, mightn't that just have been because being brought up by himself he was afraid of making a fool of himself. Oh poor Daddy. . . . Poor Mother too.

To some extent Shaffer even shows Stanley as a tragic figure, aware of his own failures as husband and father. Walter tells him he is wrong in thinking his son despises him and tries to tell him that it is bad to make a son feel he has to apologize for himself and his life. In reply, Stanley 'talks more or less to himself';

Stanley: You start a family, work and plan. Suddenly you turn round and there's nothing there. Probably never was. What's a family anyway? Just—just kids with your blood in 'em. There's no reason why they should like you . . . You go on expecting it, of course, but it's silly really . . .

Stanley makes genuine efforts to understand Clive, but it's beyond him. Equally Clive tries to state his budding attitude to people and to life, so different from his father's. One confrontation between them is worth quoting at length because it shows Shaffer's grasp of their characters and mastery of dialogue. Stanley has just found Clive drinking alone, late at night.

Stanley: If you want to drink—drink with others. Everyone likes a drink. You come over to the Club with me, you'll soon find that out. I'll make you a member. You'll get on with them in a jiffy if you'll only try.
Clive: Yes. (*Pause*) Well . . . I think I'll go to bed now.
Stanley: Just a minute. What's the matter? Aren't they good enough for you? Is that it?
Clive: (*gently*) No, of course it isn't.
Stanley: Then what?
Clive: (*gaining courage*) Well, all this stuff—right people, wrong people—people who Matter. It's all so meaningless.
Stanley: It's not a bit meaningless.
Clive: Well, all right, they matter! But what can I say to them if they don't matter to *me*? Look, you just can't talk about people in that way. It's unreal—idiotic. As far as I'm

concerned one of the few people who really matters to me in
Cambridge is an Indian.

Stanley: Well, there's nothing wrong in that. What's his
father? A rajah or something?

Clive: His father runs a cake shop in Bombay.

Stanley: Well, what sort of boy is he? What's he like?

Clive: He's completely still . . . I don't mean he doesn't
move. I mean that deep down inside him there's a sort of
happy stillness, that makes all our family rows and raised
voices here seem like a kind of—blasphemy almost. That's
why he matters—because he loves living so much. Because
he understands birds and makes shadow puppets out of
cardboard, and loves Ella Fitzgerald, and Vivaldi, and
Lewis Carroll, and because he plays chess like a devil and
makes the best prawn curry in the world. And this is him.
Well, parts of him. Bits of him.

Stanley: (*bewildered and impatient*) Well, of course I'm glad
you've got some nice friends.

Clive: (*sharp*) Don't. Don't do that.

Stanley: What?

Clive: Patronize. It's just too much.

Stanley: I'm not patronizing you, Clive.

Clive: Oh yes, you are. That's precisely what you're doing.

Stanley: That's very unfair.

Clive: (*working himself into a deep rage*) Precisely. Precisely!
'I'm very glad you have some nice chums, Clive. I did too at
your age' . . . These aren't my little play-pals, Father, They're
important people. Important to me.

Stanley: Did I say they weren't?

Clive: (*frantic*) Important! It is important they should be
alive! Every person they meet should be altered by them, or
at least remember them with terrific—terrific excitement.
That's an important person. Can't you understand?

Stanley: (*crushingly*) No, Clive. I'm afraid I don't. I don't
understand you at all.

Later, in an outburst worthy of one of Osborne's heroes,
Clive continues his attempt to assert himself and explain to
his father how he thinks people should be treated.

Clive: You think you can treat me like a child! But you don't even know the right way to treat a child. Because a child is private and important and itself. Not an extension of you, any more than I am . . . I am myself. Myself, Myself. You think of me only as what I might become. What I might make of myself. But I am myself now—with every breath I take, every blink of the eyelash. The taste of the chestnut or a strawberry on my tongue is me. The smell of my skin is me. The trees and sofas that I see with my own eyes are me. And you should want to become me and see them as I see them.

Then Clive works himself up into an emotional peroration.

Clive: I'm talking about *care*. Taking care. Care of people you want to know. Not just doing your best for them, and hoping the best for them. I mean you've got to care for them *as they are*, from blink to blink . . . Don't you see? The—the renewing of your cells every day makes you a sacred object, or it should do, in the eyes of people who care for you. It's far more important than whether you speculate in fish or furniture. Because what you do in the world and so on isn't important at all, not in the slightest, compared with what you look like and sound like and feel like as the minutes go by. That's why a question like 'What are you going to be?' is quite unreal. Do you see?

Four out of Shaffer's five characters in this play are presented with equally penetrating understanding. Walter, trying to escape from his family's Nazi background and find a 'respectable' English family for himself, is as tragic a figure as Stanley, Louise and Clive. Pamela is the most 'normal' of the quintet, and the least explored, but she is only 14 and is already protecting herself from the others by understandable and amusing role-playing.

The plot of *Five Finger Exercise* is ingeniously worked out. Clive discovers his mother in an affectionate scene with Walter and, in a drunken emotional state, tells Stanley. Louise is angry and disillusioned when Walter tells her she is like a mother to him, and gets Stanley to dismiss him on the grounds that Pamela is developing an unhealthy crush on him. She also realizes that Clive is falling in love with Walter. Stanley accuses Walter of turning Clive into a cissy with all his 'arty' talk, and of making love to Louise, though he does not really believe this charge. By the end of the play every one has confronted everyone else with a moment of truth. Walter attempts suicide and Clive is left, at the final curtain, praying for courage.

Shaffer says his life changed overnight because of *Five Finger Exercise*. He had no idea that it would be an enormous success and was completely taken by surprise to find himself suddenly earning a lot of money. Until then, he had relied on an allowance of £5 a week from his father; with *Five Finger Exercise* launched on its West End run, he was receiving about £200 a week. 'This cured my theory that I was unemployable, and the best thing of all was that it enabled me to meet people I was impressed by and wanted to meet, especially Peter Brook.'

Shaffer's next play was based on some very personal experiences in New York. 'It's a play which I've never shown anyone, about being rejected in love. But it's dangerous to write out of a narrow personal experience. After that, it was very difficult to write another play. *Private Ear* wrote itself in an hour on the train from Glyndebourne opera-house to London—of course it needed fleshing-out afterwards but essentially it was written on the train. It was given to Peter Wood, the director, without its title-page, but he knew at once that it was by me. *Public Eye* was deliberately written to go with it, as Wood wanted a second play to form a double-bill.' They were produced at the Globe Theatre, in the West End, with Maggie Smith appearing in both plays and with Kenneth Williams achieving one of his comic *tours de force* in the second. *The Private Ear* is a sensitive and touching sketch about an unsuccessful pick-up: Bob, who is shy and nervous with girls, has got chatting with Doreen at a concert and invited her round for supper. His more confident office-chum Ted has volunteered to help with the cooking, and with advice. It turns out that she is not a real music-lover, and was at the concert by accident. Bob's attempts to play and discuss classical records only bore her. She is more attracted by Ted's confident extrovert style. Shaffer makes each of the characters credible and sympathetic. Doreen eventually takes pity on Bob and allows him to kiss her; Ted has given up a free

evening to help Bob and although he grasps the opportunity to
flirt with Doreen he discreetly leaves before supper, so as to
give him his chance, and Bob finally accepts his failure, giving
Doreen Ted's phone number. He ends the play deliberately
scratching his record of *Madame Butterfly*.

The Public Eye is ostensibly a farcical comedy about an eccentric private detective hired by a middle-aged accountant to spy
on his teenage wife. The detective, rejoicing in the name of
Julian Cristo*foro*u, makes himself at home in his client's office,
and eats yogurt, sweets, raisins, waffles and treacle out of his
brief-case. He also has a good line in verbal pedantry of the
type developed by Pinter and later by Simon Gray.

Charles (the accountant): Are you trying to be humorous?
Julian: I sometimes succeed in being humorous, Mr Sidley,
but I never try.

In the course of the farcical complications there is penetrating
discussion about marriage and identity. The three characters
emerge as real, sympathetic people, not mere puppets or comic
figures. At one point Charles says that his wife, Belinda, does
not know her place, expressing the idea that we must all play
roles in life, an idea which Shaffer developed later.

Charles: Within a year I had to recognize that I had married
a child. Someone with no sense of her place at all.
Julian: Her place?
Charles: Certainly. Her place. I know that's not a fashionable word, but that doesn't mean it has no meaning. Belinda
is the wife of a professional man in a highly organized city
in the twentieth century. That is her place. It dictates that
she must live by a certain code. As I have often explained to
her, this would undoubtedly be different if she were wedded
to a jazz trumpeter in New Orleans, which she seems to
think she is, but there would still *be* a code. There is no such
thing as a perfectly independent person.
Julian: Is that what she wants to be?
Charles: I don't know what she wants to be. She doesn't
know herself. Things have got steadily worse. Three months
ago I invited a very important client to dinner: the President

of one of the largest Investment Companies in the city. My
wife presided over the table dressed in scarlet pyjamas. When
I remonstrated with her, she said she was sick of stuffy guests.
Julian: It's a fair point.
Charles: It's not a fair point. It doesn't mean my friends are
stuffy, Mr Cristoforou, simply because they do not come to
dinner disguised as motor-cyclists. Because they happen to
prefer Mozart to *Stay loose, Mother Goose*. No doubt they are
helplessly out of touch with modern living. They only read,
think, travel and exchange the fruits of doing so pleasurably
with each other. Is there anything so utterly boring and
ridiculous as the modern worship of youth?

Shortly afterwards, Belinda gets a chance to put her point of
view, in an argument with her husband.

Belinda: You always say you want me to entertain your
friends, and as soon as you can you get out the port and send
me out of the room. It's incredible, anyway, that a man of
your age should be pushing decanters of port clockwise
round a dining-table. It makes you look a hundred. When I
tell my friends, they can't believe it.
Charles: I'm sure they can't. But then, one would hardly
accept their notions of etiquette as final, would one?
Belinda: Oh, please!
Charles: What?
Belinda: Not your iceberg voice. I can't bear it. 'One would
hardly say . . .' 'I scarcely think . . .' 'One might hazard, my
dear. . . .' All that morning suit language. It's only hiding.
Charles: Indeed?
Belinda: Yes, indeed. Indeed, indeed! People don't say 'in-
deed' any more, Charles. It's got dry rot.

They get embroiled in a serious argument about their responsibilities and Charles reminds Belinda that they have made a
contract of marriage.

Belinda: Well, what about it? There's nothing in it that
says a woman must drop her friends and take her husband's.
I know it's always done, but I don't see it should be. I never
promised to cherish all those mauve old men in sickness and

in health. I love my friends; how can I be faithful to you if I'm unfaithful to them?

Charles: May I ask what that means?

Belinda: That you're not my only responsibility, that's what it means, and I'm not yours. You've got to be faithful to all sorts of people. You can't give everything to just one. Just one can't use everything. And you certainly can't *get* everything from just one. That's not reasonable to expect, is it? Just because you get sex from a man, it doesn't mean you're going to get jokes as well, or a someone who digs jazz. Oh, I know a husband claims the right to be all things to a woman, but he never is. The strain would be appalling.

Charles: Charming.

Belinda: It's true.

Charles: It's not true. You talk about people as if they were *hors d'oeuvres*; him for the herring, him for the mayonnaise, him for the pickled beetroot.

Belinda: But that's exactly it. How clever of you to think of a comparison like that. That's marvellous.

Belinda's Women's Lib view of marriage is made to seem plausible and attractive, but Charles gets back with a reasoned statement of a more conventional attitude.

Charles: Let me tell you something. Each man has all those things inside him, sex, jokes, jazz and many more important things than that. He's got the whole of human history in him, only in capsule. But it takes someone who loves him to make those capsules grow. If they don't grow, he's not loved enough.

Finally, this being a romantic comedy, Julian acts as the catalyst who brings Belinda and Charles together again, or at least tells them how to have another chance. First, in three brief speeches, he persuades Belinda that Charles is 'sick'.

Julian: He's so afraid of being touched by life, he hardly exists. He's so scared of looking foolish, he puts up words against it for barriers: Good Taste, Morality, What you *should* do, what you *should* feel. He's walled up in *Should* like a tomb.

If you hear a piece of music, you'll either love it or hate it.

He won't know what to feel till he knows who it's by. Sick.
You can say 'nigger' and have black friends. He'll only say
'negro'—but dislike them.

He's half dead, and only you can save him. The choice is
yours: walk out, and he dies. Stay, and with all your efforts
you might just bring him back to life.

Then Julian blackmails Charles into agreeing to swap
identities with him. Threatening Charles that he will tell
Belinda about his visits to a prostitute (which he in fact knows
from Belinda), he instals himself at Charles's desk and tells him
to follow Belinda around the streets for a month, not talking to
her but looking at and listening to the things she does, really
getting to know her. This is his one chance.

The Royal Hunt of the Sun is a much more ambitious and
elaborate attempt to explore the nature of men's attitudes to
each other and to life and death. It is also a big spectacular
historical pageant, which Shaffer says in his published notes is
meant to be a kind of 'total' theatre, 'involving not only words
but rites, mimes, masks and magics. The text cries for illus-
tration. It is a director's piece, a pantomimist's piece, a musi-
cian's piece, a designer's piece, and of course an actor's piece,
almost as much as it is an author's.' It was directed by John
Dexter for the National Theatre, first at the Chichester Festival
and then at the Old Vic. And it was subsequently used as the
basis for an opera with music by Iain Hamilton, which had its
première by the English National Opera at the London Coli-
seum in 1977. It tells the story of the sixteenth-century Spanish
expedition into Peru to subdue the Indians and to establish
Spanish rule. It is mainly concerned with the clash between
Pizarro, the leader of the expedition, and Atahuallpa, the
Indian leader who believes himself to be a god, and with the
inner conflicts brought out in them by their confrontation.

The play takes the form of flashbacks, narrated by the ageing
Martin Ruiz, who was Pizarro's page. Early on, the experienced
and cynical Pizarro instructs the keen young soldier Martin in
some of his rules of life, in a speech reminiscent of Charles's
views on role-playing and of Julian's attack on him for cutting
off the real world in *The Public Eye*.

Pizarro: Look, boy: know something. Men cannot just stand as men in this world. It's too big for them and they grow scared. So they build themselves shelters against the bigness, do you see? They call the shelters Court, Army, Church. They're useful against loneliness, Martin, but they're not true. They're not real, Martin. Do you see?

Martin: No, sir. Not truthfully, sir . . .

Pizarro: No, sir. Not truthfully, sir! Why must you be so young? Look at you. Only a quarter formed. A colt the world will break for its sightless track. Listen once. Army loyalty is blasphemy. The world of soldiers is a yard of un-growable children. They play with ribbons and make up ceremonies just to keep out the rest of the world. They add up the number of their blue dead and their green dead and call that their history. But all this is just the flower the bandit carves on his knife before shoving it into a man's side . . . What's Army Tradition? Nothing but years of Us against Them. Christ-men against Pagan-Men. Men against men. I've had a life of it, boy, and let me tell you it's nothing but a nightmare game, played by brutes to give themselves a reason.

Not that Pizarro allows his cynicism about war and religion to divert him from his appointed role. He is a blunt no-nonsense soldier, with the ability to inspire loyalty and obedience from his men, but with a shrewd understanding of the hypocrisy of his own words and actions. He tells his men they have got to march and look like gods, to deceive Atahuallpa, otherwise they will all be killed. His strategy works; Atahuallpa orders the Indians to lay down their arms and welcome the new god as a friend. As a result, the Indians are massacred.

When Atahuallpa realises he has been tricked, he interrogates Valverde, the chaplain to the Spanish expedition.

Atahuallpa: You kill my people; you make them slaves. By what power?

Valverde: By this. (*He offers a Bible*) The Word of God.

(*Atahuallpa holds it to his ear. He listens intently. He shakes it.*)

Atahuallpa: No word. (*He smells the book, and then licks it.*

Finally he throws it down impatiently.) God is angry with your insults.

Valverde: Blasphemy!

Atahuallpa: God is angry.

Valverde: Francisco Pizarro, do you stay your hand when Christ is insulted? Let this pagan feel the power of your arm. I absolve you all!

The Royal Hunt of the Sun is not just an attack on the hypocrisy of martial religion. It is also an exploration of the nature of power and worship and of their necessity, taken further by Shaffer later in *Shrivings* and *Equus*. Atahuallpa gets in some effective satire of Holy Communion, explaining to his high priest why Christians believe their god is inside them.

Atahuallpa: They eat him. First he becomes a biscuit, and then they eat him. I have seen this. At praying they say, 'This is the body of our God'. Then they drink his blood. It is very bad. Here in my empire we do not eat men. My family forbade it many years past.

But Atahuallpa is not allowed to have it all his own way. True to form, Shaffer sees both sides of the question. De Nizza, a sophisticated Franciscan friar, explains love and its dependence on freedom to Atahuallpa, the benevolent despot.

De Nizza: It is not known in your kingdom. At home we can say to our ladies: 'I love you', or to our native earth. It means we rejoice in their lives. But a man cannot say this to the woman he must marry at twenty-five; or to the strip of land allotted to him at birth which he must till till he dies. Love must be free, or else it alters away. Command it to your court; it will send a deputy. Let God order it to fill our hearts, it becomes useless to him. It is stronger than iron; yet in a fist of force it melts. It is a coin that sparkles in the hand; yet in the pocket it turns to rust. Love is the only door from the prison of ourselves. It is the eagerness of God to enter that prison, to take on pain, and imagine lust, so that the torn soldier, or the spent lecher, can call out in his defeat: 'You know this too, so help me from it.'

De Nizza argues that the Indians cannot know real happiness, because their despotic system denies them 'the right to hunger'.

Pizarro: You call hunger a right?
De Nizza: Of course, it gives life meaning. Look around you: happiness has no feel for men here since they are forbidden unhappiness. They have everything in common so they have nothing to give each other. They are part of the seasons, no more; as indistinguishable as mules, as predictable as trees. All men are born unequal; this is a divine gift. And want is their birthright. Where you deny this and there is no hope of any new love; where tomorrow is abolished, and no man ever thinks, 'I can change myself', there you have the rule of Anti-Christ.

This sophisticated defence of a free competitive capitalist society against a controlled egalitarian society which is superficially happier, is just one of the surprising strands in *The Royal Hunt of the Sun*. For all De Nizza's subtle apologias, the Spanish conquerors are of course unscrupulous and greedy. They want the Peruvian gold and the only way Pizarro can get it for them is by tricking Atahuallpa, promising him freedom if the Indians find and collect the gold. When the gold is duly amassed, Pizarro proclaims Atahuallpa a free man, 'but for the welfare of his country, he will remain for the moment as the guest of the army'. Pizarro's problem is that if he releases Atahuallpa, the whole Spanish army will be slaughtered in revenge for the earlier massacre. He has to break his word, and ultimately he has to accept his army's demand for Atahuallpa's death.

But Pizarro and Atahuallpa have come to understand each other, and a strange bond has grown between them. In some sense they *are* both gods, detached from their subordinates and seeing life and the world from outside. Atahuallpa agrees to die, confident that his body will be reborn in the rising sun. Before he dies, he is made to kneel to Christ—otherwise he would be burnt and have no chance of being reborn. As the sun rises, Atahuallpa's body lies on stage, remaining lifeless. By this time, the whole audience hopes for, and half believes n, a miracle. So does Pizarro, who cries out that he has been cheated. Old Martin tells us that Pizarro was killed later in a quarrel with his partner bringing up reinforcements, but 'to speak truth, he sat down that morning and never really got up again'. The play ends with Pizarro singing quietly and sadly beside Atahuallpa's body. The final stage direction is: 'The sun glares at the audience'.

From this description it is obvious that *The Royal Hunt of the Sun is* very much an author's play, as well as the many other sorts of play which Shaffer mentions. It took years to write; the first much longer draft was written before *Private Ear* and *Public Eye*. It included longer speeches for Pizarro and an extra character, Pizarro's brother, who was young Martin's guardian and who wanted to be second-in-command of the expedition. The native interpreter also had a more significant role, cheating Pizarro and Atahuallpa and finally spreading false reports of an Inca rising. Shaffer had some difficulty in getting the play produced.

'I'd always wanted to write a large epic play. I sent it to Tennents, who were dismayed by it, so I sent it to the National Theatre, where it lay around till it was spotted by John Dexter. What I learned from the production was that plays must centre on people; audiences mostly remembered the confrontations between Pizarro and Atahuallpa, though they don't meet at all in the first act and only have three scenes together in the second.'

The procession which accompanies Atahuallpa's first entry, the climbing of the Andes, narrated by Old Martin and illustrated with mime and atmospheric sound effects, and the massacre of the Indians ending with a rippling bloodstained cloth covering the stage, are among the visually memorable highlights of the play. Shaffer says that Marc Wilkinson's music is an integral part of any production of it, especially 'the final Chant of Resurrection, to be whined and whispered, howled and hooted, over Atahuallpa's body in the darkness, before the last sunrise of the Inca Empire'. This combination of visual, aural and intellectual strength gives the play its unusual appeal, a combination to be repeated, with totally different ingredients, in *Equus*.

But some lighter plays and a less visual intellectual debate

3

come first. *Black Comedy* was originally written specially for the National Theatre to stage at the Chichester Festival, where a play was needed to fill a double-bill with Strindberg's *Miss Julie*. Shaffer had just seen a visiting Chinese theatre company, with the actors in bright light pretending to be in the dark, which gave him the idea, and the play only took about two weeks to write. It is a highly professional and extremely ingenious farce. Like most farces, it's full of visual humour and stock characters who are none the less funny for being caricatures. Unlike most farces, it also occasionally touches our feelings and indicates the unhappiness lurking in superficially ludicrous people, so that the comedy is indeed 'black'.

The basic gimmick of the play, which gives the title its more obvious meaning, is that most of the action takes place in darkness, following a lighting failure. The actual stage lighting is an exact reversal of what is supposed to be happening; in other words, when the plot calls for the characters to be groping around in total darkness, the stage is fully lit. When the lights are supposed to be working, the stage is dark. This idea is carried through consistently, so that when a character strikes a match, the stage gets slightly darker. This gimmick provides spendid opportunities for visual humour.

The plot calls for a great deal of furniture moving, with the actors pretending to grope in the dark and with a lot of 'accidental' bumps and collisions. At one point a sofa is removed with someone actually sitting on it—a drunken spinster 'who waves goodbye with the haughty grandeur of a first-class passenger departing on an ocean liner'. Characters discuss each other without realizing they are present; at one point the hero describes his fiancée's father as 'a monster' only to have him grimly retort 'Good evening'; later his mistress is discussed while she is listening, and he even dances with her while listening to an angry tirade from his fiancée's father. The complications are endless.

The characters include a vacuous debutante type (the fiancée), a Colonel Blimp (her father), a teetotal spinster (the one who gets drunk, being given liquor in mistake for lemonade), a gay antique dealer, and a German refugee electrician and a rich German art collector (who are confused with each other). The plot, about the hero's efforts to impress his fiancée's father, is not to be taken at all seriously, but it works well in the theatre as a peg for bringing the characters together and for stimulating the comic business. Shaffer shows his professional grasp of the theatre by giving very precise stage instructions and even providing an alternative ending for stages without a trapdoor.

Although *Black Comedy* is mainly a farce, it still presents some of Shaffer's favourite preoccupations, particularly the clash between bourgeois and 'artistic' values, and between a conventional retired army-officer father, his society daughter, and the young experimental sculptor she wants to marry. Brindsley Miller, the sculptor, is the central character. He is trying to fool his prospective father-in-law into thinking that he is successful, has a well-furnished apartment, and would make an acceptable son-in-law. He is also fooling his fiancée about past relationships with his mistress and with the gay antique dealer, to say nothing of misleading each of them about his intentions.

White Lies was written specially to accompany *Black Comedy* at its New York production. It is also about people who are trying to fool the rest of the world about their true status and emotions. It was rewritten and retitled *The White Liars* for its first London production, and then further rewritten, as *White Liars*, for a London revival eight years later. The published version is *The White Liars*, which Shaffer at that time regarded as final; it is to be played before *Black Comedy*, 'making a complete evening's entertainment on the theme of tricks'.

In all its versions, the play is about a seaside fortune-teller, masquerading as 'Baroness Lemberg', and two young men who come to her as clients. She is a professional liar, dispensing phoney predictions, though with the ironic slogan 'Lemberg never lies'. The first version of the play concentrated on her and her memories of a former lover whom she drove away. His voice, together with her own younger voice, was heard on a tape recorder or public address system in the second version, but the focus of the play shifted to the two others. The ex-lover supplied some of the motivation for her actions and caused her to divide people into 'Givers' and 'Takers'. Shaffer decided that all this made the play too complicated and that audiences don't take in what is being said by a disembodied voice. In the latest revision she speaks to a portrait of her father, dressed in a uniform suggesting he was a nobleman, but actually a delicatessen owner who had hired the uniform to appear in an amateur operatic production, and the content of the play is divided equally between her and the young men.

They are also liars. Frank bribes the 'baroness' to warn Tom off flirting with his girl. He claims to have rescued Tom from his working-class background and from penury, and made him into a successful pop singer. At the end of the play it is revealed that Frank is really in love with Tom, not with any girl, and that his efforts were directed to keeping Tom for himself. (In the original versions of the play it is Tom who indignantly tells 'Lemberg' this; in *White Liars*, it is Frank, which is less convincing but gives the actor playing Frank more to do.) Frank has been pretending to be a heterosexual journalist when he was really gay and working in a boutique; he invented the working-class image which Tom has been enacting. Tom actually came from a conventional middle-class home. The result of Frank's intrigue with 'Lemberg', which Tom sees through, is to disillusion Tom and finish their affair.

The play thus links several of Shaffer's favourite themes—role-playing as a way of life, the revolt of a middle-class son against his family background, and the pain and loneliness of people groping for emotional relationships, especially unconventional ones. In the published version of the play, 'Lemberg's' division of people into 'Givers' and 'Takers' gives Tom the opportunity to point out that many 'Givers' are really selfish, getting their satisfaction from making other people dependent on them. 'Lemberg' has classified Frank as a 'Giver', but Tom expostulates.

Tom: They give you your role. That's what they give. They make you up, till you're just acting in a film projected out of their eyes. I was a prisoner on Wet Dream Island!

This exchange is omitted in the latest version of the play, though when it was staged in 1976, the homosexual relationship between the two men was made much more apparent

visually from the very beginning. Role-playing is still referred
to specifically when the 'Baroness' asks Tom if his parents
know that he has 'abolished' them.

Tom: No, but it doesn't matter. They've abolished *me*, after
all. How real am I to them? Dad calls me 'Minstrel Boy'
whenever I go home, because he finds it embarrassing to have
a singer for a son. And mother tells her bridge club I'm in
London studying music—because studying is a more respectable image for her than performing in a cellar. Both of
them are talking about themselves, not me. And that's fine,
because that's what everybody's doing all the time, everywhere.

Shaffer's next play has also been rewritten and retitled since
its first production. *The Battle of Shrivings* was a West End flop.
Four years later it was published under the title *Shrivings*, with
Shaffer making it clear in his preface that he considered this
to be a new play. Both plays are concerned with the clash between two formidable personalities:—Sir Gideon Petrie, a
distinguished elderly philosopher who has retreated to the
aptly named country house of Shrivings, where he has re-
nounced sex and meat and created the World League of Peace
which preaches non-violence and brotherly love, and his
former pupil, Mark Askelon, a cynical poet and bon viveur
who advertises his sexual and other appetites and comes on a
visit to Shrivings to upset its peaceful atmosphere. In some ways
their conflict is similar to that between Pizarro and Atahuallpa
in *Royal Hunt of the Sun*. The remaining characters in the
original play were Gideon's wife and his hero-worshipping
female secretary, and David Askelon, Mark's son, who makes
furniture and yearns for simple old-fashioned things, and has
been virtually adopted by Gideon. The revised version of the
play eliminated the wife, reducing the cast to a quartet.
  The battle is between Gideon's idealistic belief in human
improvability and his claim that he would not in any circumstances use violence against anyone, on the one hand, and on
the other Mark's experience of life which has made him sceptical about human nature and has convinced him that evil must
be fought, with force if necessary. Mark takes a bet, that he

can force Gideon into expelling him from the house. As usual Shaffer carefully balances the arguments and our sympathies between the characters. At first Sir Gideon and his idealistic household seem admirable, and Mark a rash intruder. But gradually he exposes Gideon's feet of clay, alleging that his pacifism and idealism are the results of weakness and that his renunciation of sex is simply a sign of his failure as a husband and of his homosexual tendencies. Several of Shaffer's regular preoccupations are introduced: David is in rebellion against his father, though they are reconciled in the end, and Gideon has a suppressed love for Mark and wishes David was his own son. Mark also has feet of clay; he was not successful as a lover with his wife, about whom he now has a guilt complex. He travels with her effigy and her ashes, and talks to them, asking forgiveness. He is unscrupulous in his attack on Gideon, torturing David with uncertainties about his parentage and about Gideon's motives, and seducing Gideon's secretary, physically and intellectually. When the secretary turns on Gideon, accusing him of having driven away his wife and of being a fraud, the philosopher abandons his principles and strikes her. In a sense it is Mark's victory, but he is appalled by what he has done to Gideon—both men are defeated by their battle, or perhaps both are shriven, and closer to the truth.

As seen in the theatre, Shaffer's attempt to marry philosophy and psychology with theatrical melodrama was not altogether successful. The father-son conflict, the discussion of Gideon's homosexuality and the hostility between him and his wife seemed almost irrelevant. The debate on human nature, though very interesting, was wordy and long drawn-out. Moreover audiences going to see West End stars like John Gielgud and Wendy Hiller were not always ready to concentrate on a fairly rigorous moral discussion. By eliminating the wife and cutting the play for its published version, Shaffer tightened it considerably. There is now just sufficient suspense and uncertainty, about Gideon's response to Mark's challenge and about his motives, to give life to the discussion.

Shaffer achieved his most complete blending of intellectual and psychological discussion with visual theatrical effects in *Equus*. It is also his biggest commercial success; following its

London production by the National Theatre, with Alec McCowen, it was staged all over the world, including a long run in New York with Anthony Hopkins, Anthony Perkins and Richard Burton among those playing the lead. The National Theatre revived it in 1976 for a West End season, and a movie was made of it in the same year, with Richard Burton repeating his Broadway success, and Peter Firth, who was in the original National Theatre production.

The first seed of the idea was planted in Shaffer's mind by the late James Mossman, who told him of hearing of a boy who had blinded a large number of horses because they had seen him being seduced by a girl. He also said that the boy's parents had been strict religious fanatics. It took Shaffer two years to complete the play. He does not remember how many times he wrote it and then tore it up. He found it impossible to find motivation for a boy blinding horses after being successfully seduced; 'I found myself thinking "he didn't actually make love" and then I had to ask myself *why* he didn't do it.' He and John Dexter, the director, agreed that it would be more interesting if the parents were reasonable, well-meaning people, not obviously repressive types that would drive any son crazy. The play only took its final form during rehearsal, with the production team collaborating in the making of crucial decisions. In his preface to the published text, Shaffer pays tribute to John Dexter, the director, who gave the play its 'vibrant and unforgettable life', and to John Napier, the designer of the horses' masks, Andy Phillips, who did the lighting, and Claude Chagrin, who arranged the mime sequences.

The conflict in *Equus* is between Martin Dysart, a psychiatrist, and Alan Strang, a teenage boy who has blinded six horses in a stable. The main plot concerns Dysart's successful efforts to get an explanation from Alan. Using various ruses, he pieces Alan's story together. The boy's father was a strict socialist who disapproved of television and regarded religion as superstition; the mother was more indulgent, allowing him to slip out to the neighbours to watch TV, and encouraging him in religious beliefs. The boy's favourite picture, of Christ being chained and beaten before the crucifixion, was torn down by his father; Alan replaced it with a life-like frontal view of a

horse. Alan's first experience of a horse had been on a seaside
beach as a small boy, when he had been given a fast ride by a
good-looking horseman. His parents had discovered this and
angrily dragged him off the horse. Alan had found the ride
sexy, and had felt for the horse, suffering with a chain in its
mouth, as for Christ. Gradually he had transferred his worship
to Equus, a god inhabiting all horses. He got a job in a stables
and took the horses out for secret night-rides, talking to them
and getting orgasms riding in the nude. Finally, his girl-friend,
working in the same stables, persuaded him to take her to a
'blue' movie. This was the first time he had ever seen a girl in
the nude. In the midst of this excitement he suddenly spotted
his father in the cinema. This was the third time his father had
interrupted a crucial sexual awakening or relationship—first,
pulling him off the horse on the beach, and then removing the
worshipped but suggestive picture of Christ in his bedroom.
While Alan was stiff suffering from the latest shock, and trying
to re-adjust to the idea that his ultra-respectable father was
really a hypocrite, the girl took him off to make love in the
stables. For him the stables were a kind of temple, so that the
sex became sacrilege; he feared he was being watched by the
horses, became impotent, drove the girl away in his shame, and
proceeded in a frenzy to blind the horses.

The story is told mostly in flash-backs. The play starts with
Alan embracing a horse, then Dysart recalls the case, and we
see the lady magistrate bringing Alan to his attention and
persuading him to undertake treatment. All the characters of
the play sit around the stage in a semi-circle, joining the action
as needed, and some of the audience sit on the stage behind
them, making the play a bit like a trial, and the audience like
a jury.

The unfolding of the story involves most of Shaffer's regular
preoccupations. Like the parents in *Five Finger Exercise*, Alan's
are socially and sexually incompatible. Alan intuitively realizes
that Dysart himself is unhappy and inadequate with his wife.
Alan's revolt against his parents, his need for worship and its
connection with his awakening sexual desires recall, in various
ways, *Five Finger Exercise*, *Shrivings* and *Royal Hunt of the Sun*.
But *Equus* is more exciting visually; each act ends with a

remarkable visual set-piece, and the two are cleverly contrasted with each other.

In the first, Alan, under gentle hypnosis, mimes undressing, climbing on horseback at night, and riding in mounting excitement till he has an orgasm, slumps off the horse and embraces it. The horses are played by actors in track suits and cage-like masks, through which their faces are visible. There is a chorus of horses humming a menacing ritualistic chant, so that the ride is at once an erotic and a religious experience. The attendant horses also revolve the platform on which Alan is riding, so that he appears to be circling the stage.

The second act ends with Alan, believing himself to be under the influence of a truth drug, having what is called an abreaction, re-enacting the crucial events of the night he blinded the horses. He and the girl actually undress and start to make love; the horses circling the stage stamp their metal hooves and their humming noise becomes very loud. Under pressure from Dysart, Alan admits that he found himself impotent and stabbed out the horses' eyes; and more horses appear on the stage, screaming. Some of them are 'archetypal images, judging, punishing, pitiless'.

After this, Dysart pronounces that Alan will be cured of his madness. But he is himself tortured by doubts about the effects of removing the boy's object of worship and purpose in life. Part of Dysart envies Alan his excitements and his visions. Even before he has 'cured' Alan, he expresses his doubts to Hesther, the lady magistrate.

Dysart: Can you think of anything worse one can do to anybody than take away their worship?
Hesther: Aren't you being a little extreme?
Dysart: Extremity's the point.
Hesther: Worship isn't destructive, Martin. I know that.
Dysart: I don't. I only know it's the core of life. What else has he got? Think about him. He can hardly read. He knows no physics or engineering to make the world real for him. No paintings to show him how others have enjoyed it. No music except television jingles. No history except tales from a desperate mother. No friends. Not one kid to give

him a joke, or make him know himself more moderately. He's a modern citizen for whom society doesn't exist. He lives *one hour* every three weeks—howling in a mist.

And Dysart admits his envy.

Dysart: All right, he's sick. He's full of misery and fear. He was dangerous and could be again, though I doubt it. But that boy has known a passion more ferocious than I have felt in any second of my life. And let me tell you something, I envy it.
Hesther: You can't . . .
Dysart: Don't you see? That's the Accusation! That's what his stare has been saying to me all this time. 'At least I galloped! When did you?'

This is the theme to which Shaffer recurs at the end of the play. In a long speech, Dysart condemns himself for being about to transform Alan from madness to dull normality.

Dysart: I'll erase the welts cut into his mind by flying manes. When that's done, I'll set him on a nice mini-scooter and send him puttering off into the Normal World where animals are treated *properly*: made extinct, or put into serviture, or tethered all their lives in dim light, just to feed it! I'll give him the good Normal World where we're tethered beside them—blinking our nights away in a non-stop drench of cathode-ray over our shrivelling heads! I'll take away his Field of Ha Ha, and give him Normal places for his ecstasy— multi-lane highways, driven through the guts of cities, extinguishing Place altogether, even the idea of Place! He'll trot on his metal pony tamely through the concrete evening —and one thing I promise you: he will never touch hide again! With any luck his private parts will come to feel as plastic to him as the products of the factory to which he will almost certainly be sent. Who knows? He may even come to find sex funny. Smirky funny. Bit of grunt funny. Trampled and furtive and entirely in control. Hopefully, he'll feel nothing at his fork but Approved Flesh. I doubt however with much passion! . . . Passion, you see, can be destroyed by a doctor. It cannot be created.

You won't gallop any more, Alan. Horses will be quite safe. You'll save your pennies every week, till you can change that scooter for a car, and put the odd 50p on the gee-gees, quite forgetting that they were anything more to you than bearers of little profits and little losses. You will, however, be without pain. More or less completely without pain.'

As in all Shaffer's plays, the arguments are fairly balanced. Hesther, the magistrate, puts the case for 'cure', and for putting a teenager out of his agony. Alan's parents, though quarrelling and responsible for his state, both mean well and are deeply upset by what has become of him. The father shows himself capable of compassion and understanding when his wife gets distraught. But the central unanswered question posed by *Equus* is whether we need an element of mysticism to give our lives meaning. It is, as Shaffer says, a play about worship.

Some critics have taken the view that the conflict between worship and psychiatry in *Equus* is phoney and irrational, effective in the theatre but not worthy of serious consideration. They have thought it self-evident that a young man should be released from his anxieties and fears, and have suggested that Dysart's doubts about the cure are suspect and sentimental. Many psychiatrists have taken the play as an attack on their profession. It is not intended to be, but is rather an attack on our society and our standards of 'normality'. Shaffer recognizes the Dionysiac forces in all of us, especially the young, and the need for beliefs and excitements beyond everyday experience, and he draws attention to the dangers of suddenly destroying such beliefs and excitements without providing any replacements. When I asked him if he himself longed for a faith, he enthusiastically answered 'oh, yes' but immediately added that he had not made much effort to find one. 'I do realize that what we call ordinary everyday experience is very far from ordinary or everyday, and that a lot of it is mysterious and miraculous. I feel that, and I want to feel it more. And I do believe that if life seems to have lost its savour, you can restore it by an effort of will.'

I also asked him about the apparent inconsistency between

the fully-dressed miming of the nude night ride at the end of the first act and the actual nude re-enactment of the climax. He pointed out that the difference in the text is between describing an earlier experience under hypnosis and having an abreaction, re-living the experience under an alleged truth-drug. But Shaffer admits that there were also compelling theatrical reasons for the difference. It was found in rehearsals that the night-ride in the nude actually looked silly; also it would have robbed the final scene of its surprise and shock value. Shaffer noted that the fully dressed scene is actually the more erotic. 'I wanted the end of the first act to be erotic and the end of the second anti-erotic and clinical, which is why the lighting is bright. In any case it's not necessary to be logical—it's an aesthetic choice. It's much more exciting this way and why not? After all, we are in the theatre.'

How much does Shaffer feel he owes to the new permissiveness, without which *Equus* could hardly have been written or staged in its present form? '*Five Finger Exercise* might seem a bit evasive now but Clive himself was genuinely confused about what he wanted. I don't believe all that much has changed with the change in sexual attitudes. The agony of discovering the truths of life for yourself remains much as ever. I could have written *Shrivings* before the abolition of censorship, except for a few words. After all, we had *Oedipus* and *Hamlet* when we had censorship, so not all that much has been gained. But it is good to be free to write anything one likes.'

Although rebellion against family, social and sexual conventions, and idealistic searchings for faith and wider experience recur in Shaffer's plays, they are never propaganda pieces. As we have seen, even the most narrow and conventional characters are always presented with sympathy and understanding, and Shaffer seems to see every conflicting point of view. 'The theatre must be concerned with ambiguity, because it's concerned with life,' he told me, 'and yet there must be clear images and ringing statements to make for drama.'

Shaffer is unusual among modern British dramatists in the breadth of his sympathies; he is also unusual in starting in the commercial theatre, before he graduated to the National. He has graduated back again:—*Black Comedy* was staged in the

West End after it had been dropped by the National and
Equus, also dropped by the National for a long time, was staged
on Broadway and then eventually, by the National, in the
West End. 'I'm very grateful to the National for giving me John
Dexter and such marvellous rehearsal conditions; we had
twelve weeks' rehearsal for *Royal Hunt*. And it's a great honour
to be produced there—I'm very proud of having been produced
there more than any other living playwright. But I'm also disappointed by the cavalier way they treat plays, dropping
successes much too quickly. Basically, I prefer subsidized to
commercial theatre. I like the repertory system, which keeps
actors fresh by giving them a change from day to day. I'd be
perfectly willing to devote myself to writing for the National,
if I could have a regular salary, keeping pace with the cost of
living, regular holidays and a pension. Then I would abandon
commercial motives forever.'

For most of his life Shaffer has been hesitant about labelling
himself 'a playwright'; rather, he thinks of himself as someone
who has written plays. 'I wrote my first play when I was 14 or
15, about Abraham and Isaac, and a long novel when I was
17, which I've never shown to anyone and never looked at
since. My mother stimulated my interest in the theatre—she
still goes as often as possible—but for a long time I didn't
think it was really respectable. My father regarded writing as
a leisure activity, not central to life and not a profession. He
thought I should have a definite profession and should go into
the family business. As I was always very lazy, and covered
it up by trying to be very industrious, and as I've always
regarded myself as totally unemployable, I did that. I was
able to live at home, making gestures of defiance but with
security. Then I was attracted by the idea of going to New
York, where I had lots of friends. The quota for English immigrants was never full in those days and I was able to get a job
in 1951. By 1954 I'd had enough of New York, for the time
being, I'd written my first play—*The Salt Land*—for television,
and I went back to London and worked for Boosey and Hawkes.
When they wanted me to learn all about brass band music, I
left. My father said he would support me while I tried to write.
My first plays were for television; *The Salt Land* was actually

one of the first plays to be presented on a British commercial channel. At the same time I was writing *Retreats*, which eventually became *Five Finger Exercise*.

'I have very little recollection how I wrote *Five Finger Exercise*; the experience of writing disappears once you have lived through it. It's a semi-autobiographical play, and it's what's called 'well-made'. I don't think a play can be 'well-made' enough; but you should conceal your own cleverness, your own 'making' of the play. I like plays to be like fugues—all the themes should come together at the end.'

This determination to make his plays work as precisely as possible is what led Shaffer to re-write so many of his plays. In addition to the three versions of *White Liars* and two versions of *Shrivings*, he also rewrote *Royal Hunt of the Sun* for a touring production in Britain. 'As soon as someone tells me they want to stage one of my plays, I start wondering how I should improve it. I'm aware of what seemed wrong with it before. For example I thought some of Pizarro's speeches were too prosey and too rhetorical, so I rewrote his role. It's easier to rewrite a play than to write a new one, because the structure is already there and you know what the problems are. On the other hand, it's dangerous because your style changes over the years, and your attitudes change too, so if you aren't careful the new bits stick out. You find yourself rewriting more and more, to make it work.'

It is very unusual to find a writer so concerned with ideas and psychological relationships who is also so skilful at creating striking visual and theatrical effects. Shaffer believes the theatre should be visual as well as verbal, though mainly verbal. He has become very interested in helping with the revivals of his plays, attending auditions and rehearsals and keeping a close eye on performances. He became virtually a co-director of *Equus* in the United States, wrote the film script, and was present on location throughout the filming. He would like to direct a play on his own, though probably not one of his own.

Four: Peter Nichols

Born: Bristol, England, July 31 1927.

Father: a commercial traveller in groceries for the Co-operative Wholesale Society; he did not approve of the theatre as a career. Mother had been an amateur singer and had wanted to be a professional. She took young Peter to perform with her in wartime concert parties. Uncle worked for a theatrical agent and often sent them free tickets to Bristol music-halls.

Education: Bristol Grammar School, where he wrote and staged revue sketches and entertainments but did not take part in official school plays. National Service in Royal Air Force, including Combined Services Entertainments in the Far East, where he was in a concert party with Kenneth Williams and Stanley Baxter, an experience which inspired *Privates on Parade.*

After National Service, got a state grant to study acting at Bristol Old Vic Theatre School. ('I did not want to be an actor, but they had no courses in writing plays.')

Was an actor for 5 years, then decided he was not good enough and went to Trent Park Teachers' Training College—spent two years as a teacher.

Married in 1959—four children—the first, a daughter, died at the age of ten and was the model for 'Joe Egg'.

Started writing plays while serving in R.A.F. in India. First plays were destroyed without being submitted to anyone; first plays produced were on television.

Plays:

The Hooded Terror (Bristol 1965). *A Day in the Death of Joe Egg* (Glasgow and London 1967; New York 1968). *The National Health* (London 1969; Chicago 1971; New York 1974). *Forget-Me-Not-Lane* (London 1971; New Haven, Conn. 1973). *Chez Nous* (London 1974). *The Freeway* (London 1974). *Harding's Luck* (children's play adapted from Nesbit story—London 1974). *Privates on Parade* (London 1977).

Arts Council bursary 1961. *Evening Standard* Awards 1967, 1969.
Plays and Players Award 1969. Resident dramatist, Tyrone
Guthrie Theatre, Minneapolis, U.S.A. in 1976.

NICHOLS FIRST ACHIEVED fame and success in the theatre
by the unlikely means of making a comedy out of the plight of
parents with a spastic daughter who is little better than a
vegetable. He followed it up with a play set in a National
Health Service hospital, and managed to make music-hall
humour out of illness and death. It seemed as if an obsession
with illness and a penchant for black comedy were to be his
hallmarks. However, his later plays, until *Privates on Parade*,
deal with more conventional aspects of life—marital squabbles,
family relationships, social inequalities and class rivalries.
They too are amusing, and reveal a sharp ear for colloquial
dialogue and a strong sense of theatre. But they are less original
and have on the whole been less highly praised and less successful. *Privates on Parade* marks a return to music-hall style and
to sick humour—there is even a comic military funeral—and
was an immediate success on its first production.

A Day in the Death of Joe Egg starts with a device which was
still fairly unusual in the British theatre in 1967 and which
Nichols, like many of the new British playwrights, uses regularly—the music-hall technique of having actors step out of
character and speak directly to the audience. In *Joe Egg*, Bri
starts by addressing the audience as if they were the class he is
teaching at school. In a sense he is in character, and his speech
serves the double purpose of establishing him as a harassed
schoolteacher and of getting the audience to quieten down for
the play to begin.

Bri comes on without warning. Shouts at audience.
Bri: That's enough! (*Pause. Almost at once, louder.*) I said
enough! (*Pause. Stares at audience.*) Another word and you'll
all be here till five o'clock. Nothing to me, is it? I've got all
the time in the world.

This opening speech continues for some time; then the stage lights brighten and we see Bri returning home to his wife Sheila. Their dialogue speedily establishes their jokey relationship, their frank, trendy lifestyle, Bri's sexual desire for Sheila, her cool appraisal of him, and Nichols' mastery of sharp and lifelike conversation.

Bri comes home with a comic black spider on his face, which frightens Sheila.

Bri: I confiscated it. From Terry Hughes.
Sheila: Vicious sod!
Bri: He *is*. For thirteen.
Sheila: You, I mean.
Bri: In Religious Instruction.
Sheila: It's not funny.
Bri: What I told *him*.

A few seconds later—

Bri: Let's go to bed.
Sheila: At quarter to five?
Bri: I came home early specially.
Sheila: The usual time.
Bri: Yeah, but I was *going* to keep them in.
Sheila: Who?
Bri: Four D.
Sheila: Did you *say* you would?
Bri: Yes.
Sheila: To them?
Bri: Yes.
Sheila: Then why didn't you?
Bri: I kept imagining our bed, our room, your legs thrashing about—
Sheila: When *are* you going to learn?
Bri: My tongue half-way down your throat—
Sheila: You must carry out your threats—
Bri: —train screaming into tunnel—
Sheila: They'll never listen to you if you don't—
Bri: —waves breaking on rocky shore.
(*She moves out of his reach. Pause. He sips tea. Winces.*) Sugar. (*He helps himself.*)

Sheila: You want bromide.

Bri: I want you. It's you I want. (*Turns, makes a joke of it, pointing to her like the advert.*) I want you, Kitchener, look. I want you. (*She smiles. He sits and drinks.*)

Sheila: You should have kept them in.

Bri: I did for a bit. Then I left them with their hands on heads and went to fetch my coat and suddenly couldn't face then any more, so I never went back. Wonder how long they sat there.

Sheila: Brian—

Bri: Terry Hodges, Fatty Brent. . . . Glazebrook, the shop-steward—he's got a new watch. And of course Scanlon—(*shakes his head at the idea.*) the Missing Link. Pithecanthropus Erectus.

Sheila: Has he flashed it lately?

Bri: Not at the teachers anyway.

Sheila: Only that once.

Bri: That once was the only time it was reported.

Sheila: Poor girl.

Bri: Some of the older women might keep quiet. Hope for more.

Sheila: What happened to that girl?

Bri: Never heard of since.

Sheila: Not surprising.

Bri: Shortest teaching career on record. Thirty-five minutes.

The relationship between them having been established, their child Joe is brought on. She is ten, mostly lies supine in an invalid chair, and only makes a noise transliterated as 'Aaaah!' Bri and Sheila cover their pain with a jocular manner, even inventing conversation for the baby and taking it in turns to mouth 'her' dialogue.

Bri: See the Christmas trees, Mum.

Sheila: Did you see the Christmas trees? *What* a clever girl!

Bri: And Jesus.

Sheila: Jesus?

Bri: Bathed in light, in the sky.

Sheila (*aside, to Bri*): She got a screw loose, Dad?

Bri: No, Mum.

Sheila: Seeing Jesus?
Bri: On top the Electricity Building.
Sheila: (*relieved*) Oh yes! Thought she was off her chump for a minute, Dad.
Bri: Seeing Jesus in a dump like this? No wonder, Mum. But no, she's doing well, they say.
Sheila: Daddy's pleased you're trying, love. What with your eleven-plus on the way.
(*Bri gives a short burst of laughter, then resumes*)
Bri: You want to get to a decent school.
Sheila: I don't want to be shunted into some secondary modern slum, she says.

This dialogue reveals another of Nichols' specialities, the way he relates his characters and plots to topical issues. The argument about the selective eleven-plus examination as a result of which children were 'streamed' into different types of schools was a key issue in British politics for many years, while shop-stewards and trade union leaders like Hugh Scanlon were stock targets for abuse in middle-class homes. The comedy is also the sugar around the central pill of *Joe Egg*. It soon transpires that Joe has been having fits at the Spastics Centre because they ran out of the special anti-convulsant medicine; they also let her sit in wet nappies all day. Bri and Sheila are suffering from the strain over Joe. Sheila has a guilt complex about her promiscuity and wonders if it could in some way have caused Joe's abnormal birth. She thinks that Bri is self-indulgent and mother-dominated. Bri is suffering from sexual starvation. Both of them explain their attitudes in direct addresses to the audience. Bri even shows awareness of the audience by asking, when describing Sheila's sexual habits, 'How shall I put it in a way that will prevent a sudden stampede to the exit-doors?' or by interrupting Sheila's speech with 'What are you telling them?'
Nichols takes music-hall technique further, with sketches in which Bri impersonates a hearty doctor who only paid half-attention to Joe's problems, a heavily German-accented psychiatrist who tells them 'your daughter vos a wegetable' and a vicar who offers the 'laying on of hands'. Even when they

are re-enacting these scenes, Bri and Sheila improvise new jokes and are amused by each other's ingenuity. Bri, as the psychiatrist, tries to explain why Joe's brain does not work.

Bri: Imagine a svitchboard. A telephone svitchboard, ja?
Sheila: I worked as a telephone switchboard operator once.
Bri: Das ist wunderbar! Vell. Imagine you're sitting zere now, facing ze board. So?
Sheila: So.
Bri: Some lines tied up, some vaiting to be used—suddenly brr-brr, brr-brr—
Sheila: Incoming call?
Bri: Exactly! You plug in.
Sheila (*mimes it, assuming a bright telephone voice*): Universal Shafting.
Bri (*coming out of character*): What?
Sheila: That was the firm I worked for.
Bri: You've never put that in before.
Sheila (*shrugs*): I thought I would this time.
Bri: Universal Shafting? Story of your life.

At the end of the first act Sheila confesses to the audience that she only joins in these jokes to please Bri, to help him live with the situation. She still has faith that Joe may improve, Bri has none. In the second act, they are visited by another couple, Freddie and Pam, and by Bri's mother, Grace. Freddie attacks their jokes and suggests they are symptomatic of a British malaise: 'the whole country giggling its way to disaster'. They think the child should be placed in an institution but are horrified by Bri's support of euthanasia. Bri pretends to have suffocated Joe while Sheila was out, and later he gives her an overdose of medicine. Then he leaves her out in the cold to die of exposure, but she is found and saved in hospital. Bri decides to leave Sheila, who thinks he has just gone to arrange for Joe to be admitted to a residential hospital. The play ends with Sheila alone on stage, planning a second honeymoon, and talking maternally to her goldfish, her caged bird—and Joe. For all the laughs, it is a hopeless situation.

The 'message' of *Joe Egg*, if there is one, is that only euthanasia could have made life really tolerable for Sheila and Bri.

Euthanasia is also favourably mentioned in Nichols's next play, *The National Health*. This was commissioned by the National Theatre, following the success of *Joe Egg*, and incorporated Nichols's television play *The End Beds*, a study of life in the general ward of a large hospital, based on his own experiences with a collapsed lung. For the stage he added fantasy scenes, parodying television soap-opera, and a compere, Barnet the hospital porter, to comment on the action and defuse moments of emotional tension with camp music hall comedy.

His first entry, pushing a wheel chair and addressing the audience though ostensibly talking to the *male* patients, is typical.

Barnet: Come along, ladies, come along. Knickers on and stand by your beds. Those that can't stand, lie to attention. No, it's wicked to laugh. I said to this old man in the next ward, I said, 'Dad, you better watch your step,' he said, 'Why?', I said, 'They're bringing in a case of syphilis.' He said, 'Well, it'll make a change from Lucozade.'

The fantasy part of the plot is concerned with a West Indian nurse's affair with a young hospital doctor; his father, a senior surgeon, disapproves of racially mixed marriages, drives his son near to collapse and then saves his life in a dramatic operation. All this is presented in the larger-than-life terms of a sentimental serial or a B-movie. A plea for racial tolerance comes through the parody, just as Barnet's camp remarks contain a plea for sexual tolerance. The more serious part of the play is centred on the various contrasted characters seen in the ward.

Mackie: The early Socialists thought . . . if we achieved this, the rest would follow.
Foster: Achieved what?
Mackie: This state we're in. This ward. Where men are prevented from death by poverty or curable sickness even the least intelligent . . . least healthy or useful . . .
Foster: You've got to do what you can for people—
Mackie: Can't cure loneliness—boredom—ugliness . . . but at least you can see they're lonely on clean sheets . . . ugly on tapioca pudding . . .

Foster: Why can't you try to look on the bright side?

Mackie: I'm dying of a stomach cancer and the pain's only bearable with pethidine and morphine. I've asked them to let me die . . . but because of their outdated moral assumptions they have to keep me going . . .

Foster: Isn't life precious though?

Mackie: *Good* life. Useful life. Good *death's* precious too, when the time comes. If you can get it. My heart's stopped once already, which used to be called death . . . now they bring you back . . . I've had it written in my records, don't bring me back again.

Mackie also conducts his argument with the ward Sister.

Sister: Wouldn't you like a chat with the Chaplain?

Mackie: I parted company with organized religion some years ago . . . when I saw it was being used to justify the activities of cretins . . . Jesus Christ lived in a largely unpopulated world . . . disease and natural hazards killed off multitudes every year . . . kept the balance of nature . . . if He came back today, He wouldn't say, 'Thou shalt not kill', He'd advocate mass euthanasia . . .

Sister: We can't estimate the value of a life.

Mackie: Time we could. Not enough kidney machines, someone's going to have to . . .

Sister: I'm not going to stand here listening to all this childish nonsense.

Mackie: If somebody doesn't let us die—or prevent others being born—there are going to be seventy million British by the turn of the century—

Sister: I shall get you a sedative.

If there is an effective answer to the argument for euthanasia, Nichols does not provide it. He does provide a tragi-comic picture of hospital life, as a microcosm of society, which ends as ambiguously as *Joe Egg*. There are only two patients left in the ward, a young man who has been reduced to playing like a baby, following brain damage in a motor-bike crash, and a melancholy ex-teacher, who has made himself at home in the hospital and talks endlessly and nostalgically to everyone about 'my boys', and about the old days of 'grace' and 'style'. The serious and fantasy elements of the play are brought together in a wedding finale : the surgeon and the ward sister, the surgeon's son and the black nurse lead a wedding march and Barnet reappears as a black-faced minstrel to speak the last words.

> Barnet: It's a funny old world we live in and you're lucky to get out of it alive.
> *(A black-face band marches on playing a cakewalk and Barnet joins them with a tambourine or banjo. At once the whole company dances to the music. CURTAIN. Curtain rises and dance continues. Each group comes down to bow; bridal quartet first, next nursing staff, then patients. Music and dance stop suddenly. A silent tableau, the patients frozen in their attitudes. CURTAIN.)*

Nichols's next two plays, *Forget-Me-Not-Lane* and *Chez Nous*, are much more conventional in content, focusing on family life and personal relationships. *Forget-Me-Not-Lane* is unconventional in form, being part-play and part-revue, but its concern with the frustrations of marriage and its interest in changing attitudes to education, class, and race are typical of many plays of the period. Nichols is more sympathetic to the past, and to the human foibles of the present, than many of his contemporaries, poking tolerant fun at social institutions rather than launching all-out attacks on them. The play is largely auto-biographical, casting a nostalgic eye back to his youth and contrasting Britain in wartime and twenty-five years later.

The nostalgic mood is set before the play begins, with a recital of wartime pop music from Vera Lynn to the Squadronaires. Frank, a middle-aged lecturer at a technical college, wanders on and off the stage during the introductory music and then launches into a monologue of reminiscence. As he recalls his parents, they come on, to be joined by Frank's younger self, a 14-year-old boy, and Urse, his girl-friend who later becomes Ursula, his wife. The opening domestic scene is set in Shaffer's psychological territory, though in a lower social stratum. The father, a commercial traveller, criticizes his son for being un-tidy, sloppy about language, and idle, and criticizes his wife for spoiling the boy. The mother complains about not being allowed to follow her career as a singer, and the boy calls his father a cruel tyrant and sings at wartime concert parties with his mother. The middle-aged Frank stays on the sidelines as a commentator, and the action switches frequently between past and present.

The 14-year-old Frank sides unequivocally with his mother against his father; the middle-aged one is less certain, reflecting on his childish certainties about his parents in a soliloquy.

Frank: How could I possibly understand them at fourteen? Their complicated middle-aged game of regret and recrimination? My own experience was confined to chasing high-school girls through the city museum at lunch-time. Oh, those stuffed kangaroos! Those tableaux of British wild-life! That scent of gravy! I took a party of students last week and I'm glad to say it's resisted all attempts at modernization. The hippopotamus still yawns beside the fire buckets. (*Screws his eyes tight shut and claps his hands*) Stick to the point, man! The point was that I couldn't understand the sophisticated war my parents were conducting—either the issues or the strategy. But I was in the line of fire. So instead of understanding I took sides. Dad was a monster, Mum a martyr. But it might have been just as true the other way; Mum a shrew and Dad henpecked. What did my own boy make of it when at thirteen he watched Ursula and me growling and roaring at each other? Yes, that's one of the reasons I left her. Having seen my parents like cat-and-dog year after year, I wanted to save my son that spectacle.

Just as the brief description of the city museum immediately conjures up a typical picture of one of those dreary establishments, so Nichols fills in a great deal of detailed wartime background which brings the period back to all who lived through it. Young Frank recalls his father's black market deals, and the sexual excitement aroused in him, as in so many young men and women, by American soldiers, 'skidding about the semis in their sexy jeeps with tight-arsed trousers and Hollywood names'. Like many of Shaffer's heroes, Frank has a gay or bisexual streak. At one point Young Frank dresses up in his mother's clothes and gets wolf whistles from an American sentry, at another he is nearly seduced by a phoney Chinese conjuror. He makes a further confession in conversation with Ivor, a school-friend.

Ivor: Hey, man, you know when you toss off—
Young Frank: Yeah.
Ivor: —d'you pretend you're a man or a woman?
Young Frank: I keep changing about. Sometimes I'm a slave girl like Hedy Lamarr and my master whips me a lot and I cringe and beg for mercy. Then I come in as the brave bloke—
Ivor: Alan Ladd?
Young Frank: Yeah. And beat up this cruel bloke and then I'm Hedy Lamarr again and terrifically glad I shan't be whipped any more . . . so I take me in my arms and surrender . . . then I'm the brave bloke and hold her tight . . . keep changing round.
Ivor: I pretend I'm the bloke all the time.

This frank dialogue, which would have been unthinkable only a few years earlier, not only captures some typical masturbatory fantasies but also evokes a period when most young people in Britain were modelling themselves on Hollywood. Nichols similarly uses conventional schoolboy smut and sexual exploration to comment on the way wartime youth was brought up in isolation from Nazi-occupied Europe and given a traditional education which was later to seem largely irrelevant.

Young Frank: Hey, you know Jacobs in Four A.
Ivor: Terrific swot, yeah.
Young Frank: I saw his tool when we changed for gym. You seen it?
Ivor: No.
Young Frank: It's different to everyone else's.
Ivor: More like a knob?
Young Frank: Yeah.
Ivor: I've seen some like that.
Frank: We knew so little about the Jews.
Ursula: They were in the Bible and Shakespeare.
Frank: But that was nothing to do with Jacobs of Four A.
Ursula: And my uncle sometimes made a veiled remark about band-leaders.

Frank: There was Dad's Ikey Cohen . . . but when you think
what was happening a few hundred miles away!
Ursula: And our history lessons were still about Clive and
Wolfe and Arkwright's Spinning Jenny.

Later we see Young Frank aged about 20, just back from
National Service in India with a new 'posh' accent, more
intellectual interests and a political awareness of the emerging
'Third World'. He has grown away from Ivor and from Amy,
his mother.

Having done National Service instead of having a teenage
period of irresponsibility, wild oats and fun, the middle-aged
Frank is to some extent jealous of his son, Bill, for enjoying
freedom and affluence, without having had to struggle for it.
Bill is in rebellion against society, but still comes to his father
for money. Frank ironically tries to dissuade him from relying
on such an unegalitarian, bourgeois institution as the family.

Frank: The family presupposes preference. Means people
put their nearest and dearest first. Surely your new paradise
won't allow that degree of discrimination. The family will
have to go, Bill, along with nation, class, creed, won't it?

Frank also delivers a long diatribe against marriage and the
family, but ultimately he is not a revolutionary, and recognizes
that it cannot be avoided.

Frank: We're all in the genetic trap. However highly we
regard ourselves, we owe our being to some unlikely people
we meet at Christmas. We struggle at the end of our strings
but here we are with our father's hands . . . our mother's
sneeze . . . their middle-aged indigestion . . .

Forget-Me-Not-Lane ends with Frank and Ursula about to go
off on a 'second honeymoon'. She nags him, as before, and goes
off, slamming the door, leaving him to finish the packing. He
asks himself if he can stand much more of this and immediately
answers 'Oh yes, much more.' While packing he sees a vision
of the young Ursula, showing him her naked schoolgirl body
for the first time. He closes the suitcase and follows his wife to
the bedroom, as the curtain falls. In a final stage direction,

Nichols says: *After their bows, the actors sing* Forget-Me-Not-Lane *and go off severally by the doors.*

Chez Nous is described by Nichols as 'a domestic comedy' and is a frank account of the sexual activities of two married couples who share a holiday home in France. They are successful professional people—Dick, a pediatrician and the author of a book on child care, and his wife Liz, and Phil, an architect, and his wife Diana. In the first act of the play it emerges that Dick's and Liz's latest baby is not actually their child at all, but an illegitimate grand-child. Their daughter has not revealed the identity of the father, who turns out to be Phil. Later Dick and Diana think of eloping together. There is talk of Phil adopting his baby, but this is resisted by Liz. Finally everything remains much as it was at the beginning, but with everyone having a fuller knowledge of the situation and having faced up to its various consequences.

The plot is just a thin thread on which Nichols hangs very 'permissive' conversation about personal relationships and the nature of marriage. The characters are successful and trendy professional people, and therefore this conversation is plausible. At times the play appears to be an attack on marriage, the family and conventional morality, but actually it is a study of the frustrations of middle-age, and of the way people generally accept their lot and give up trying to change it.

The Freeway was Nichols's second play for the National Theatre, following the success of *The National Health*, but the success was not repeated, either with the critics or with the public. Nichols had an original and interesting idea—a gigantic traffic-jam, stretching for miles, in a slightly futuristic Britain. The motorists and their families cannot escape, and are cut off from food, water and essential services. This idea builds up all sorts of expectations which are not fulfilled, and the second act is an anti-climax. The characters are a kind of cross-section of present-day British life, from James, an aristocrat full of high-sounding phrases but not above bribing the police and getting preferential treatment for himself and his eccentric but surprisingly practical mother, to Les, a solid and successful trade unionist, and his generous, warm-hearted wife, May. Les supports the right-wing government, which won an election on the promise of 'a car for every family and enough roads to drive them on'; the play shows this policy breaking down, in a society where the roads are blocked and have to be guarded by a new-style militia.

> May: Well, tell me, how are we going to live without the Cherokee? How shall I get to the corner shop the far side of the motorway with the nearest bridge a mile off? If I want a bag of sugar or a dozen eggs, Les takes me on the fly-over, drops me by the shop—
> Les: There's nowhere to pull in, so I keep circling the roundabout while she's in the shop till I see her waiting at the kerb.

The futuristic picture is painted early in the play by a newsreader heard over loudspeakers.

> Newsman: The Autoclubs report that travellers on the Royal Freeway may experience some delay. The cause is apparently another demonstration by the Scrubbers, the anti-motor group whose avowed aim is to paralyse the Freeway. The incident began with two ordinary collisions, each involving less than thirty vehicles, but rescuers arrived to find the terrorists already occupying the wreckage. Mobile mercy teams were given access to clear the dead and wounded although the Scrubbers have remained in position, blocking the Northbound Freeway, chanting slogans and, as these pictures show, exposing their private parts to the watching newsmen. A spokesman says the situation is not so far regarded as serious, through travellers are advised to avoid the Freeway and its linkroads. Those with unavoidable journeys might, at their own risk, try exploring the old A-roads and motorways. In this case, drivers should be armed and are advised to keep their windows firmly closed against marauding bands of lorry-drivers.

However Nichols does not supply many further details of the nature of the society, or of the struggle between various armed groups, nor does he show any eruption of violence. Instead the play is a fairly gentle comedy, poking fun at class distinctions and familiar patterns of social behaviour. Some of it is very funny, such as the scene when Barry Potter, the Minister of Movement, visits the jam. He is discussing the situation with James and Les, who is a strong supporter of the road programme, and who says the crowd would skin Barry alive if he tried to order them to leave their cars. At that moment they are interrupted by Barry's pre-recorded announcement of the evacuation, which was not meant to be broadcast till after his departure.

Barry (*speakers*): Tally-ho, all freewheelers! This is the Minister of Movement, fresh from a traditional walkabout.
Barry: Not yet!
James: Oh, Lord!
Barry (*speakers*): Now I've had a chance to see for myself the sacrifice you're making to help us deal with the crisis. A crisis brought about by two very different groups of extremists.
Barry (*over this, moving to Security Man*): Get through and tell then to turn that fucking thing off—
Barry (*speakers*): And I know from what you've said to me that when someone waves the big stick, you don't want us to wave the white flag.
Barry (*back to fence*): I'll have that man on a charge so fast his feet won't touch the ground.
Barry (*speakers*): And when I tell you that in the interests of public health, we must now begin to evacuate the Freeway, I'm sure you'll accept—
Les (*same time*): What's that he's saying?
Barry (*speakers*): that it's one of those irksome things that sometimes have to be done.
Barry: Potter here, are you receiving me? Over.
Barry (*speakers*): Operation Dunkirk will begin immediately with Phase One: leaving the linkroads. I can't promise that the Long Walk ahead will be without its hazards.
Les: Long Walk?
Barry (*speakers*): But as you leave your keys in your vehicles and gather your essential hand baggage, you will know that
—(*Suddenly cut off, Barry comes down to fence and stares over at speakers*)

Barry: I'll throw the book at that dopey bugger!

The contrast between the smooth public Barry heard on the speakers and the bad-tempered out-of-control one seen on the stage is very funny, and recalls the technique Nichols used in *Forget-Me-Not-Lane*, when middle-aged Frank confronted his own younger self. It also reflects a strong public feeling in Britain at the time—that politicians are unreliable hypocrites, always abandoning or breaking their election promises. The play ends pointedly, theatrically and amusingly, with James and his mother being evacuated by helicopter from the roof of Les and May's caravan. James excuses himself ('public duties') for abandoning his friends and pompously tells Les what a pleasure and privilege it has been to share the experience with him. While the others are left to slog away on foot, and forced to abandon their cars, Nichols provides a final touch of cynicism —two policemen prepare to drive James's car to his game lodge. Wally, a working man who has declined promotion and opted out of the materialistic rat-race, remains alone on the road, with a wood-pigeon he has trapped, singing a song.

Wally (*sings to himself*):
>So what care I for my goose-feather bed
>With the sheet turned down so bravely-oh—
>Tonight I shall sleep in the cold open field . . .
>(*Crash of thunder as Wally puts up his hood and drops to roll under fence. Hear rain falling heavily. Curtain.*)

Privates on Parade takes a wry look at the British army in Singapore during the terrorist emergency which began in 1948. Primarily it is an extremely funny representation of a service concert party, run by a Captain Dennis who specializes in 'drag' impersonations of Marlene Dietrich and Carmen Miranda and even off-stage addresses his fellow-officers and soldiers by girls' names. There are a lot of 'camp' jokes and doubles entendres; several of the characters are obvious homosexuals. It is possible to take the play merely as brilliant, outrageous light entertainment. But it also reveals a number of critical social attitudes. If the homosexuals are faintly ridiculed, so is the commanding officer, Major Flack, with his crusading Christianity and anti-Communism. There is a quietly ironic and moving scene at the end, when a Sergeant-Major is killed by terrorists. In a funeral oration, Major Flack announces that he had arranged for the dead man's wife to come from England to join him as a surprise. At the same time, at the back of the stage, we see the dead man's male lover giving him a farewell kiss. A recurring theme throughout the play is racism; the British soldiers treat the natives as less than human. The final disaster, when the concert party is ambushed, is caused by Major Flack totally ignoring his native servants, discussing troop movements in front of them as if they did not exist. To some extent *Privates on Parade* is a nostalgic evocation of a lost world; to a greater extent it is a condemnation of past attitudes and life-styles.

Michael Blakemore's production for the Royal Shakespeare Company contributed powerfully to the play's success, with a great variety of lighting effects and techniques for the numerous revue numbers. He blended these numbers into the rest of the play to give it a coherent, quasi-music-hall style throughout. Denis Quilley's remarkable performance as Captain Dennis was also a key ingredient in the play's popularity, which seems destined to be widespread and long-lived. The management's rather coy description of it as 'possibly not suitable for children' seemed a little dated in an age when children are exposed to frank discussion of sexual problems and aberrations on television. Like all Nichols's plays, *Privates on Parade* is based on people and situations he himself has experienced, though in some cases the experience has been vicarious, derived from a play or a film. 'I can only write dialogue when I hear people's voices in my mind; my writing is not really creative—it comes from memory and imitation—I've always been a good mimic. And I write comedies because I just don't see things tragically. My characters meet adversity cheerfully and humorously, as I try to do.

'*Joe Egg* is based on the experience of our first child, who died when she was ten. Somehow it never seemed as terrible to us as it did to our friends. My wife and I have seen much worse cases; our child was more like a pet cat than a human being. We came to accept the situation, and to joke about it, like the parents in the play. But the parents in the play are not me and my wife, though they were originally, in my first draft.

'*The National Health* was partly written before *Joe Egg*, as a television play called *The End Beds*, which was not shown because it was considered too depressing. It concentrated entirely on realistic scenes in the ward; the fantasy scenes and the music-hall character of the porter were added for the stage. The play was based on my experiences in hospital when I had a collapsed lung, before and during the early years of my marriage. *Forget-Me-Not-Lane* is autobiographical too, with both parents closely modelled on my own. *Chez Nous* owes its setting to the fact that we have a house in the Dordogne, where we go every school holidays. It's about the irksomeness of marriage and the family, and the way people grow out of one family only to will themselves into another. All my married men are a bit like that—they feel trapped, and want to be free, but realize they probably couldn't make it on their own. So they generally settle to stay with what they've got. I'm not at all like Whitehead, trying to destroy marriage and the family. It's another thing my characters find they have to accept. Originally *Chez Nous* ended with Dick going upstairs to type a farewell note—he was actually going to leave. But that didn't seem right and also it didn't make a good ending—nothing happening on the stage, just the sound of an off-stage typewriter. So I altered it during the previews. I suddenly got the idea that he could try to break an egg again, and find he couldn't, just like he couldn't break the grip of his family.'

Nichols thinks that in some ways *The Freeway* is the most honest of his plays. 'It's the one I'm most satisfied with. I felt strongly about the fraud of the motor-car, the claim that it gives people greater freedom when it really provides them with a new form of captivity. But perhaps I made a mistake setting it in the future. I wanted to exaggerate and parody the present, but I didn't want audiences to opt out, thinking it was nothing to do with them. All the characters are real, based on people I know. The second act turned out to be something of an anticlimax. I should have made it about mobility, to contrast with the immobility of the first act; I should have shown the people being forced to travel up the road, seeing contemporary England, in a kind of epic. It's not meant to be a grim play, but jolly, with people carrying on happily, ignoring the threat in the background. People live with horror, and accept it fairly cheerfully. In fact I wanted the set to be much more attractive, with trees in the background, not grim or sinister.'

Like many modern playwrights, Nichols leaves his plays fairly open-ended, with the audience free to draw its own conclusions. Bri leaves Sheila at the end of *Joe Egg*, but we wonder if he will return, and what would really be best for them. Nichols himself is not certain, or dogmatic, which is why he can so frequently alter the plots of his plays while writing them. 'It usually takes me about a year to finish a play; the first draft takes three or four months and then there are one or two complete re-writes. Each of these is also altered and revised quite a lot. I often wonder if it's worth all the trouble, whether the final version really is better than the first. But ideas do occur in the rewriting. And Michael Blakemore, who has directed four of my plays, works a lot on the scripts and makes constructive suggestions. I don't rewrite my plays once they have been produced, though my stage work does incorporate quite a lot of material I originally wrote for television.'

Five: E. A. Whitehead

Born: Liverpool, England, 1933.

Father: a linotype operator on the local newspaper; mother was employed in a tin works. Parents were both Roman Catholics, but only married when he was 19.

Education: Roman Catholic elementary school and Jesuit grammar school. Was one of the first to benefit from the Education Act providing greater educational opportunities for working-class children. Won a classical scholarship to Christ's College, Cambridge, where he read English. Brought up as a Roman Catholic and passionately interested in theology, he joined the Heretics Club at Cambridge, discovered Sartre and the Existentialists, and had a deconversion, deciding that 'the universe is empty'.

Two years national service in the infantry as a corporal, having been rejected for a commission, partly because he declared himself an atheist. After the army, a series of menial jobs for short periods—bus conductor, milkman, postman—'perhaps to show I was part of the "beat" generation or perhaps to stay true to my working-class origins and to avoid the white-collar ladder, which I despised.'

Married in 1958 and, needing more money to support his wife and two daughters, took a white-collar job as a sales promotion writer for a mail-order firm. Later worked as an advertising copy-writer in London and in Liverpool. A colleague in the London office lent him texts of plays by Osborne and Pinter, and introduced him to the new drama. Until then he had no interest in the theatre. On finding that plays could be successfully written about present-day people and problems, in modern colloquial speech, he started writing dramas intended for television but never produced. Only after the success of *The Foursome*

did he settle in London and become a full-time writer.
Divorced 1975, married again 1976.
   1971–2: Resident dramatist, Royal Court, London.
Evening Standard Award 1971. Arts Council Fellow in
Writing, Bulmershe College, Reading, 1976–77. Drama
critic of the *Spectator* 1977.
Plays: The Foursome (London 1971; Washington, D.C. 1972;
New York 1973). *Alpha Beta* (London 1972; Washington and
New York 1973). *The Sea Anchor* (London 1974). *Old Flames*
(Bristol 1975; London 1976). *Mecca* (London 1977).
(Until 1977 Whitehead always used his initials rather than his
Christian names but *Mecca* was published under the name 'Ted
Whitehead'. He never uses his full names—Edward Arthur.)

ALL WHITEHEAD'S PLAYS are concerned with the battle
between men and women—in and outside marriage—and the
destructive effects on both sexes of trying to live up to traditional social norms. In particular they are concerned with the
ambivalence of human desires to have lasting relationships and
at the same time to be free. This ambivalence is summed up in
Old Flames by a dialogue between the only male character,
Edward, and his mistress, Sally:

Edward: I want to be fused with somebody else and I want
to be free. And I want them to be fused with me and I want
them to be free.
Sally: Do you mean free to fuck?
Edward: I mean free to have other relationships.

The *Foursome* takes place on a beach near Liverpool. There
are just four characters—two young men and the two teenage
girls they picked up in a pub the night before. When the play
was first produced, at the Theatre Upstairs and at the small
Fortune Theatre in the West End, it was notable for the set, a
floor covered in mounds of real sand. It is also notable for
extremely frank dialogue, including references to toilet and
hygiene habits not previously discussed even in the permissive
theatre, and for its apparent misogyny. The girls were depicted
as brainless, forever daubing themselves with cosmetics, never

washing, giggling inanely and leading the two men on to expect
sexual fulfilment without providing it. The men were also
depicted fairly unflatteringly; at the end of the play they tell
the girls to go on ahead to the van and then escape by another
route, leaving the girls stranded. They also indulge in quite a
lot of horseplay together, including a mock striptease, which
causes the girls to suggest that they are 'queer'.

One of the biggest *frissons* felt by the audience was when the
girls returned to the beach from 'going for a piss' and came on
wiping their legs saying, 'Sorry, lads . . . it's the drips!' Words
like 'fuck', 'arse', 'piss' and 'shit' occur frequently, the girls
constantly refer to the men as 'dirty buggers' and early on in
the play there is a colloquial reference to menstruation:

> Tim: She looked a bit shy.
> Harry: I think she had the rags up.
> Tim: And how would you know?
> Harry: I had a bit of finger pie.
> Tim (*laughing*): Did you lick your fingers after? (*Harry laughs
> and lies, loudly sniffing his fingers.*) The van smelt like a fish shop
> after.
> Harry (*wry*): It smells like a bloody scent counter this
> morning.

The dialogue also contains some local dialect: 'pipping' for
peeping, 'butties' for sandwiches, but the plot is universal. The
play consists mostly of realistic, earthy, colloquial talk, but
there is some action. At the end of the second act, the men
force the girls to play a ball game, getting more and more violent in their persuasion. Harry holds Marie down and pours
sand over her face, she kicks him between the legs, and then
Tim starts throwing away the contents of Marie's handbag,
including false eyelashes, artificial suntan, and face cream,
shouting, 'Muck, muck, muck.' He grabs Bella's stockings and
burns them while telling the girls, 'You reek of piss and powder.'
This act ends with the men forcing the girls down towards the
sea, to scrub 'the muck' off them.

Alpha Beta has only two characters, a married couple called
Mr and Mrs Elliot. It opened at the main Royal Court Theatre

and then transferred to the larger Apollo, in the West End. It
had an all-star cast, Albert Finney and Rachel Roberts, and is
simply a duologue in which it becomes apparent that they are
destroying each other.

Alpha Beta opens with the husband making coffee but not
offering it it his wife. When she asks why, he says, 'When I
want to crap, do you want to crap?' In an argument with her,
he denounces working-class morality as 'rigid and depraving':

> Mrs Elliot: Depraving?
> Mr Elliot: Yes, because it's stallion-style morality—the
> principle is very simple: the male pokes everything he can
> get until one day he inadvertently pokes himself into wed-
> lock; after that he stops poking and starts lusting. The
> morality is rigid because, once married, the male never
> actually pokes anything else; and it's depraved because he
> lusts his life away in masculine obscenities and dirty jokes.

Actually the discussion would apply at least as aptly to
'middle-class morality'. Mr and Mrs Elliot, like the characters
in the other Whitehead plays, discuss morality in an intellectual,
middle-class way, and although the language of the girls in *The
Foursome* and *Sea Anchor* is working-class, the ideas they formu-
late are not. The exact social status of Whitehead's characters
is often obscure.

Mr Elliot's friends, like the men in other Whitehead plays,
are happiest boozing and swopping dirty stories in the pub and
clubbing together to show 'blue' movies, while ill-treating and
bullying their wives at home. He resents this way of life, and
would prefer mixed company for the 'blue' films, but his
friends won't hear of it. They are 'like the First XI mastur-
bating in the locker room'. The argument between Mr and
Mrs Elliot flares up when he suddenly announces that he wants
a separation, and reminds her that she only got him to marry
her by threatening suicide. She totally denies this, leaving the
audience uncertain which of them is lying. In a great outburst
of hate, which ends the first act, Mr Elliot pleads for freedom:

> Mr Elliot (*desperately*): I have got to get out of this trap. I
> can't stand it! I want to live, to grow, to thrive. . . . I want
> to be free!

Mrs Elliot: Free for what?

Mr Elliot: I want to fuck a thousand women! (*He stares furiously around the room. Turns towards the wallpaper.*) This house . . . it's dead. There's no life in it, no life at all. And this room . . . white, all white. . . . It's all cold and sterile and lifeless! There's no love in this room or in this house. NO LOVE! It's DEAD!

He starts tearing down the wallpaper, and destroying the parcels containing birthday presents from his children, shouting, 'I hate this house and I hate you and I hate the brats!' He bursts into tears as the curtain falls.

The second act takes place in the same room, four years later. Mr Elliot has agreed to stay on for the sake of respectability and the children. Mrs Elliot is plying him with jealous questions about his 'slut'. She finally attacks the whole notion of marriage and breeding children, saying their children might be better off 'queer'. But she won't agree to a divorce, and continues to hound his girl-friend with offensive phone calls. She made him what he is and is not going to let another woman have the benefit; she declares that she has resigned herself to the marriage and he will have to do so too. At the end of this act she breaks down in a hysterical fit, screaming, 'Sluttysluttyslutty-slutty,' as the curtain falls.

The last act takes place five years later still. Mr Elliot has now left home, and Mrs Elliot has let the house go to rack and ruin. He comes on a visit and in the course of another argument, from which the play gets its title, he attacks her for telling the children about his infidelity.

Mrs Elliot: They had a right to know.

Mr Elliot: They had a right *not* to know! Christ . . . we're off again. You say alpha, I say beta, you say gamma, I say delta. . . . The dance of the dead language.

He urges his wife to accept the situation, to find herself a new man, so that they can both live freely and honestly. She claims that because they are married, she is entitled to cling on to him forever, even if it means keeping him in misery. He pleads for a new morality.

Mr Elliot: I don't know whether we're going to develop some concept of 'serial marriage' where everyone *expects* to have a series of partners . . . Hollywood-style. Or whether we're just going to develop a new-style relationship that's permanent as long as it lasts . . . but with a hell of a lot more honesty from the beginning. But one thing is certain . . . in future, men and women are going to share free and equal unions that last because they want them to last. Not because they're forced! And not because anybody *owns* anybody. Nobody can *own* anybody. Free men . . . will live freely . . . with free women.

Mrs Elliot: And who's going to look after the children?

Mr Elliot: Professionals.

Mrs. Elliot: Professional what?

Mr Elliot: Pedagogues. People who choose freely to look after children.

Mrs Elliot: You mean . . . you'd put the children in a home?

Mr Elliot (*explodes*): I'd put all the children in the world in a home! To learn to love. And I'd put all the adults in the world *in the world*. To learn to live.

Mrs Elliot, who has been made the more unreasonable of the two for most of the play, rounds on him and accuses him of picking up women, making them dependent on him, and then abandoning them. Finally, when he starts to leave, she says she will kill herself and the children if he goes. He hesitates but goes, she hesitates over the three glasses of poison she has prepared, then throws them down the sink. Like all Whitehead's plays, *Alpha Beta* is open-ended.

The Sea Anchor is in some ways a continuation of *The Foursome*. Again there are two men and two girls, this time on a jetty in Dublin waiting for a friend who is attempting to sail alone from Liverpool. Again there is frank discussion about sex and hygiene (one of the girls tells the other she can't use Tampax because 'I'm too tight.') And again there is discussion of a man who drinks and ill-treats his wife. Towards the end of the play there is a serious debate about sexual freedom and permissiveness and this time there is a note of warning that permissiveness may not be all it is cracked up to be.

Andy (*discussing Nick, the friend who is sailing*): There he was
. . . with a good wife, lovely kids, a good job. And he threw
it all away. Why? He was always carrying on about being
free. 'Free', what the hell is that? He forgot the basic values
. . . lost touch with his roots. Went haywire. I mean, you can
take a drink without being an alcoholic. Any of you can have
sex without being a sex maniac. But Nick—Nick really
swallowed all this rubbish about permissiveness. Huh! Permission to what? Permission to ruin your life? Because that's
what he did. . . . Anyway, people are fed up with it now. It's
not human, it's not real, it's just a fad. The pendulum is
swinging back. It's already happening in America!

The play ends with the news that Nick's boat is coming in;
Jean, his girl friend, is delighted, but the other characters know
that the boat is coming in empty—it's been riding about on its
'sea anchor'.

Old Flames has a very different plot, and is much more
obviously favourable to the feminine point of view; in fact, it is
almost a piece of Women's Lib propaganda. Edward has gone
to supper with Sally, his mistress, on her houseboat, when he
learns that she has invited other people. At first he is disappointed, then he reconciles himself to meeting her friends,
then she reveals that they are *his* friends. He is mystified, saying
he has not got any friends. When they arrive, one at a time,
they turn out to be his wife, his previous wife, and his 'first
love'—his mother. In conversations with each of them separately (a somewhat contrived device) it is revealed that he had
treated them all badly. He has not visited his wife in hospital,
though he kept meaning to, he left his first wife without means
of support for herself and their children, and he did not even
enquire after his father when he was dying of stomach cancer.
His mother is a devout Roman Catholic and his very first love
was the Pope, his first desire to be 'Saint Edward'. But as a
teenager he fell in love with a girl, thinking she was a Madonna.
One night he and the girl took shelter from the rain in a barn.

Edward: We stayed in the barn and we fucked. So at least
I'd fucked the Madonna . . . and nothing was ever quite the
same afterwards.

Sally: What happened?
Edward: I left her.
Sally: Why?
Edward: I didn't worship her any more.
Sally: Tough!
Edward: Oh, it was tough all right. So tough I got sick of
the whole business and dedicated myself to the brotherhood
of men. Socialism.
Sally: That does surprise me.
Edward: Well . . . I couldn't worship her, my first love . . .
and I no longer worshipped my mother . . . and the Pope
and I had fallen out, so . . . I needed a new idol.

However Edward has not given up women, though he now
asks them to hit him and punish him when he tries to get them
too quickly. Like Andy in *The Sea Anchor*, he has doubts about
too much easy sex:

Edward: I don't really like the idea of everyone just jumping
in and out of the sack with different partners.
Sally: Why not?
Edward: What'll happen to ecstasy? Could you still feel
ecstatic if you were climbing in and out of the sack every
night with a different partner?

And later on:

Edward: I'm still stuck with the old marriage of true minds,
love's mystery, the ecstasy of soul speaking to soul in the
wedding of flesh. I'm a sucker for the old sweet agonies . . .

At the end of the first act Edward impatiently asks what's for
supper; the three women turn on him and tell him that *he* is.
When the second act begins, he has vanished, and the women
are finishing their supper, discussing men. They attack men
from every point of view, for their possessiveness, their selfishness, their sexual habits, and their lack of hygiene.

Diana: When Edward walked out on me I was desperate.
I mean, I was a fucking housewife, had no job, no friends,
no contact with anyone. Completely isolated. And I was so
angry and humiliated that I was determined to get myself

fucked by the first man I could. But could I? I couldn't even meet a man. I mean, I wasn't invited out, the other wives I knew treated me as if I was a fucking leper or something. So finally I had to force myself to go and sit in a pub. I got a drink, looked around, and then went and sat next to the least repellent male in there, I chatted him up and then I took him back to the house. I'd got everything ready in advance . . . I'd left the kids at my mother's so we had the place to ourselves . . . and we sat on the couch and started snogging. Well . . . I don't know if it was all the snogging or what but I chickened out. I told him I couldn't make it . . . because I knew he thought I was on the game. Somehow that thought turned me right off. I said maybe if we could meet again I might feel different, might feel better than then. You know what he said? He said he couldn't make assignations because then he'd feel like he was betraying his wife but if he banged me on the spot then he wouldn't feel so bad about it. What a fucking hypocrite! I told him to bugger off. Then he asked me . . . well, if I wouldn't fuck, could he go down on me and wank himself off? That shook me . . . I'd never heard of anything like that before! . . . Anyway I was curious so I told this bastard to go right on with it. You know what he said? He said, 'OK, you go and wash it.' Wash it! Christ, it was all right to stick his dick in me but not his precious tongue! But I was stupid enough to trot to the bathroom and do it! After he'd gone I could have kicked myself. There was come all over the couch and I could never get rid of the stains.
Julie: That sickens me.
Diana: What?
Julie: The smell of come.
Diana: I used all sorts of cleaning stuff but I just couldn't get those stains out.
Julie: I remember once fucking a bloke and afterwards he rushed straight out into the bathroom and washed his cock. But really thoroughly. He peeled the skin back and gave it a really good wash. Then he dabbed it all over with cotton wool and then he shook talcum powder all over it. He wouldn't clean it before he stuck it in me but he had to give

it a bloody good wash afterwards. And when you think of the fortune that women spend on purifying their cunts . . !

Diana: Like we were dirty or something.

Julie: We bombard ourselves with chemicals. Sprays and perfumes and vaginal deodorants. Why?

Diana: Because we're terrified of offending some delicate male nostrils.

Julie: Yes.

Diana: It's men who ought to worry about hygiene. Have you noticed they never even wipe their cock after a piss? They just give it a shake, for Christ's sake! They just shake it and let it hang down and drip dry.

Edward's mother confesses that she has never discussed sex before, and that her generation thought sex was something to be endured, not enjoyed. She believed women were guardians of morality, to curb men's appetites. But she confesses envy for the freedom of the younger generation. Sally confesses that she is so disgusted with men that she has become a Lesbian, and she makes good progress towards seducing Julie, Edward's widow. The play ends with the ritual serving of red wine and meat, clearly suggesting the eating of Edward and a parody of the Holy Communion. The ladies each say, 'In memory of Edward.' Before departing, Julie says she would love to come and see Sally again.

Mecca is partly a comment on puritanical attitudes to sex, partly a questioning of the effect of western tourism in under-developed countries. A group of British tourists in a small Moroccan seaside town squabble among themselves, make love, and discuss their attitudes to Women's Lib, the family, and the native Arabs. There is some typically frank dialogue about feminine hygiene and sex. Violent action is precipitated by Sandy, a cool, 'liberated' girl of about 20 who goes out with an Arab boy and is assaulted and raped by two other Arabs. There is some debate about whether she is responsible for her own rape, and the other women are shocked by her comparatively easy acceptance of it. Several of the tourists beat up the Arab boy whom they wrongly suspect of having attacked her, and the boy later dies from his injuries. The tourists bribe the manager of their holiday camp not to call the police and to arrange for them all to fly home.

Whitehead cheerfully admits that his plays are autobiographical, starting with an actual incident in his own life and then building on it. He turns ideas over in his mind for a long time, but sometimes writes the plays quite quickly. *Alpha Beta* only took three weeks but *The Sea Anchor* took six months. For years he wrote plays at weekends while working in an office all the week. 'I felt trapped by the need to support my family, and I hated both the work I was doing and the Liverpool suburbs in which we lived. The whole thing seemed a huge 'con', and I soon found that most men around me felt the same, living lives they didn't like, to maintain families they had acquired almost by chance. The wives felt marooned and the children wanted to escape as quickly as possible. The escape routes for the men were booze, soccer and sexual 'promiscuity'—awful word. I dived into all this and started questioning the whole society that made it necessary. A friend and I took two girls to a local beach one day, found they were prick-teasers, promising sex but not providing it, and got bored with them. We made a date to see them again in the evening, but we didn't turn up.' This incident was the inspiration of *The Foursome*.

Whitehead's plays reflect the failure of his own marriage and his disillusion with marriage as an institution, as well as his reaction against the Roman Catholic Church in which he was brought up. The eating ritual at the end of *Old Flames* is deliberately designed to suggest the cannibalistic nature of Holy Communion, in which Roman Catholics believe they are actually eating the flesh and blood of Christ. But his main concern is reforming society. His living room is filled with the feminist writings of authors from Alexandra Kollontay to Germaine Greer, Kate Millett and Betty Friedan. He regards the attack on sexual stereotypes, marriage and the nuclear family as an essential first stage in the attack on privilege and injustice in our society.

'My obsession with sex is not Strindbergian, but social and political. My plays are meant to show how men and women are driven into exaggerated positions of jealousy and hostility by the present system, and how awful their lives are as a result.

The family breeds the ideas of ownership, inheritance and class structure, and you won't get rid of those till you get rid of the family. Husbands expect to own their wives and parents expect to own their children. The number of 'battered' wives seeking shelter and children leaving home, and the constantly rising divorce rate, are proofs that marriage and the family as institutions are breaking down. Unfortunately we keep trying to patch them up, and there is still strong social disapproval of free love and of people living in communes. Children are repressed from an early age; if they could have sex freely from the age of 11 or 12, they might grow up liberated and happier. It's a great pity that Women's Lib in Britain has been driven into alliance with traditional left-wing political movements, which are usually committed to conservative social values and upholding family life. In the United States there aren't any strong left-wing movements, so Women's Lib is much more radical.'

Asked about the constant preoccupation of his characters with toilet and hygiene functions, Whitehead explains: 'Part of the hypocrisy of our culture is the way women have been put on a pedestal, as if they were not flesh and blood That's why the women in my plays refer to 'drips', and make clear they do shit.'

Whitehead admits to some uncertainty about sexual freedom, and that is why some of his characters question it. 'For the first six months I lived in Chelsea I thought it was liberated and free, but this was superficial. Most of the "free" relationships turned out to be as possessive and agonized as the old ones. Are jealousy and possessiveness ineradicable, or are they a result of our social conditioning?' There is no doubt that he leans strongly towards the second explanation.

Six: Christopher Hampton

Born: Fayal, The Azores, 1946.

Father: Cable and Wireless engineer who became an administrator and manager of branches in the Middle East. 'We lived rather grandly when I was a boy, enjoying a kind of colonial life with servants and smart houses and flats, provided by the company. We caught the last boat home from Egypt, at the time of Suez.'

Education: Kindergarten in Aden and the British Boys' School in Alexandria. 'Although it was a British school, it followed rather a French system of education, so we were very advanced, especially in languages, compared with normal English education. We had drama classes, and we all had to write plays, at the age of eight! I enjoyed it very much —Edgar Allan Poe was my source and enthusiasm at that time.'

Preparatory school in Reigate, England—'a dying school, picked out of the prep. school directory by my parents with a pin. But I produced my plays in the dormitory at the end of term.'

1959–63: Lancing College. 'I did not write plays there, though I started working with David Hare and others on a play which they eventually finished without me. I went in a school party to see Peter Brook's *King Lear*— that was what made me want to work in the theatre. It was a fantastic experience, I've never been so moved since! I left school as soon as I could, at 17, and wrote a novel about it which has not been published—it was rejected by several publishers. Between school and Oxford I did various jobs, at home and abroad, in a factory, wrapping examination papers, etc., like the characters in *When Did You Last See My Mother?* which I wrote during that year. Otherwise the play was not autobiographical as I had no emotional life at all at that time. The plot just came into my head in the course of half an hour.' 1964–68, New College, Oxford. 'I wanted to be an actor, and auditioned for parts in undergraduate plays, but never got any. I did act in my own play *When Did You Last See My Mother?* when it was produced by the O.U.D.S. I wrote a half-hour version of *Faust* for my college freshmen to act in the inter-college 'cuppers' competition. And I had a year off from Oxford in mid-course, to write *Total Eclipse* and do some work—I got a job at Hamburg Schauspielhaus, which was supposed to be for the whole year but I discovered that I was not going to be paid, so I left after six weeks. Then I went to Brussels and Paris, where I translated lectures for a French novelist, Jacques Borel, who was going to the United States to lecture on James Joyce. After Oxford I went straight to the Royal Court as resident dramatist, and I've been a full-time playwright ever since. I've written five plays, 8 adaptations and 8 or 9 film scripts which never became films. I always got fired!'

Married in 1970.

Plays:

When Did You Last See My Mother? (Oxford and London 1966; New York 1967). *Total Eclipse* (London 1968; New York 1971). *The Philanthropist* (London 1970; New York 1971). *Savages* (London 1973; Los Angeles 1974). *Treats* (London 1976). Numerous adaptions from Ibsen, Chekhov, Molière, Feydeau, etc. *Evening Standard* and *Plays and Players* Awards 1970.

CHRISTOPHER HAMPTON SHOWED exceptional promise as a dramatist while still a university student; since then, his plays have become more complex and more ambitious, but it is arguable that his full promise has not yet been fulfilled. Certainly his most recent plays have not been as satisfying or as successful as the early ones. All of them were first produced at the Royal Court and all except *Total Eclipse* were transferred to the West End. Only one of them, *The Philanthropist*, had a really long run—just over three years at the tiny Mayfair Theatre. It also ran for three months on Broadway.

It is not surprising that Hampton's first play, staged when he was only 20, should clearly show the influence of Osborne's

Look Back in Anger, nor that it was first staged at the Royal Court. It is more surprising that such a young man's play should be so 'well-made' and the emotional content so powerful and disciplined. It speedily won a transfer to the West End. The plot concerns Jimmy and Ian, who were at public school together and are now sharing a bed-sitting-room. Jimmy is comfortably off, from a middle-class family, and is trying to grow out of his homosexual schooldays; Ian is poor, an orphan and in love with Jimmy.

Like Jimmy Porter in *Look Back in Anger*, Ian is inclined to self-pity, angry outbursts and long nostalgic anecdotes intended to point a moral. Also like Jimmy, his partner is torn between two life-styles and, just as Jimmy Porter gets involved with his wife's parents, so Ian gets involved, though in a very different way, with his friend's mother. She even slaps Ian before making love, a direct counterpart to the scene in Osborne's play where Helena slaps Jimmy, before becoming his mistress.

Hampton's Jimmy is not at all like his namesake in Osborne's play, but more like Cliff, reacting to outbursts and occasionally puncturing them. He accuses Ian of being tactless.

Ian: Tactless? Yes, I am tactless. I come from a tactless family. Take my father. He was a very tactless man: (a) because instead of having me educated on the house he nearly broke himself giving me the inestimable benefits of a public-school education, and (b) because he went and caught, nasty, rotten, lumpy cancer and, tactlessly as ever, timed his death for my sixteenth birthday. My mother was also tactless enough to die, when I was twelve.
Jimmy: Oh, spare us the poor orphaned me spiel for Christ's sake.

Ian and Jimmy give a party, after which they have a big row. Ian, bad-tempered at failing to get anywhere with a schoolboy called Dennis, refuses to leave the bed-sit to enable Jimmy to have sex with his current girl friend. He also insults her. When Dennis and the girl have gone, Ian kisses Jimmy, who is furious and promptly leaves, to live with his parents. In the second act, Jimmy's mother comes to visit Ian, saying that

Jimmy is being very difficult and argumentative at home, and will not reveal why he and Ian quarrelled. Ian complains to her about his boredom and loneliness, and tells her the touching story of his mother's death. Eventually they kiss and make love, an outcome which might easily have seemed melodramatic and incredible but is so skilfully led up to by Hampton's dialogue, that it seems entirely natural and credible.

Later, Jimmy's mother calls on Ian again, apologizing for what happened and saying she must have been drunk. Ian is naturally hurt, and confesses that it was his first sexual experience with a woman. She is surprised and touched, but still can't understand how she came to do what she did. Thinking aloud, she tells him he is nothing special and confesses her anxieties.

Mrs E: I've commited adultery, gone back on twenty years of happy marriage, made myself feel guilty and miserable . . . for you it was just experience. You didn't take it seriously. It was just the first of many notches. So . . .

Ian: Listen, I don't know about you, but I think it's very important, losing your virginity. I wouldn't waste it on any old can, you know. It counts for me too, what we did. Do you think I enjoy breaking up your marriage? I like your husband a hell of a lot. What do you think I feel like?

Mrs E: It's not so important for you.

Ian: I don't count.

Mrs E: It's not so important . . . Oh, God, I can't understand why I did it. I'd never do a thing like that again.

Ian: Then why did you come back for more?

(*Mrs E slaps Ian hard. Then she collapses into his arms*)

Mrs E: Because I want you so much.

Ian: You're as bad as your son.

Mrs E: What?

Ian: Never mind. And now you've had your little catharsis, do you want us to make love?

Mrs E (*amazingly enough with some dignity*): Yes please.

But they do not. Mrs Evans continues to question her motives and is uncertain what she wants, causing Ian to repeat his devastating, revelatory accusation.

Ian: You're just like your son.

Mrs E: Why? Why do you keep bringing him into it? I don't know what you're talking about. Why am I just like him anyway?

Ian (*nervously*): Don't ask me. Don't keep asking me.

Mrs E: I will. You can't just make remarks like that out of the blue. Why am I just like him?

Ian (*blurts out*): Because you don't understand why you're saying yes, and he didn't understand why he said no.

Mrs E (*after a brief, shocked silence*): What do you mean?

Ian: You know what I mean. And its ironical isn't it? Mm? Salty in the wound. Irony rubbed right in. (*Shouting*) Doesn't it make it just about bloody unbearable?

Mrs E: It's not true.

Ian (*blazing suddenly*): Of course it's true. Do you think I'd have made love to you if I didn't see him in you?

Mrs E (*agonized*): IT'S NOT TRUE!

Ian: IT IS TRUE! (*Sudden aching silence*) Oh, God, I'm sorry . . . I . . . (*He stretches out his hand to her*)

Mrs E (*avoiding him*): Just . . . (*She grabs her coat and handbag and rushes to the door. Ian tries to stop her. She runs out.*)

In the next and final scene, Jimmy returns to tell Ian that his mother was killed in a car crash. Jimmy does not know that his mother visited Ian, or what took place between them, or that the crash was immediately afterwards. Ian of course does, and almost tells Jimmy the truth, but thinks better of it. Instead he makes conversation to help Jimmy relax, and repeats a long anecdote he told at the beginning of the play, this time with the true ending instead of the invented one he had always used before. Jimmy tells him that he was going to return to Ian, but now he must stay at home with his father. Jimmy thanks Ian for his help and leaves. Ian is alone.

Ian (*his voice full of bitter pain*): Always pleased to help people whose mothers I've seduced and killed. (*Silence. Then, with disgust*) And before long, doubtless I shall be back to go to bed with you.

(*He presses his hands over his eyes for a moment, groans softly. Then*

he drops his hands and goes over to pick up the paper. Empty, hollow)
What's on the telly?
Curtain.

Hampton pursued his study of emotional relationships in modern Britain, and also developed a sophisticated style of verbal humour, in *The Philanthropist*, his most successful and in my opinion his best play. Sub-titled 'a bourgeois comedy' and with a programme quotation from Humpty Dumpty's speech in *Through The Looking Glass* about making words mean whatever he wants them to mean, it is a modern counterpart to Molière's *The Misanthrope*. Whereas Molière's protagonist disapproves of most people but feels obliged to tell them the truth when asked for his opinion, Hampton's Philip approves of people instead, and assumes that they all try to live by rational principles as he does. When he dislikes them or their activities, he tries to avoid telling the truth, so as to spare their feelings. The result is the same: both of them antagonize most of the people they meet. Philip's determination to be pleasant may be simply the expression of a fear that he is essentially boring and unlikeable.

Towards the end of *The Philanthropist*, Philip, a university teacher, gets involved in discussion with Donald, another teacher, about the break-up of his engagement.

Don: You see, I always divide people into two groups. Those who live by what they know to be a lie and those who live by what they believe, falsely, to be the truth. And having decided that Celia belonged to the first group and you to the second, I concluded that you weren't compatible, and that furthermore that was what attracted you to one another. But, I mean, trying to make elegant patterns out of people's hopelessness doesn't really work. It's only a frivolous game.
Philip: Seems to have worked on this occasion . . . But why . . . why do you say I live by what I believe, falsely, to be the truth?
Don: Because you do. Your whole behaviour is based on the assumption that everyone is like you.
Philip: Isn't everybody's?

Don: No. Of course not. Most people's behaviour is based on desperate hope that everyone isn't like them.
Philip: And why do you think Celia lives by a lie?
Don: Because her vanity demands it.
Philip: I'm not sure about that.
Don: I am.
Philip: Well, no doubt if you go on about it long enough, you'll persuade me to believe it. I haven't even got the courage of my lack of convictions.
Don: Oh I wish I'd said that.
Philip: Why?
Don: I don't know, it sounds good.
Philip: That's not really why I said it, believe it or not.

That dialogue is typical of Hampton's style, as well as revealing Philip's detached, critical approach to his life. Earlier on, in an argument with Celia, he has summed himself up with unconscious humour.

Philip: I'm sorry. I suppose I am indecisive. My trouble is, I'm a man of no convictions. (*Longish pause*) At least I think I am ... (*Celia starts laughing*) What's the joke?

The Philanthropist is mainly concerned with the break-up of Philip's engagement. Celia has decided to leave him anyway, but her excuse to do so is provided by a sexy girl called Araminta, who spends a night with Philip. The night means nothing to either of them; she sleeps around with everyone and he is simply too polite to refuse her advances. In the event he is impotent. Trying to explain this in the morning, and refusing Araminta's invitation to try again, his attempt at gentle honesty only makes matters worse.

Philip: I know it was my fault, I was very weak-minded.
Araminta: Weak-minded, was it?
Philip: I should never have agreed, I knew it would be a disaster.
Araminta: Well, I could see you were thrown by the directness of my approach.
Philip: It wasn't that. It was just, I didn't really want to.
Araminta: I know. It's funny how important fidelity is to

some people. I mean, it's something that never occurs to me.
Philip: It wasn't that, the truth is, I don't really find you attractive.

Araminta gets more and more upset, ending the conversation with a wounding *double entendre*.

Araminta: A lot of people do find me attractive.
Philip: I'm sure. It's just me. I can't seem to like women unless they're . . .
Araminta: There's no need to go into it.
Philip: No, all right.
Araminta: Not that you did.

Perhaps because he is writing about university teachers, Hampton indulges in a lot of play with words. Philip is fascinated by words and anagrams, and more interested in pedantry about how they are used than in what is actually being said— that is why he teaches philology rather than literature. In the first scene of *The Philanthropist*, parallelling the opening criticism of a poem in *The Misanthrope*, he and Don bring their respective forms of criticism to bear on a play written by John, a young student. Their discussion of the play is a witty parody of certain sorts of modern drama and modern criticism.

John: Tell me what you don't like about it.
Don: Well, one thing is that character who appears every so often with a ladder. The window-cleaner. What's his name?
John. Man.
Don: Yes. Well I take it he has some kind of allegorical significance outside the framework of the play. I mean I don't know if this is right but I rather took him to signify England.
John: No, no, erm, in point of fact he signifies man.
Don: Ah.
John: Yes.
Don: Hence the name.
John: Yes.
Don: I see.
John: Although now you come to mention it, I suppose he could be taken to represent England.

Philip: Is that two ns?
John: What?
Philip: In Man.
John: No, one.
Philip: Ah, well you see, I thought it was two ns. As in Thomas.
John: Thomas?
Philip: Thomas Mann.
John: Oh.
Philip: So I thought he was just meant to represent a window-cleaner.
John: Well . . .
Philip: Under the circumstances, I think you've integrated him into the plot very well.
John: Thank you. (*He seems displeased.*)

This scene starts *The Philanthropist* with a real *coup de théâtre*, and prepares the way for an equally striking final curtain. As the play opens, John is reading a suicide speech from his play, but not until he has put the revolver to his head, said 'curtain', and smiled, does the audience know they are watching a play within a play, not a real suicide. However the scene ends with John repeating his demonstration; this time the gun goes off and he is killed instantly. In the last scene of the play, when Philip's loves have all gone wrong, he tells Don on the phone that he is about to do something terrible. He points a pistol at himself and pulls the trigger—but it is a cigarette lighter disguised as a pistol. Philip is merely resuming smoking, which he had given up because of the cancer risk. If he is committing suicide, it is not in the melodramatic way the audience was momentarily led to expect. Curtain.

In addition to this main plot, and these characters, *The Philanthropist* has two minor characters and some passing references to politics and violence. Elizabeth is a non-speaking part; she appears in just one scene, sitting silently during the after-dinner chit-chat which leads up to Araminta's night with Philip; her only function is to be someone for Philip to think of turning to when he is deserted by Celia. But by then, she is with Don. The other subsidiary character is Braham, a successful and trendy novelist who makes money and a reputation as a popular pundit. He provides an excuse for satire about fashionable television personalities, and for some of the mildly shocking language which is almost obligatory in serious modern drama. He describes his job as subsidized masturbation, and masturbation as the thinking man's television. And he is cynical about generally approved good causes.

Braham: Nowadays, if I get one of those things through my letter-box telling me I can feed an entire village for the price of a prawn cocktail, I tear it up, throw it in the waste-paper basket, go out to my favourite restaurant and order a prawn cocktail.

Don: And do you find that amusing?

Braham: Oh, come now, the next thing you're going to say is what if everybody was like me. Fortunately for the world and even more fortunately for me, not everybody is. Look, if I actually get a concrete chance to help people, then I do.

Araminta: Yes, I saw that TV appeal you did a few weeks ago.

Don: What was that for?

Braham: Twenty-five guineas.

Don: I meant, on behalf of whom.

Braham: I know you did.

Don: Well?

Braham: Oh, I don't know. It was an appeal on behalf of spavined children, or something equally sordid.

Don: And did it raise much money?

Braham: Enough to cover my fee.

Don: I'm sorry . . . I find that rather disgusting.

Braham: That's perfectly all right. Most people do . . . Obviously my living depends on disgusting a certain percentage of people. If I didn't disgust at least a substantial minority, I wouldn't be controversial, and if I wasn't controversial, I wouldn't be rich.

This is as near as Hampton gets to direct criticism of our society. At one point early in the play Don tells Philip that the Prime Minister and most of the Cabinet have been assassinated in the House of Commons but the characters then continue to discuss their personal problems as if outside events do not concern them. It is not clear whether Hampton wants to show the irrelevance of political events to our lives, or our foolish egocentricity. Either way, the point is not really made.

However he obviously likes this device, which he uses again in *Treats*, a similar but less satisfying play. In the first act, a noisy demonstration is heard offstage and is said to be an Irish protest against the Home Secretary, but no further reference is made to this and the three characters who make up the cast of the play ignore it completely. The second act opens with one of the characters taking no notice whatever of a radio news bulletin.

Treats is about a *ménage à trois*, or rather about a girl who cannot decide between two men. One of them, Patrick, is very similar to Philip in *The Philanthropist*. He is indecisive and a bit of a bore, but kind-hearted and well-meaning, anxious not to hurt or upset anyone. Ann complains about his lack of passion.

> Ann: You're so cautious and rational, anything as crude as a wish or a whim or a desire dies before you ever get your mouth open.

Patrick finds it difficult to understand why his rationality and good intentions so often prove irritating. Their incompatibility is neatly summed up in the following dialogue.

> Patrick: Someone once accused me of being too happy.
> Ann: I don't see what that's got to do with it.
> Patrick: Well, by and large it's true that I'm a . . . happy man. Consequently, I don't expect very much from people, and consequently, I never quite know what it is they expect from me. To that extent, I'm totally maladjusted. That's why I find people, or at any rate women, so bewildering.
> Ann: You make a distinction, do you, between women and people?
> Patrick: No, don't let's get off on all that, you know what I mean. I mean, when someone says to me, I want this or that, or I feel this or that, I always try to respond accordingly. And it's only later that I realize that's not what was meant at all.

When Ann asks Patrick to leave, telling him their affair is

over, he irritates her by meekly agreeing and proceeding to discuss practical matters like what he should do with the keys. He is being decent and civilized; she yearns for some show of emotion.

Ann: If you were even vulnerable.
Patrick: I'm sure I bleed as much as the next man.
Ann: Maybe you do: but very neatly, I suspect.

Dave, on the other hand, provides all the emotional storms and tantrums she could wish—too many in fact. When *Treats* opens, she has chucked him out because she can't stand any more of his violent moods and bullying. At the end, she takes him back, though for how long is left in doubt. Dave is a self-centred but charming journalist, a philanderer and a bit of a con man. He manipulates Ann and Patrick, talking to one of them while ignoring the other, or steering the conversation in directions designed to expose Patrick's dreariness and to increase Ann's irritation. He also succeeds in ingratiating himself with Patrick, which annoys Ann still more. His cool audacity and rudeness, used to conceal and cover his basic insecurity, in true 'angry young man' style, provide some of the most amusing and theatrical scenes in the play. At one point he actually proposes marriage to Ann, which is what she says she wants, but she rejects him. Instead she offers immediate sex and undresses; then it is *his* turn to change his mind—he slaps her and walks out. The trouble with this series of battles is that Ann, who should be the central character, is nebulous. We are not told enough about her, or what she wants, and her indecisiveness, unlike Patrick's, remains uninteresting and unconvincing.

As with *The Philanthropist*, Hampton makes *Treats* almost circular in construction. At the beginning, Dave breaks through a window to interrupt Ann and Patrick; at the end, it is Patrick who breaks in. However Ann turns on Patrick, abuses him and tells him to get out for good. Then she runs after him, leaving Dave (and the audience) wondering if she has changed her mind yet again. Finally, she comes back and sits opposite Dave. Her exit seems artificially theatrical and her return inconclusive. It leaves us feeling irritated with a play which has to some extent aroused our curiosity about Ann, and then failed to satisfy it.

Between writing this trio of plays about personal relationships in present-day Britain, Hampton produced two works with more remote settings and with more historical themes. *Total Eclipse*, which was produced at the Royal Court and off-Broadway, is a study of the relationship between the French poets Verlaine and Rimbaud. It is Hampton's own favourite among his plays. 'I was obsessed by Rimbaud and from the age of 16 I'd always wanted to write something about him.' Written in twelve short scenes, it covers the twenty-one years from the two men's first meeting in 1871, to Rimbaud's death. The play opens extremely promisingly with the uncouth, rude, 17-year-old Rimbaud's arrival at the respectable 27-year-old Verlaine's home. Rimbaud shocks Verlaine's wife and antagonizes her father, who owns the house, but his unconventional behaviour immediately attracts Verlaine, who adopts rough dress and aggressive behaviour. Later, Hampton gives Rimbaud a self-analytical soliloquy.

Rimbaud: When I was in Paris in February this year, when everything was in a state of chaos, I was staying the night in a barracks and I was sexually assaulted by four drunken soldiers. It wasn't a particularly agreeable experience, but when I got back to Charleville, thinking about it, I began to realize how valuable it had been to me. It clarified things in my mind which had been vague. It gave my imagination textures. And I understood that what I needed, to be the first poet of this century, the first poet since Racine or since the Greeks, was to experience everything in my body. I knew what it was like to be a model pupil, top of the class, now I wanted to disgust them instead of pleasing them. I knew what it was like to take communion, I wanted to take drugs. I knew what it was like to be chaste, I wanted perversions. It was no longer enough for me to be one person, I decided to be everyone. I decided to be a genius. I decided to be Christ. I decided to originate the future. The fact that I often regarded my ambition as ludicrous and pathetic pleased me, it was what I wanted, contrast, conflict inside my head, that was good. While other writers looked at themselves in the mirror, accepted what they saw, and jotted it down, I liked to see a mirror in the mirror, so that I could turn around whenever I felt like it and always find endless vistas of myself.

This analysis of a writer suggesting how closely Hampton identified himself with Rimbaud at one time, is Rimbaud's prelude to asking Verlaine to leave his wife. The later scenes of the play, in which their relationship deteriorates and they fall into poverty and drunken quarrels, make good descriptive narrative but are more predictable and less interesting, though there are further flashes of psychological insight.

Rimbaud: My search for universal experience has led me here. To lead an idle, pointless life of poverty, as the minion of a bald, ugly, ageing, drunken lyric poet, who clings on to me because his wife won't take him back.
Verlaine: How can you bring yourself to say a thing like that?
Rimbaud: It's easy. It's the truth. You're here, living like this, because you have to be. It's your life. Drink and sex and a kind of complacent melancholy and enough money to soak yourself oblivious every night. That's your limit. But I'm here because I choose to be.
Verlaine: Oh yes?
Rimbaud: Yes.
Verlaine: And why exactly?
Rimbaud: What to you mean, why?
Verlaine: Why exactly did you choose to come back to London with me? What was the intellectual basis of your choice?
Rimbaud: That is a question I repeatedly ask myself.
Verlaine: No doubt you regarded it as another stage in your private Odyssey. Only by plunging even deeper, if I may mix my myths, will you attain the right to graze on the upper slopes of Parnassus.
Rimbaud: Your attack is unusually coherent this morning.
Verlaine: My theory differs from yours. My theory is that you are like Musset.

Rimbaud: What?

Verlaine: Rather a provocative comparison, don't you think, in view of your continual attacks on the wretched man?

Rimbaud: Explain it.

Verlaine: Well, I simply mean that like Musset or one of Musset's heroes, you tried on the cloak of vice, and now it's stuck to your skin. You came back here with me because you wanted to, and because you needed to.

Rimbaud: Well now, that's quite original for you, even though you have made your customary mistake.

Verlaine: What's that?

Rimbaud: Getting carried away by an idea because its aesthetically plausible rather than actually true.

Verlaine: Oh, there are less subtle reasons for your putting up with me.

Rimbaud: Such as?

Verlaine: Such as the fact that I support you. (*Silence.*)

Rimbaud: Your mind is almost as ugly as your body.

Towards the end of the play, Rimbaud and Verlaine discuss their philosophies and there is a revealing exchange about the function and purpose of writing. Verlaine has had a religious conversion and tries to interest Rimbaud in God, to help him to achieve his aims. Rimbaud counters that he has no aims, and that he no longer writes.

Verlaine: Yes, but why not?

Rimbaud: Because I have nothing more to say. If I ever had anything to say in the first place.

Verlaine: How can you say that? (*Rimbaud laughs at Verlaine's unhappy choice of words.*) How can you?

Rimbaud: Well, as you know, I started life as a self-appointed visionary, and creator of a new literature. But as time wore on, and it took me longer and longer to write less and less, and I looked back at some of the absurdities of my earlier work, at some of the things I thought were so good when I wrote them, I saw it was pointless to go on. The world is too old, there's nothing new, it's all been said. Anything that can be put into words is not worth putting into words.

Verlaine: The truth is always worth putting into words.
Rimbaud: The truth is too limited to be interesting.
Verlaine: What do you mean?—Truth is infinite.
Rimbaud: If you're referring to the truth that was revealed to you in prison by an angel of the Lord, you may be wrong. After all, what makes you think it's any truer than the rather different views you asserted with equal confidence three years ago?
Verlaine: Well, obviously one develops.
Rimbaud: And have you developed?
Verlaine: Yes. (*Long silence.*)

Despite this kind of analysis, touching on many writers' nightmares and on age-old questions about the relativity of truth, *Total Eclipse* fades away inconclusively. It is too episodic, with only passing references to Verlaine's imprisonment for drunkenly wounding Rimbaud, to his religious conversion, and to Rimbaud's fatal illness and death-bed confession. This is reported by Rimbaud's sister, who visits Verlaine to ask him to suppress the unpublished poems, and return them to Rimbaud's family. *Total Eclipse* ends with Verlaine drinking absinthe in a bar, seeing a vision of the young Rimbaud, and recalling their love. But Hampton has not enlightened us sufficiently about what brought them together or what went wrong, and although the play holds the audience's attention, it leaves disappointingly little behind.

Savages is Hampton's most overtly political play: instead of using political events as a hazy background to personal relationships, he presents political arguments as his main theme, with the characters' private problems only lightly sketched in. The plot was originally suggested to Hampton by a *Sunday Times* article about the extermination of the Brazilian Indians. In particular his imagination was caught by the description of a tribe being massacred during a spectacular ritual feast, the 'quarup', which Hampton at once saw as full of theatrical possibilities. In his published notes, he says 'more than any other of my plays, *Savages* is a director's play'. Its subject-matter is obviously similar to Shaffer's *Royal Hunt of the Sun*, produced at the National Theatre ten years previously, and

Hampton may have imagined his play having a similar impact. But the resources of the Royal Court are much more modest, fire regulations made his opening and closing scenes impossible to stage as originally envisaged, and Robert Kidd, the director, did not find such striking visual or aural images as John Dexter did for Shaffer. The political argument in Hampton's play is more didactic and less sophisticated, and the characters are not presented in such depth, though Paul Scofield filled out the central role with his personality.

Savages concerns a British official, Alan West, who is kidnapped by left-wing extremists in Brazil as a hostage for the release of political prisoners. Hampton clearly brings out the irony that these left-wing revolutionaries are no more concerned about the fate of the Indians than anyone else. They merely want to replace a right-wing dictatorship by a left-wing one. Scenes showing West in captivity alternate with flash-backs to his previous life, including scenes with his wife, with an anthropologist and with an American missionary, and with views of the Indians preparing for their ceremonial. West himself is of a philosophic temperament; he writes poetry and collects Brazilian folk myths, which he recites as commentaries during the Indian scenes.

The play begins with one of these recitations—a legend about how human beings first antagonized the jaguar and made it cruel. Then we see West being kidnapped, while changing into evening dress, and being harangued by his pleasant and humorous kidnapper, Carlos, on capitalist exploitation. The fifth scene is a flash-back to West's conversation with Crawshaw, an anthropologist, who is cynical about the efforts allegedly being made to help the Indians and about the 'scientific' way anthropologists remain detached from what is going on. This scene includes two further flash-backs, flash-backs within a flash-back, in which a Brazilian general instructs the Attorney-General to deposit all the evidence dealing with the exploitation of the Indians at the Air Ministry and then calmly announces that a mysterious fire has destroyed it. There is also a fragment of dialogue between West and his wife, hinting at their marital problems and showing some of Hampton's flair for barbed exchanges. While Crawshaw is out of the room, Mrs West remarks that he is not a bit like his father.

> West: I shouldn't think our children would be anything like us, if we had any.
> Mrs West: What's that supposed to mean?
> West: Nothing.
> Mrs West: He wasn't very nice about your poetry, was he?
> West: You're not very nice about my poetry.
> Mrs West: I've never said anything about your poetry.
> West: Exactly.

Savages includes several detailed descriptions of atrocities and tortures committed against Indians, and also shows supposedly civilized people like Mrs West and the American missionary treating them as half-wits or savages. The scene in which West visits the Rev. Elmer Penn's mission is actually very amusing, in a grim way. Penn is full of slightly phoney bonhomie, calling West by his Christian name and taking for granted that he will share his assumptions—that the natives must be taught Christian sexual morality, that it's very amusing to hear a native failing to pronounce the name of an English footballer, and that training them to sing hymns and play the harmonium is really worthwhile.

A large part of *Savages* is taken up with accounts of conditions in Brazil, accounts which are so horrifying and extreme that they smack of propaganda. Hampton visited Brazil, and did considerable research; most theatregoers will of course have no way of judging whether his version of events is fair. But they do not *seem* fair, and a few attempts to make the presentation more balanced are inadequate. For example, Carlos tells West that the people are starving because of American capitalist exploitation. His speech ends emotionally and demagogically.

> Carlos: You may think all's fair in love and commerce, but some of us take it personally when our children starve to death so that somebody in Detroit or Pittsburg can buy themselves a third car.
> West: That's a ludicrously oversimplified way of putting it.
> Carlos: Well, as it so happens, it's a ludicrously oversimplified

process, starving. You don't get enough food to eat and, by an absurdly oversimplified foible of nature, it makes you die.

Savages is often more like cheap political polemic than fair exposition. Nor are we told enough about the background and motives of the characters. Carlos is gentle, and constantly promises West that he will be released. But there is a change of plan and Carlos has to shoot West. Before doing so he tells him that his wife has gone back to England. None of these things are explained. The play as originally written ends with the burning of the massacred Indians; as presented at the Royal Court, it ends with newspaper headlines about West's death being flashed on a screen, followed by pictures of the piles of Indian bodies.

Hampton admits that *Savages* is easily misunderstood, because audiences tend to identify with West and to assume that he represents the author's views. West represents standard western liberal values and attitudes, but is forced to modify his views by his experiences during the play. 'If anyone in the play represents *my* views, it is Carlos. His priorities are absolutely right— he was disgusted by all the Western liberal fuss over the Indians, ignoring the fate of the majority of Brazilians. Most Brazilians don't even know there are any Indians! It's true I started with West's attitudes, more or less, but I was cured by going to Brazil.' He hopes the audience will modify its views as he and West did. 'In some ways West is the audience, and the play is actually about the audience.'

But, like many British playwrights today, Hampton is very anxious not to preach, not to 'spoon-feed' the audience, and not to devise characters and plots to get a predictable response. 'What upsets me most in the theatre is over-simplification, and the sound of an author baying out his beliefs. Theatre is about ambiguity and the richness of a play relates to the thickness of its texture.' Hampton thinks that even Ibsen is the weaker for deliberately pushing a point of view, and he dislikes the way Brecht 'leads an audience by the nose'. What drew Hampton to the work of Horvath, two of whose plays he has adapted for the National Theatre, was that 'he puts forward a complex picture and leaves the audience to sort out what it feels.'

In *Total Eclipse*, Hampton does not tell us what he thinks, or what we should think, about Rimbaud and Verlaine. His own sympathies shifted, as he wrote the play. 'At first I thought Rimbaud was absolutely right to think that a writer must be a genius or nothing, and I was not very sympathetic to Verlaine carrying on once he had realized he was a mediocre writer. In the end I found Verlaine's attitude more admirable. And of course I admired him for preserving Rimbaud's work, despite the great pressure put on him by Rimbaud's family. (He did not actually meet Rimbaud's sister, but they corresponded.) The appearance of Rimbaud to Verlaine in a kind of vision at the end shows the way Verlaine sentimentalized their relationship in his old age, and his sentimentality generally.'

Apart from his childhood enthusiasm for Rimbaud, and identification with him, Hampton was drawn to write *Total Eclipse* as an investigation of what it means to be a writer, 'what are his hopes and responsibilities'. He finds it strange that people always seem to identify the views of the central character with those of the author. '*Treats* is about a misogynist, but I'm not one. I'm not interested in preaching my views through a central character, as Osborne did in *Look Back In Anger*, though of course I was influenced by Osborne when I was at school. He showed that it was possible to write serious plays about real people today. But I'm quite a different kind of writer.'

It is not easy to be sure what kind of writer Hampton is. Like David Hare, he deliberately varies his style and his subject-matter. 'I have a violent urge not to repeat myself. Also there is a great danger of orthodoxy in the theatre, of fitting in with the prevailing wind. It's easy to see what is going to be acceptable at any given moment, even if what is acceptable is not what has usually been considered acceptable.' Nor is Hampton worried if his plays are not immediately understood, rather the reverse— 'it's a danger signal when what you are doing is too readily assimilable'.

At times Hampton seems ready to agree that his plays are deliberately open-ended, or ambiguous. 'It's true that I don't believe in tying up loose ends.' But he denies that *The Philanthropist*'s ending is uncertain. 'Philip will obviously become a
5

kindly bachelor don.' Hampton first had the idea of writing
The Philanthropist while studying *Le Misanthrope* at Oxford;
Molière was one of his special subjects. 'I wanted to create a
character who was entirely the opposite of Molière's—but
exactly the same things happen to him, which shows how times
have changed. A different kind of person is unpopular now.'
The play is full of literary jokes, and references to Molière.
For example, Elizabeth, the silent character, corresponds to
Elionte in *Le Misanthrope*. 'In Molière she is decent and honest
and only says boring things, so I decided she should say nothing
at all.' Another of Hampton's conceits in writing the play was
to think of each of the characters as representing one of the
seven deadly sins.

The political events which are briefly referred to in Hampton's
plays reflect what he calls 'the lack of politics' in Britain. 'I
became aware of this at Oxford. To come from France in 1967
to England in 1968 made a very strong contrast. People here
don't take a definite line, and don't seem to care one way or
another. That's why the political events in the backgrounds of
my plays are virtually ignored by the characters, and why I've
tried especially to convey apathy and despair in *Treats*. I'm
trying to describe the prevailing atmosphere and feeling. *Treats*
was the result of a deliberate decision to take a very commonplace situation, and link it to the apathy and perversity of
today. I also wanted to break various theatrical superstititions,
such as the one that it is fatal to write a play for three characters.
It's been a very useful play for me to write—it may be a tran-
sitional play. I decided to make it much more laconic and
enigmatic, and less explicit, than anything I'd done before.
There are no long speeches and the characters are not exactly
explained or defined. I want to move further in that direction.
I work entirely by instinct, and in fact I'm quite pleased with
the result.'

I asked Hampton why Ann rushes out after Patrick at the
end, only to return to Dave almost at once. 'It's partly to show
what happens to Dave when she goes—his fear that she may
not return, and then his disgust at his hollow victory when she
comes back. Ann is really the central character—her tragedy
is that she doesn't get rid of both of them. Dave should generate

fear and terror in the other two, and in the audience, but maybe that wasn't quite brought out at the Royal Court— perhaps James Bolam was too likeable.'

Hampton does not write for particular actors, but he is very conscious of the way casting affects plays. 'Victor Henry's Ian in *When Did You Last See My Mother?* helped very considerably with the play's West End run, while *Savages* only got into the West End because of Paul Scofield. I always wanted Charles Gray to play Braham in *The Philanthropist*, and Gray had to be persuaded back to the stage, which he had abandoned for several years.' Hampton has always taken an active part in the rehearsals of his plays and his role in them has increased with experience. He has worked with Robert Kidd, the director, regularly for ten years. 'We trust each other. Rehearsals are never calm, and one must know the director well enough to be able to have rows with him.'

Part 3

Laughter in Court

ALAN AYCKBOURN, Simon Gray and Tom Stoppard are famous mainly for their highly individual forms of humour. Their plays are so funny that it is easy to dismiss them as nothing more than farces or comedies. In fact they bring wit and laughter to bear on many of the problems that concern the dramatists in part 2; their plays are indictments of many of our social attitudes and customs, indictments which are none the less serious for being brilliantly disguised.

Seven: Alan Ayckbourn

Born: London, England 1939.

Father: Horace Ayckbourn, a violinist in the London Symphony Orchestra.

Mother: Mary James, a writer of novels and magazine stories. Stepfather was a bank manager. Maternal grandfather was a Shakespearian actor-manager and maternal grandmother (Lillian Morgan) was a male impersonator in music-halls.

Education: Haileybury School, where he wrote poetry and belonged to the drama club, and was encouraged by a master who was keen on theatre. On leaving school, worked as a stage manager for Sir Donald Wolfit's touring company, as a result of an introduction arranged by the master at school. Later, through the actor Robert Flemyng, an Old Haileyburian, was employed at the Connaught Theatre, Worthing, as a stage manager, doing some acting. Subsequently worked as stage manager and actor in various theatres. Joined Stephen Joseph's company in Scarborough, moving with them as a founder-member to the Victoria Theatre, Stoke-on-Trent. Gradually realized that as an actor he 'would only be average, at best' and was encouraged by Joseph to direct and to write plays.

1964–1970: Drama producer for the British Broadcasting Corporation in Leeds. Started directing the Scarborough Theatre in the Round while working in Leeds, becoming full-time artistic director in 1970.

1959–1963: Wrote plays under *nom de plume* 'Roland Allen', subsequently using his own name.

Married in 1959: Two sons.

Plays (as 'Roland Allen'): *The Square Cat* (Scarborough 1959). *Love after All* (Scarborough 1959). *Dad's Tale* (Scarborough 1961). *Standing Room Only* (Scarborough 1962).

(In his own name): *Xmas* v *Mastermind* (Stoke-on-Trent

1963). *Mr Whatnot* (Stoke 1963; London 1964). *Meet my Father*
(Scarborough 1965; retitled *Relatively Speaking*, London 1967;
New York 1970). *The Sparrow* (Scarborough 1967). *How The
Other Half Loves* (Scarborough 1969; London 1970; New York
1971). *Countdown* (one-act play in *Mixed Doubles*, by various
authors, London 1969). *Me Times Me* (Scarborough 1970). *The
Story So Far* (Scarborough 1970). *Ernie's Incredible Illucinations*
(children's play: London 1971). *Time and Time Again* (Scar-
borough 1971; London 1972). *Absurd Person Singular* (Scar-
borough 1972; London 1973; New York 1974). *The Norman
Conquests* (Scarborough 1973; London 1974; New York 1975).
Absent Friends (Scarborough 1974; London 1975). *Confusions*
(Scarborough 1974; London 1976). *Jeeves* (book and lyrics for
the Andrew Lloyd Webber musical; London 1975). *Bedroom
Farce* (Scarborough 1975; London 1977). *Just Between Ourselves*
(Scarborough 1976; London 1977). *Ten Times Table* (Scar-
borough 1977).

Evening Standard Awards 1973, 1974—*Plays and Players* Award
1974.

Mr Whatnot, Ayckbourn's first work to reach London, was
largely a mime play with a complex taped sound track. His
first big success was *Relatively Speaking*, which established him as
a writer of ingenious farcical comedy, with an ear for dialogue
and with a penchant for complex situations and misunderstandings, and ingenious plots. His delight in playing games
with the English language is evident from the play's punning
title, which aptly describes the plot. There are just four characters: Greg and Ginny who are having an affair, Philip, an older
man who was Ginny's previous lover, and Sheila, Philip's wife.
After an introductory scene in Ginny's London apartment,
with Greg getting suspicious that she still has other men and
not understanding why he can't go with her to her parents'
for the week-end, the scene shifts to Philip and Sheila's country
cottage. Greg, having found the address lying around Ginny's
apartment, arrives to surprise her, assuming that he is visiting
her parents. Ginny arrives to try to persuade Philip to stop
pestering her with his attentions. The main humour of the play
derives from Greg's continuing misconception that he is visiting

Ginny's parents and the various misunderstandings that result. In addition to the amusement generated by these, there is also some mild social satire. The play ends with a typical Ayckbourn twist. Greg has earlier shown Sheila a pair of men's slippers which he found under Ginny's bed; Sheila recognized them as Philip's and thus learnt of his affair with Ginny. But at the final curtain Philip discovers that they are not his slippers: Ginny had yet another man.

The opening scene of *Relatively Speaking* is a slightly contrived way of preparing for the main action of the play; with greater experience Ayckbourn would probably have started the play differently. In the rest of the play, however, he is astonishingly skilful in maintaining various permutations of his basic situation and holding the audience's attention, an achievement which is all the more remarkable when one considers that in real life either Sheila or Philip would surely have asked Greg what he was doing in their house and who he was, or he would have discovered that they were not actually Ginny's parents.

How the Other Half Loves—another punning title, a variation on 'How the Other Half Lives', refers both to different social classes and to the stage set which is a mixture of two different living rooms. It has a cast of six—three married couples. The ingenuity of this play is that two of the couples have their living rooms on the stage at the same time, sometimes passing without seeing each other. The set is partly 'smart period reproduction' furniture, for the home of the successful and wealthy company boss Frank Foster, and partly 'more modern, trendy and badly looked after' for his underling Bob Phillips. Fiona Foster and Bob Phillips are having an affair, and when questioned about where they were the previous evening they both seize on a luckless couple called the Featherstones as their alibi. William Featherstone works for the firm too, and is about to be promoted, so Frank Foster invites him to dinner. Terry Phillips also invites the Featherstones to dinner, to help them out of their alleged marital problems. The play consists mainly of the two dinner parties, at which every possible misunderstanding and disaster occur, and which provide Ayckbourn with opportunities for social satire at the expense of three different life-styles and at employer-employee and husband-wife relationships.

Time and Time Again, the next of his plays to be presented in London, shows Ayckbourn getting more interested in pillorying the manners and social conventions of the middle classes. This time the cast consists of two couples and an odd man out, Leonard, who is the central character. He is a 'pale, alert, darting' young man who is bored by the idle chit-chat of those around him, and who has a disturbing effect on them with his mixture of selfishness and naïveté. His sister Anna is downtrodden by her husband Graham and has retreated into a routine of domestic chores. Leonard talks to the garden gnome, hides in cupboards and lusts after Joan, the fiancée of Graham's employee Peter. Graham a cold, practical bully, impatient of Leonard's fantasies and keen to get him out of the house, has invited Joan and Peter to tea. The action takes place in a garden with the back of the house at one end and a sports ground at the other. The plot is not quite so elaborate as in the earlier plays, while the characterization is deeper. But a great deal of fun is extracted from the misunderstandings when Leonard contrives to make Peter think it is Graham who is flirting with Joan. In the end Leonard pretends to have no idea what has been going on, Joan leaves in disgust with both Leonard and Peter, who make it up and go off to play football together. Ayckbourn regards this as a happy ending, as Leonard would have been 'trampled to death' in a few years if he had married Joan. Peter, a typical Englishman of a certain sort, is happier 'playing the game' than in emotional relationships.

Absurd Person Singular has Ayckbourn returning to punning titles and to an ingenious symmetrical plot-scheme. It also marks a further development in his trend towards social satire. The cast consists of three married couples, and the three acts of the play take place at successive Christmases in their respective kitchens (The last act is called 'Next Christmas' but there is no suggestion that the action is less real than in 'Last Christmas' or 'This Christmas'.) The first kitchen is modest but modern and spotlessly clean, well equipped with gadgetry; it belongs to Sidney and Jane Hopcraft, a suburban couple. He is another of Ayckbourn's fussy, bullying husbands and she is obsessive in her endless cleaning and dedication to domestic duties. They have invited Ron, a banker from whom Sidney wants a loan for his architectural business, and his wife Marion, an alcoholic, as well as two old friends, Geoffrey and Eva. Geoffrey is 'the life and soul of a party', endlessly telling funny stories, while Eva is a suicidal depressive. The humour of the first act is mainly farcical. Jane mislays the tonic water and goes out in rubber boots and an old raincoat to buy more; Sidney accidentally locks her out of the kitchen so she has to come back through the front door and walk right through the party. Ron and Marion inspect the kitchen, with Marion pretending enthusiasm for the gadgetry but whispering asides to Ron that they must leave as soon as possible as she can't stand Geoffrey's jokes. The act ends with Jane cleaning the kitchen yet again, singing loudly.

The second act is closer to black comedy. It takes place in Geoffrey and Eva's untidy, old-fashioned kitchen, and all through the act she is trying to commit suicide. But when she puts her head in the gas oven, Jane enters and offers to clean the oven for her. When she tries to take pills she drops them down the sink. Sidney finds her trying to dig them out of the waste pipe, thinks she is trying to clean it and offers to do the job for her. When she tries to hang herself from the ceiling light, Ronald thinks she is mending it and gives himself a bad electric shock taking over that job. This act ends with Eva leading everyone in singing the canon 'On the first day of Christmas'.

The last act is in Ronald and Marion's Victorian, partly-modernized kitchen. Ron doesn't realize that Marion is an alcoholic, but Eva tells him. Sidney and Jane have not been invited but just 'drop in'; one of the funniest scenes occurs when the others hear them outside and switch out the lights, pretending to be out. Sidney and Jane burst in, complete with false noses and unsuitable presents, and Sidney proceeds to organize a ghastly game of 'Musical Dancing'. Marion comes in, very drunk, and the play ends with Sidney leading the others into wilder and wilder dancing, with Jane imposing forfeits ('apple under the chin', 'orange between the knees').

This was Ayckbourn's most savage act to date; as audiences laughed they were also aware of the horror of humans bound up in themselves and in a meaningless dance symbolizing the social round or life itself.

The Norman Conquests was a much more ambitious undertaking and hardly seemed destined for the commercial success it achieved. Its punning title misled many people into thinking it was a historical play; actually it is a trilogy set in the same country cottage on the same weekend with the same cast of three couples. The three plays can be seen in any order and each stands up on its own, though extra interest and humour is generated by seeing all three within a short time of each other. *Table Manners* takes place in the dining room, *Living Together* in the living room and *Round and Round the Garden*, obviously, in the garden. The cottage belongs to Annie who looks after her ageing bad-tempered mother. Neither the mother nor the upstairs bedrooms are shown, which caused some critics to suggest that Ayckbourn might eventually add fourth and fifth plays!

Annie has been planning a weekend away with Norman, a dreamy and lecherous young man who is not so very different from Leonard in *Time and Time Again*; both parts were originally played in London by Tom Courtenay. Norman is married to Ruth, a successful career woman who supports him financially and who doesn't join the house-party until half-way through the weekend. He not only flirts with Annie who is Ruth's sister, but also with Sarah, the bossy prissy wife of Reg, who is the brother of Ruth and Annie. At the end of the garden play, which is in some ways the conclusion of the trilogy, the women leave Norman to himself, as he shouts, 'I only wanted to make you happy' at all three of them. The plays contrast his innocent desire to have unemotional therapeutic sex with their emotional needs and social hang-ups.

The way Ayckbourn has interwoven the three plays is extremely ingenious. Events occurring in one are referred to in another, and the audience gets a comfortable glow of recognition as they discover what was happening in the living room that caused comment in the dining room or vice versa. Apart from Norman, the most memorable character is Sarah, constantly trying to manage events, and constantly failing, but all the characters are well contrasted and easily recognizable types. In addition each play contains a set-piece which must be among the funniest in contemporary drama.

Perhaps the funniest of all is the dinner-party in the second act of *Table Manners*. Sarah is determined to have a happy family gathering and tries to arrange the seating with formal precision. The effort to avoid two women sitting together and to split up the various couples leads to an endless shifting of places, with Sarah getting more and more irritable and near-hysterical, and with Ruth at one point asking if it would be easier if she ate in the kitchen. Just when all except Norman are finally seated, he enters 'in an old ill-fitting suit and collar and a floppy tie. His jacket has a row of medals on it.' He sits between Reg and Tom, and is promptly told by Sarah he can't sit there because 'it's wrong'.

> Norman: Wrong? Is it wrong to sit between my old pal Reg and the dwarf on my left? (*Patting the top of Tom's head*) Hallo, little chap.
> Tom: Hallo.
> Ruth (*hissing*): Norman.
> Sarah: Norman!
> Annie: It's all right, Sarah. I'll sit here. It's fine.
> Sarah: But . . .
> Annie: This is fine.
> Reg: Fine.
> Ruth: Fine.
> Tom: Fine.
> Sarah: Oh well, it's not correct.
> Norman: Is this lettuce leaf all for me? I can hardly believe my good fortune.
> Annie (*hissing*): Norman.

There is similar confusion in *Living Together* when coffee is served after dinner.

> Annie: What's everybody want? White or black?
> Sarah: No, I'll do it.
> Annie: It's all right.
> Sarah: No, I'm doing this.

Annie: I'm already doing it.

Sarah: You're not already doing it. I'm doing it.

Annie: Oh don't be so ridiculous, Sarah.

Sarah: I'm not being ridiculous. This is your week-end to rest.

Annie: Oh, forget that.

Sarah: Will you please give me that coffee pot?

Annie: What's the use of . . .

Sarah: Annie, will you give me that coffee-pot at once or I shall lose my temper.

Annie (*thrusting the coffee-pot at Sarah*): Oh, go on have the damn thing then.

Sarah: Thank you. Now then, everyone. Black or white?

Tom: Um? (*he considers*).

Sarah: Annie?

Annie: No thank you.

Sarah: Oh, don't be so silly.

Annie: None for me. I couldn't drink it.

Sarah: Reg?

Tom: Black, I think.

Sarah (shrilly): I'm asking Reg.

Tom: Oh, sorry.

Reg: White.

Sarah: Please.

Reg: Please.

Sarah: At last. White for Reg. Black for Tom. None for Annie.

Tom: I think I'll change mine to white on second thought.

Ayckbourn's skill in satirizing an everyday social situation leads him from coffee muddle to party game. Reg bullies the other guests into playing a complicated board game he has invented. It is interrupted by Norman's snoring and then by Norman phoning Ruth and being rude to the sick mother upstairs who picks up the phone extension. Reg's game is about police and crooks in a city. There is endless misunderstanding and confusion as he explains it.

Reg: Police cars can run on the roads but not in the buildings . . .

Sarah: That's a relief.
Reg: Look, do you mind, do you mind? The police cars can see up to twenty spaces ahead of them and up to four spaces each side. They can't see behind them and they can't see round corners.
Sarah: Why can't they see behind them?
Reg: Because they can't, that's why.
Tom: Motto, don't drive behind a police car.
Norman (*loudly for a second*): Love? What do you know about love? (*With an apologetic look at the others, continuing in a lower tone*) Have you ever felt love for a single human being in your life?
Reg: The police also have the Chief Superintendent. (*Holding him up.*) This chap—he can see up to three spaces ahead of him and three spaces round a corner.
Tom: Useful chap in a crisis.
Sarah: Oh, this is absurd.
Reg: What's absurd?
Sarah: How can you have a man see three spaces ahead and three round a corner?
Reg: Because he's got a very long neck. I don't know, it's a game, woman.
Sarah: It's not even realistic.
Reg: What's that got to do with it?
Sarah: It's not much of a game if it's not even realistic.
Reg: What are you talking about? Realistic? (*Leaping up*) What about chess? That's not realistic, is it? What's wrong with chess?
Sarah: Oh well, chess . . .
Reg: In chess, you've got horses jumping sideways. That's not realistic, is it? Have you ever seen a horse jumping sideways?
Sarah: Yes. All right . . .
Reg (*leaping about*): Like this (*imitating a knight's move*) Jumping like this. Jump, jump-jump. Jump, jump-jump. That's very realistic I must say.
Sarah: You've made your point.
Annie: Reg . . .
Reg: And bishops walking diagonally (*demonstrating again*)

You ever seen a bishop walking like this? Well, have you? I'm asking you, have you ever seen a flaming bishop walking like this?

Sarah: Reg, will you please sit down and get on with it?

Reg (*sitting triumphantly*): Well then.

Round and Round the Garden is slightly different in character from the other two plays. Most people liked it less, though a minority which did not much enjoy the other two plays, liked the garden play better. It is less obviously farcical, and goes in for deeper exposure of the characters of Norman and his wife Ruth. But it also has some very amusing scenes, starting with Norman trying his new pyjamas on a garden statue and then being discovered by Tom.

Tom: Good Lord, what on earth are those?

Norman: Ssh. They look like wild pyjamas. Don't disturb them, they're nesting.

Tom: Yours, are they?

Norman: Yes. I better put them away before they savage someone. (*Snatching them, pretending they are attacking him, then cramming them back in the suitcase*) Go on, get in you brutes. In, in—get in. (*He slams the lid triumphantly*) The tops are all right, it's the bottoms you've got to watch.

In the second act there is a hilarious misunderstanding when Ruth tries to tell Tom to be more aggressive in his wooing of Annie but Tom imagines she is confessing her own love for him. This scene ends with Norman and Annie on the ground in an embrace, Tom and Reg discussing motor cars, Tom telling Ruth he loves her, and Sarah shrieking at all of them.

The social satire, and the sense of the thoughtless cruelty of people to each other, especially within families, come out even more strongly in Ayckbourn's next play, *Absent Friends*. This is about three married couples and their old friend Colin, whose fiancée recently died in a drowning accident. The couples have not seen Colin for years, but have invited him to tea to cheer him up. In fact he is quite happy with his memories, his photos and his romantic expectations of what his marriage would have been like; they are all unhappy in their marriages, and are soon made worse by *his* efforts to cheer *them* up with memories

1 Tom Stoppard's *Jumpers* (*photo* Zoe Dominic)

Above **2** David Storey and **3** Edward Bond (*photos* John Haynes and Laurence Sparham/IFL)

Below **4** David Storey's *The Changing Room* (*photo* John Haynes)

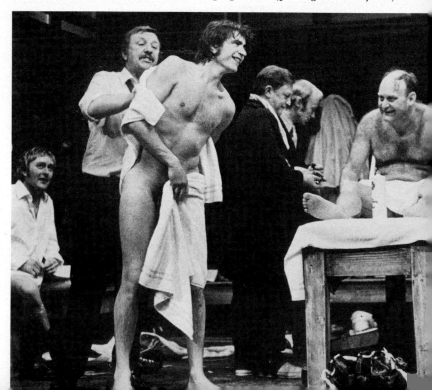

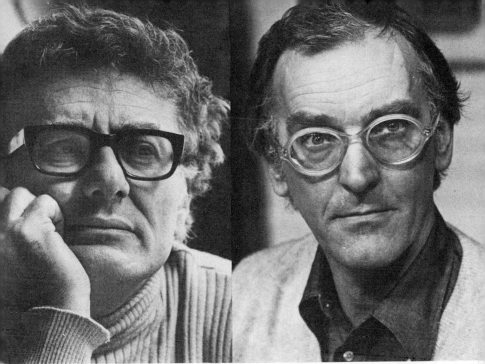

Above **5** Peter Shaffer and **6** Peter Nichols (*photos The Guardian* and Sophie Baker)

Below **7** David Dixon in Peter Shaffer's *Equus* (*photo* Zoe Dominic)

Above **8** E. A. Whitehead and **9** Christopher Hampton (*photos* Mark Gerson and John Haynes)

Below **10** Paul Scofield and Tom Conti in Christopher Hampton's *Savages* (*photo* Chris Davies/Report)

Above **11** Alan Ayckbourn and **12** Simon Gray (*photos* Colin Davey/Camera Press and Fay Godwin)

Below **13** Tom Courtenay and Felicity Kendal in Alan Ayckbourn's *The Norman Conquests* (*photo* John Haynes)

Above **15** Tom Stoppard and **16** David Hare (*photos* Mark Gerson)

Below **17** Helen Mirren and Hugh Frazer in David Hare's *Teeth 'n Smiles* (*photo* John Haynes)

Above **18** Howard Brenton (*photo* Chris Davies/Report) and
19 Howard Barker

Below **20** Tim Woodward, Constance Cummings and Michael
Hordern in Howard Barker's *Stripwell* (*photo* Chris Davies/Report)

Above **21** Trevor Griffiths and **22** Stephen Poliakoff
(*photos* John Haynes and Mark Gerson)

Below **23** Jonathan Pryce in Trevor Griffiths' *Comedians*
(*photo* John Haynes)

of their youth. *Absent Friends* is mainly a study of the way people can deteriorate in marriage. It also shows how well-meaning but insensitive people, trying to help others, can easily upset them further—a favourite Ayckbourn theme.

The hosts at the tea-party are Paul and Diana, materially well-off but now emotionally far apart. Diana suspects Paul of being unfaithful to her. The second couple, John and Evelyn, also squabble; she nags him for being mean and despises him for toadying to Paul for business reasons. He accepts her infidelities. The third husband, Gordon, does not appear; Marge has left him at home sick. He is always suffering from some minor ailment and has become very dependent on Marge, who fusses over him continually. He even rings up to say he has spilt cough mixture over his pyjamas and to ask what he should do.

The dialogue is spiced with dry humour, as when Marge interrogates Evelyn.

Marge: Have you been—having—a love affair with Paul?
Evelyn: No.
Marge: Truthfully?
Evelyn: I said so.
Marge: Oh. Well. That's all right then.
Evelyn: We did it in the back of the car the other afternoon but I wouldn't call that a love affair.

But on the whole *Absent Friends* is less funny and less ingenious than Ayckbourn's earlier plays, and not at all gimmicky. Its humour concentrates on the characters themselves, and is near the bone and slightly chilling. The play's climax is provided by Colin, refusing to accept that the marriages around him are on the rocks. Trying to assure Diana that Paul must still love her, he recalls that when they were courting Paul took a table-napkin from Diana's home as a souvenir. Marge and Diana are quite touched by this story. Paul promptly smashes their mood by saying he has still got the napkin—and uses it for cleaning the car. Diana promptly gets up from the tea-table and pours a jug of cream all over him. This, done in silence, is very funny; it is also an immediate prelude to Diana's breakdown, in which she screams her regret for marrying Paul and not following her childish ambition of joining the Mounted Police. This outburst is funny in its absurdity, but laughter is quickly killed by the pain of its revelation.

Ayckbourn is clearly trying to develop a new blend of laughter and social criticism. *Absent Friends* is a bit slow in developing, and people accustomed to the lighter Ayckbourn plays did not always know how to take it. His picture of married life is almost as savage as those painted by Osborne and Whitehead, but it is deceptively framed in cosiness. It became even more savage in *Just Between Ourselves*.

Confusions, five one-act plays loosely strung together to make a two-hour evening, marks a return to Ayckbourn's lighter manner, though spiced with a strong element of social satire and with a vague linking theme of man's loneliness and selfishness. The last of the five plays epitomizes this theme and the central 'confusion' of the evening:—five strangers sit close to each other on park benches and each in turn unburdens his worries to his uninterested but mildly irritated neighbour. The final line is spoken in frustration, when the wheel has come full circle and the first speaker realizes that his neighbour is not listening: 'You might as well talk to yourself.' That, in effect, is what the characters of *Confusions* all do.

Ayckbourn shows his customary ingenuity in using just three actors and two actresses to play twenty-one characters, arranging their costume and make-up changes so that one play follows another with scarcely any break. The first two are linked in the sense that the husband of the central character in the first actually appears in the second. Similarly, a woman whom we see quarrelling with her husband in the third play reappears without her husband in the fourth. The second and third plays feature waiters, who were originally played by the same actor, but this link was not maintained in the London production. Ayckbourn says that a character in the last play who refers to her husband running a pub can be assumed to be the ex-wife of Gosforth in the fourth play, but this link is certainly not at all evident to the audience. The plays can in any case be performed separately, and Ayckbourn hopes they will be, when they are done by amateur groups.

Mother Figure, the opening sketch, is about Lucy, a woman

so obsessed with her children that she also addresses her neighbours in baby talk and treats their marital squabbles with an old-fashioned nanny's mixture of bullying and cajolery. She succeeds in making the husband apologize to his wife, while forcing them to drink milk and orange juice, and she stops the wife crying by holding up a toy and asking if she wants it to see her cry! The result is amusing, and strangely moving. *Drinking Companion*, the least successful of the five plays, shows Lucy's husband trying to pick up two girls in the bar of a provincial hotel; he persists in thinking they are going to come to his bedroom, and gets drunker and drunker while forcing them to accept drinks. The play takes rather too long to reach its inevitable denouement, when they walk out on him.

Between Mouthfuls, which ends the first act of *Confusions*, has a typical Ayckbourn gimmick. Two couples are dining in a restaurant, but the audience can only hear as much of their conversation as is overheard by the waiter. As soon as he leaves one of the tables, the conversation there reverts to dumb show. One couple is quarrelling, with the wife demanding to know what her husband was doing while allegedly on business in Rome. The man at the other table is an employee of the man at the first, while the second man's wife was the boss's mistress in Rome. A great deal of laughter is extracted from this situation, from the sudden interruptions of conversation as the waiter moves from table to table and to the kitchen, and from the waiter's 'tactful' hoverings and occasional deft intrusions with the food and wine.

Gosforth's Fate, which opens the second act, is the funniest of the five sections. Everything goes wrong at a village fête:—one couple discuss their affair and the girl's pregnancy over the public address system by mistake, the lady councillor who opens the fête gets her dress ruined in the mud, the tea urn cannot be switched off, so that a manic procession of tea cups is carried to it while the councillor is trying to make her speech. The sound system short circuits and nearly electrocutes the councillor, while the pregnant girl's fiancée gets drunk and bawls obscene songs over a megaphone. The climax, when most of these things are happening simultaneously, is hilarious.

Finally *A Talk in The Park* has five solitaries in turn complaining to their neighbours that they have just been bored by their other neighbours, though of course they would never do such a thing themselves. It sums up the self-centredness and confusion of the entire evening, and of most of the characters in Ayckbourn's plays. As with the other plays, it is possible to enjoy *Confusions* without noticing its social satire or its implicit criticism of our behaviour, but nevertheless it is much more than the mere commercial farce which it superficially resembles.

So, despite its deceptive title, is *Bedroom Farce*. Traditionally a bedroom farce is a romp in which various characters jump in and out of bed together, or are caught in embarrassing circumstances in the same bedroom. Ayckbourn's play is set in three bedrooms, shown side by side on the stage, and involves four couples, but the married couples stay together and never get sexually intermingled, while their characters and problems are probed much more deeply than is usual in farce. Trevor and Susannah are infuriatingly self-absorbed; they think nothing of having a row in their hosts' bedroom at a party or of visiting their friends in the middle of the night to pour out their troubles. This couple provides the link between the others and the three bedrooms; their own bedroom is never shown. Nicky, another of the self-pitying characters that Ayckbourn loves to pillory, lies in bed with backache, demanding constant attention and sympathy from his wife and visitors, and also provoking truly farcical laughter with his clumsy and unsuccessful attempts to avoid falling out of bed. Trevor's parents, trying to recapture their youth by eating pilchards-on-toast in bed, tolerantly give advice to their daughter-in-law in the small hours of the morning. Malcolm and Katie play 'amusing' tricks on each other, like hiding shoes in their bed; Malcolm, a 'do-it-yourself' fanatic, sits up most of the night putting together a desk as a present for his wife. There is a lot of humour, especially at the end when the desk falls to pieces, but it is wry humour. *Bedroom Farce* is mainly notable for the sympathetic irony of its characterizations and for the ingenuity with which Ayckbourn links his couples and keeps the action —consecutively and sometimes simultaneously—in their bedrooms.

This was the first production that Ayckbourn himself directed in London, jointly with Peter Hall. There was nothing but praise for the skill of the production, but some criticism that such a 'commercial' piece should be staged at the National Theatre. It could equally well have been a West End success, but the National aims to have been the best plays of all kinds, not just non-commercial ones. *Just Between Ourselves*, in which a husband drives his wife into a catatonic trance, or *Absent Friends*, might have been more obvious choices for the National, being Ayckbourn's most serious plays. He describes *Absent Friends*, as a calculated risk, a deliberate slowing-down. 'I broke all my own rules in doing it, avoiding conventional comic set-pieces, etc. Most writers start with intense autobiographical works; I started with broad farce and I've been getting more and more gloomy ever since. Farce came to me naturally—the first ones were very derivative—and then I got interested in trying to enlarge my boundaries. You have to have been through at least one unhappy relationship to enjoy my plays now—married couples usually enjoy them particularly, recognizing their own problems and their relations and neighbours in the stage characters. They hardly ever recognize themselves. You can at most make people see their fellows in a new light, and you can make them feel for the characters, without loving them.'

Laughter is the main thing Ayckbourn wants to stimulate. 'There is nothing I want to say that can't be said through laughter, though of course other writers may have things they want to say that can't be said that way. I've been asking myself what sort of laughter I want. I find laughter arising from understanding and recognition between the audience and the stage characters is the most rewarding. I aim towards the audience—to do something to them. And I want to move further into the Chekhovian field, exploring attitudes to death, loneliness, etc.—themes not generally dealt with in comedy. The actors should be exploited, stretched, used, and the audience drawn in. However, *Bedroom Farce* goes back to traditional comedy a bit; it's a comedy though it's called a farce, and it's a study of the British in bed, with everything except sex!'

He dislikes modern forms of theatre in which the audience is directly assaulted or bullied into some form of participation.

'This makes me feel uncomfortable and disturbed when I'm in the audience myself, and a disturbed audience isn't a very receptive audience. If I'm disturbed my mind slows down and I don't respond.' No doubt Ayckbourn's style of writing and awareness of audience response are partly the result of writing and directing all his plays for his own company in Scarborough before they are staged elsewhere. They are never written as star vehicles or for particular actors. The only work he did specifically for London was the book and lyrics of the musical *Jeeves* which was, deservedly he thinks, an artistic and commercial disaster. He had no experience of writing a musical, and his first version was so long that it allowed no time for the music. (He hopes to make another attempt.) His plays have to be easily understood by a seaside audience, drawn from many walks of life and not consisting mainly of regular theatregoers. Apart from that, being a professional man of the theatre, Ayckbourn believes that plays should be skilfully put together.

'I was brought up in an intermediate era, when "well-made play" was not a dirty word, though new talents like Osborne and Pinter were overthrowing things. I've got a tidy mind and I like symmetry and shapes. If the structure is right, you can sustain an evening. After all, "playwright" suggests the craft of making a play, and why shouldn't it be well made? Growing a writer is like growing a rare plant—it often takes many years and many plays. Directing other people's plays concentrates my mind on why scenes do or don't work, and is very useful.' He encourages new writers to come and work in his theatre, even if only in a humble capacity, and is a keen supporter of the new tendency for theatres to have 'playwrights in residence'. 'Actually being in the theatre and meeting the actors is very valuable.' He himself often mulls over an idea for a play for a long period, perhaps a year, while getting on with his other duties in the theatre. 'The final draft can then be written in a week—it's a very quick affair.'

Ayckbourn admits to having been influenced by conventional writers like Coward and Rattigan, as well as by Pinter, who once directed his *Birthday Party* in Scarborough. 'During rehearsals we thought he was mad, but the first night was electrifying and frightening. Some aspects of Pinter appear in my work, especially a love for the bizarre use of the English language.' Ayckbourn also admires Simon Gray, 'ninety-eight per cent of Peter Nichols and a lot of Shaffer. I'm alarmed by people who state categorically that a play is no good unless it has a definite commitment to something, like Marxist revolution. I think a play can only be good if it's balanced. I dislike plays that preach, though marvellous plays do of course preach sometimes.'

Ayckbourn's progress from traditional farce 'into the Chekhovian field' remarkably parallels the development of the American playwright Neil Simon. Both seem increasingly interested in the comic side of the more bitter and tragic aspects of modern society. Perhaps because they are so closely concerned with their own societies, both of them have had difficulty in crossing the Atlantic. An attempt was made to 'translate' *How the Other Half Loves* into American, 'but the result was more like bad English than good American.' However, a lot of Ayckbourn's characters have American equivalents and with *Norman Conquests* it was decided to let American actors play the text as originally written. Even so, it ran for only six months in New York, compared with nearly two years in London.

Eight: Simon Gray

Born: Hayling Island, Hampshire, England, 1936.
Father: a medical practitioner, eventually specializing as a pathologist, mother a housewife. Paternal grandparents Canadian, and he was evacuated to Canada during Second World War.
Education: Westminster School, Dalhousie University, Nova Scotia, and Trinity College, Cambridge. Between taking B.A.s in English at both these universities, he taught in a French university (Clermont-Ferrand). After graduating, held university teaching jobs in Cambridge, at the University of British Columbia, Vancouver, and since 1966 at Queen Mary College, London University.
Married in 1965. Two children.
Has written various novels and television plays.
Plays:
Wise Child (originally written for TV but not considered suitable, London 1967, New York 1972). *Spoiled* (television 1968), (Edinburgh 1970, London 1971). *Dutch Uncle* (London 1969). *The Idiot* adapted from Dostoievsky, (London 1970). *Butley* (London 1971, New York 1972). *Otherwise Engaged* (London 1975, New York 1976). *Dog Days* (Oxford, England 1976). *Molly* (based on *Death of a Teddy Bear*, written for TV, Charleston, U.S.A., 1977).

Evening Standard Awards 1971, 1975. *Plays and Players* Award 1973. New York Drama Critics Circle Award 1977.

GRAY'S COMEDIES all show his interest, not surprising in a teacher of English, in the precise use of language. There is a lot of verbal humour, often achieved by one character taking literally another's loose use of words, and querying the meaning in a mocking or pedantic fashion. Butley, for example, himself a university English teacher, deliberately pretends to misunderstand the application of carelessly used relative clauses.

When a new student tells Butley that her predecessor didn't get to see him often, owing to administrative tangles, Butley promptly ripostes with 'Mrs Grainger got into administrative tangles?' Similarly when his colleague Joey tells him that a student has complained about another teacher's seminars in a pub, Butley says: 'Edna holds her seminars in a pub? I shall have to report this,' but of course it was the student's complaint that was made in a pub. In *Otherwise Engaged* Simon's wife tells him about her relationship with another man and says that they want to be husband and wife to each other. 'Husband *and* wife to each other? Is Ned up to such double duty?' Simon retorts. When Simon's brother accuses him of being indifferent, he answers, 'In what sense? As a wine is indifferent, or propositionally, as in, say, indifferent to . . .'

Gray also uses language to achieve various double meanings, usually with sexual undertones. In *Wise Child*, 'Mrs Artminster' is ostensibly showing her supposed son, Jerry, how to fix an ear-ring for the simple West Indian servant girl Janice.

> Mrs A: Just pop it into the hole and screw, dear, you can work it out for yourself.
> Janice: Ow! (*giggles*)
> Mrs A: Closer, my dear, closer, you look as if you're fishing without a pole. You've good eyes, don't worry about pricking her. You move in on him, girl.

And again, in *Dutch Uncle*, when the chiropodist Godboy is trying to get rid of a patient's husband, allegedly so as to remove her corns, he uses phrases like 'we were getting down to it' and 'we'll have it off'.

Many of Gray's characters have their own idiosyncratic phrases, which they use repeatedly. Godboy keeps saying 'merely' and Joey in *Butley* constantly says 'in point of fact'. Humour is derived from these repetitions, which are also revealing about the characters concerned. Similarly both Butley and Simon frequently repeat what someone else has said to them, but in the form of a question, a common habit of a certain type of mind, playing for time while thinking how to reply to an awkward remark.

Gray's humour is not simply verbal; it is also often visual, sometimes almost farcical. *Dutch Uncle* in particular attempts to obtain laughs from Godboy trying to gas his wife, when he thinks she is in a cupboard, while in fact she has already left it, in full view of the audience. *Spoiled* extracts farcical humour from Howarth, a schoolteacher, trying to give French dictation to a pupil who is still fumbling around with satchel, pencils and papers, and *Wise Child* has a classical farcical setting—two adjoining bedrooms in a hotel—with the kinky twists that 'Mrs Artminster' tries to get Janice to strip in one room while Mr Booker, the manager of the hotel, makes homosexual advances to 'her son' Jerry in the other.

These plays are also much more than mere farces. They are essentially about psychological and emotional relationships, about people's attempts to dominate and possess each other or, in the case of *Otherwise Engaged*, about efforts to avoid being possessed or involved. *Wise Child*, the first of Gray's plays to reach the London and New York stages, seemed very kinky when produced in 1967. 'Mrs Artminster' was originally played by Sir Alec Guinness. At first the audience is kept in doubt whether the other characters know they are dealing with a man in drag and whether 'Mrs Artminster' is a transvestite and her relationship with Jerry a homosexual one. Indeed there is even doubt whether we are watching a real woman, who happens to be played by a man. This kind of sexual ambiguity, not always so explicitly stated, is characteristic also of Gray's later work.

Wise Child, like all except one of Gray's plays to date, was produced in the West End commercial theatre. 'Mrs Artminster' and Jerry are crooks on the run, hiding out in a sleazy provincial hotel and posing as mother and son. They have conned Mr Booker, the manager, with talk of a country house being prepared for them and they pretend to have mistaken his hotel for the town's posh one. Jerry earns money by applying for jobs, making himself thoroughly unsuitable at the interviews, and claiming lavish expenses for attendance. He also flirts teasingly with Booker, while his 'mother' flirts with Janice. There are hints of a sado-masochistic sexual relationship between 'Mrs Artminster' and Jerry, but these are never made explicit. At the end of the play, when 'Mrs Artminster' reverts to his real identity as Jock Masters, Jerry dresses in Janice's clothes, so their ambivalent relationship is presumably to continue.

Gray's next play to reach the London stage, *Dutch Uncle*, was the only one to be presented by a publicly subsidized company, the Royal Shakespeare Company at the Aldwych. It had the prestige of being directed by Peter Hall, had the well-known television actor Warren Mitchell in the lead, and was a complete flop, being withdrawn after only twelve performances. Reading the text confirms my impression at the time that the fault was mainly in the production and performance, rather than in the play. Gray himself would like it produced in his original text, rather than in the considerably rewritten version he eventually produced for the Aldwych. It could perhaps be 'rescued' rather as Joe Orton's *What the Butler Saw* was rescued by the Royal Court several years after its disastrous West End production. Essentially it requires a magnetic star actor as Mr Godboy, a homicidal chiropodist.

Dutch Uncle has been compared to Orton's *Loot*, as both plays are black farces dealing with death. The plot concerns Godboy's efforts to gas his wife in a cupboard, specially bought and prepared for the purpose, and to have an affair with Doris, the wife of the upstairs neighbour. Complications are provided by Godboy's Raskolnikov-like infatuation with murder, as a means of achieving celebrity, and his attempts to interest Inspector Hawkins in his proposed crime. Inspector Hawkins is on the trail of an actual rapist and murderer, who turns out to be Doris's husband. After various false alarms and farcical twists, including Hawkins flirting with Doris, the play ends with Godboy's wife casually shutting him in the cupboard. The audience is left, in Gray's typically open-ended manner, unsure whether Godboy will ever emerge.

Several of Gray's other favourite themes appear in *Dutch Uncle*, but in a minor way. Hawkins is assisted by a policeman who has to put on drag in an attempt to decoy the street rapist; Hawkins talks about religion and sin while fondling Doris, and Godboy himself is in some ways similar to Simon's brother Stephen in *Otherwise Engaged*, in that they are both 'greyish' characters who realize that they make no lasting impression on their fellows and are desperately trying to remedy this, though in very different ways.

THE NEW BRITISH DRAMA

Gray denies having any special interest in religion, one way or another. But Donald, in *Spoiled*, a teenage boy of uncertain sexual tastes, also suffers from a religious upbringing and a consequent sense of guilt affecting his sex life. *Spoiled* was presented in London at the large Haymarket Theatre, mostly associated with rather conventional plays, did not have a very big star in the cast, and lasted for only thirty-seven performances. Simon Ward, an actor who specialized for a long time in playing very good-looking youths, and who had already played Jerry in *Wise Child*, appeared as Donald and Jeremy Kemp as Howarth, the schoolmaster giving him extra tuition at home. *Spoiled* is more conventional than *Wise Child* and *Dutch Uncle*, daring only in that it hints at a homosexual relationship between the teacher and pupil. However it does not really face up to the problems posed by such a relationship. Howarth's nocturnal visit to Donald's bedroom, to comfort him in his distress, is presented as accidental, and not to be repeated, while Donald actually breaks off a friendship with another boy when Howarth tells him that the boy had to leave school because of homosexual activities. The effect of all this on Howarth's marriage is left uncertain. The relationship between his problems as a schoolmaster and his marital problems recalls Storey's *Arnold Middleton*; as in the earlier play, the ending is enigmatic. Howarth tells Donald he will not coach him any more and his wife hands him the cake Donald left behind. *Spoiled* is theatrical, with a particularly effective first-act curtain when Howarth unexpectedly goes into Donald's bedroom. There are some shrewd psychological insights, but because of its failure to face up to the big issues it raises, *Spoiled* left most people dissatisfied.

Butley was Gray's first big success, running for over a year in the West End, with Alan Bates, Richard Briers and Alec McCowen successively playing the title role, and winning the *Evening Standard* Award for the best new play of the year. Ben Butley is a lazy, cynical London University teacher, a master of the arts of getting out of his duties and of being wittily unpleasant to his friends and colleagues. One student is told, 'I can't give tutorials during the first week after the break, I'm afraid. Too much administration.' Another asks Butley what he should write his essay about and is fobbed off: 'You must decide for yourself, can't expect spoon feeding.' But the play is mostly about Butley's relationship with Joey, an ex-pupil and now a junior colleague with whom he shares his home and the office where the action of the play takes place. He keeps Joey on tenterhooks about his promotion and he is merciless in prying into his private life. When Joey is clearly reluctant to tell Butley anything about Reg, with whose family he has been staying, Ben starts an interrogation.

> Ben: Tell me, what does he do, Reg's dad? (*Smiles*) But we're not ashamed are we?
> Joey: (*pause*) He owns a shop.
> Ben: What sort of shop?
> Joey: Just a shop.
> Ben: Just a shop? Just a shop like Harrods, for example. What does he sell?
> Joey: (*after a pause*) Meat, I think.
> Ben: You think. Did you ever see the shop?
> Joey: Of course. Why?
> Ben: Was there meat on display?
> Joey: Yes.
> Ben: In that case he either owns a meat museum or if it was for sale you're quite right, he owns a shop that sells meat. He's what's called a butcher.
> Joey: That's right, he's a butcher.

Ben discovers later that it's not right at all; Joey has been stung into totally deceiving him about Reg. During the play all Ben's world collapses. He not only loses Joey, but also his wife, and he is under increasing suspicion from his colleagues for his laziness and malicious tongue. The play ends with a new student, whom Ben has 'poached' from one of the other teachers, coming to read poetry to him. It looks as if Ben is about to embark on a new relationship like the one with Joey. But he suddenly thinks better of it, in the very last words of the play: 'I'm too old to play with the likes of you.' The curtain falls as Ben sits at his desk trying unsuccessfully to get the reading light to work.

It is difficult to account for the great success of this play. It is both witty and psychologically interesting, but one might have expected that its appeal would be limited to middle-class intellectuals. Obviously many other people identify with Butley's emotional and professional problems, and enjoy the outrageous way in which he treats people. Something of the same formula was repeated in Gray's next play, *Otherwise Engaged*, which also won the *Evening Standard* Award, among many others, and which again starred Alan Bates for the first months of its long London run. Like Butley, Simon in this play is an intellectual, this time a publisher. There is even less plot than in *Butley*: *Otherwise Engaged* is a series of duologues between Simon and various visitors who interrupt his attempt to listen to a complete recording of *Parsifal*: the upstairs lodger, a student who thinks the world owes him a living, Simon's brother Stephen, a veteran schoolteacher desperately worried about whether he will become a deputy headmaster, Jeff, a trendy literary critic who launches tirades against 'literature', Australians, women, homosexuals, his wife and almost everyone and everything else, Jeff's mistress who tricks him into thinking his wife has attempted suicide and who suddenly strips 'topless' in an unsuccessful attempt to seduce Simon, Wood, a faintly sinister stranger who recalls lusting after Simon when they were at school and who now accuses him of seducing his girl, and finally Beth, Simon's wife, who insists on telling him the details of her affair with another man.

At first *Otherwise Engaged* seems like a series of witty and sometimes outrageous revue sketches. Simon listens to his visitors with apparent solicitude and endless patience, but his interest in them is superficial. He asks questions which are often trivial and irrelevant. When Stephen complains that his rival for the job had the unfair advantage of being educated at Oxford, Simon asks, 'Which college?', and when Stephen describes having to drink his headmaster's herbal coffee, Simon wants to know what sort of herbs. His equanimity is disturbed, first by Davina's striptease and then by Wood. The first act ends, on a typical Gray note of uncertainty and suspense, with Simon admitting he had sex with Wood's girl. Simon is under the impression that the girl is Wood's young daughter and the audience is left wondering whether Simon

is telling the truth. In the second act, Simon's character becomes clearer. Wood explains that the girl is not his daughter
but his fiancée, and that she sleeps around a lot anyway.
Simon admits that he has regular sex on a couch in his office
and explains his techniques for avoiding VD and detection by
his wife. But he refuses to be unfaithful at home and wants to
preserve his marriage. He suspects his wife's affair but does not
want to know about it. When Beth says to him, 'In other words,
you do know', his answer is, 'In other words, can't we confine
ourselves to the other words'. He is fairly happy with the life
he has organized for himself, and does not want it disturbed
by unnecessary complications.

However it *is* increasingly disturbed. Wood expresses a wish
to kill him, Stephen accuses him of being indifferent and of
despising his job, the student launches a furious tirade against
him and then installs two further lodgers in the upstairs flat,
and Beth tells him she is expecting a baby and does not know
whose. The play ends with Simon cutting off a recorded phone
message in which Wood is announcing his suicide; Simon then
persuades Jeff to settle down to listen to *Parsifal*. (He has even
forgotten that it was Jeff who first introduced him to Wagner.)
Perhaps Simon does not love or care about anyone, except
himself; perhaps he cares about them too much and has to
distance himself from them to avoid intolerable suffering. He
certainly helps people as much as he can, and tries to avoid
saying anything to hurt them. Equally, he does not want to
hear anything that will hurt him unnecessarily. Both Simon
and Ben Butley are similar in many ways to Philip in Hampton's *The Philanthropist*. They all share the same sort of detachment and pedantic verbal humour. Indeed the scene in which
Simon rejects Jeff's mistress and tells her that fidelity means
more to him 'than a suck and a fuck with the likes of you' is
astonishingly reminiscent of Philip's rejection of Araminta's
advances.

Some people would regard Simon's behaviour as thoroughly
sensible and civilized. Paul Johnson, in a political article in the
New Statesman, even suggested that Simon represents western
civilization, giving aid and comfort to the rest of the world and
getting nothing but abuse in return.

Gray does not intend any such parallel, and he certainly understands why Simon is disliked. 'I like all my characters. But of course if you are Simon's brother, then Simon is intolerable. If you are Simon, then you are doing your best to help people, without getting over-involved with them. Somehow it does nowadays seem selfish and disreputable to be so well organized, and as little involved with others as possible'. Gray rejects the suggestion that he particularly identifies with Simon, to the extent of giving the character his own name. 'The choice of names is pure laziness; some of the characters are simply called after people I'd recently met. I only identify myself with Simon in the sense that I identify with all my characters.'

Peter in *Dog Days* is another character in the Butley/Simon mould. Like Butley, he uses verbal pedantry to discomfort and upset his friends and relations; like Simon, he is a publisher with a schoolteacher brother whom he despises. He is more outspokenly rude than either of them, and more obviously unhappy. Although it was not produced till 1976, *Dog Days* was written around the same time as *Butley* and before *Otherwise Engaged*. In fact Gray describes it as the source of *Otherwise Engaged*, and of two of his television plays. He was dissatisfied with it, thinking it insufficiently structured, and refused permission for it to be performed on several occasions. His final agreement was reluctant and, in the first instance, only for a provincial try-out. Contrary to his usual practice, he did not attend rehearsals, fearing that his lack of enthusiasm for the play might infect the cast.

The characters and plot of *Dog Days* exactly parallel those in *Otherwise Engaged*, but with interesting and significant differences. Peter is more openly hostile to his brother, and his quarrels with his wife are shown in greater detail. On the other hand he is nice to Joanna, the artist who brings him her work, instead of brusquely rejecting her as Simon rejected Davina. While Simon refused to have sex with Davina because he was married and their meeting was in his home, it is Joanna who refuses Peter for the same reasons. Instead of sitting at home refusing to alter his life, Peter moves out to a flat of his own and attempts an affair with Joanna there.

Peter is as fastidious about language and as clever at using it to make other people uncomfortable as any of Gray's heroes. The mood is set in the very first scene, when Joanna is looking at a family photo.

Joanna: Your Dad's a fine figure of a man. I love his balaclava, is it from the war or something?
Peter: Actually that's my mother in her gardening gear. But you're right, she was a fine figure of a man. That's my father there, on the edge of the picture as usual. In the fine figure of the little husband.
Joanna: He's got a really nice smile.
Peter: Hasn't he? A positive advertisement.
Joanna: For what, your mother you mean?
Peter: No, drunkenness.
Joanna: Oh. Did he drink too much then?
Peter: He did, yes.
Joanna: But he gave it up?
Peter: Oh, nothing so drastic. He got killed in a car crash some years ago.
Joanna: Oh God, I'm sorry. How terrible.
Peter: For whom?
Joanna: Well, your mother. . . .
Peter: Not at all.
Joanna: You mean she didn't mind?
Peter: She didn't have time to, as she was driving.

There is not quite as much of this witty dialogue as in *Butley* or *Otherwise Engaged*, but what there is, is vintage Gray. Here is Joanna rejecting Peter's attentions:

Joanna: Get off me! What sort of fool do you think I am?
Peter: My sort, I hope . . .
Joanna: You're married!
Peter: Good God, who to?
Joanna: That landlady of yours.
Peter: Scarcely.
Joanna: Scarcely what?
6

Peter: Scarcely eight years.

Joanna: And that little boy's your son. Well, isn't he?

Peter: If I answer that question with too much confidence, I'll destroy the promise of a whole tragic literature. Besides, he's very little, if you stare straight ahead, you won't even see him.

Joanna: I don't sleep with married men, I'm afraid.

Peter: Of what? We're very well trained.

Joanna: Jesus, what a prick!

Peter (*angrily*): What a *what*?

Joanna: Prick, that's what you are, a prick!

Peter: Oh, thank God, I thought you said *prig*.

Apart from the same kind of dialogue, *Dog Days* is clearer and sharper in its psychological observation than Gray's other plays. It is possible to take *Otherwise Engaged*, for example, simply as a witty comedy, and to ignore its compassionate study of Simon. *Dog Days* is less funny and more moving. Not only is Peter more fully exposed than Simon, but his brother and his wife display their feelings more than their equivalents do in *Otherwise Engaged*. There is a particularly touching scene when Charles, the brother, admits that he always assumes people are thinking the worst of him. Peter mocks him unmercifully for his innumerable children and his toadying to the headmaster but finally agrees that they are true brothers 'under the skin' when he himself toadies to the directors of his firm after insulting them and their authors while drunk. (The description of the trendy literary party at which this happens is a very amusing and accurate bit of satire.) Charles is secretly in love with Peter's wife, and envies him his various affairs, which are actually fantasies. The play ends with Peter offering to return to his wife, who does not want him back, and with an enigmatic final scene in which Peter and Joanna resume exactly as they were at the beginning of the play.

Despite the differences between the character and plots of *Butley*, *Otherwise Engaged* and *Dog Days*, the similarities are much more apparent.

Gray says there is no particular reason why certain characters and themes recur in his plays, except that they are characters and themes familiar from life. When it is pointed out that many of his characters are sexually ambiguous, he replies that that is how many people are. 'Howarth in *Spoiled* is in some ways still a boy, only really relaxed with a younger boy, not with his wife.' Similarly, 'Butley has some of his most emotional and possessive relationships with other men, but these relationships are not necessarily sexual.' Gray is surprised that people see Butley as homosexual; 'he might have been happier if he *had* had a homosexual relationship with Joey, and then he might have preserved it. It's because Butley is unhappy that he uses language to irritate or embarrass others. Simon in *Otherwise Engaged* is the opposite, in a way; he applies his verbal dexterity and pedantry to little games which are mainly designed to amuse himself.'

Gray has always written, since he was a boy, but did not at first think of writing plays. At first he wrote novels; it was only when he adapted one of his short stories for radio that he decided it was easier and more lucrative to write plays. 'I was not a theatregoer, and had only been to three or four plays when I wrote my first. Although I've been told that my work shows the influence of Orton, actually I didn't know Orton's work at all till Peter Hall suggested I should read some of his plays when we were rehearsing *Dutch Uncle*. The main influence on me as a writer has been Charles Dickens, who had a marvellous eye for unusual and grotesque characters—like Sarah Gamp and other women who are almost men. Dickens really caught the new sex, the sexual ambiguities we think we have discovered today.' Gray denies having any message, any particular views about politics, religion or human behaviour which he wants to put across. 'Writing a play is like writing a poem or a story—one has a responsibility to one's audience or one's readers, a clear obligation to entertain or interest them. On the other hand, I wouldn't write if I thought my sole function was to keep the audience happy. I want to give people a new perception of life, different from their own. I certainly don't set out to shock them; indeed I'm surprised when they are shocked.'

His plays start, not with a group of characters or with a plot, but with one person in a room saying something. 'Who does he say it to, and why? The play usually follows on from there.' The plays are not planned in Gray's mind but take shape in dozens and dozens of drafts, written and rewritten in gaps between teaching. In an article in the *New Statesman* shortly after *Dutch Uncle* had flopped in London, he amusingly described how it was rewritten several times during the pre-London provincial tour. The ending was altered several times and 'a comedy that covered the audience in a vast shroud of depression' was turned into 'a farce as witless as it was macabre, that would goad the audience into an irritated restlessness'. The plays are not written with any particular cast in mind; when he wrote *Otherwise Engaged*, Gray at first thought Alan Bates would be unsuitable for Simon. In fact he had a triumph in the role, though the play works equally well when Simon is played by other actors; Michael Gambon, who succeeded Bates in London, was much colder and more withdrawn, while Tom Courtenay, who opened in the play on Broadway, had even more defensive charm. Following some unhappy experiences earlier, Gray does now insist on control over casting being inserted into his contracts. He has a friendly relationship with Michael Codron, his producer, and with Harold Pinter, who directed *Butley* and *Otherwise Engaged*; the casting and production of those plays was planned between the three of them. Gray attends nearly all rehearsals; *Butley* and *Otherwise Engaged* were both cut by him during the rehearsal stage.

He enjoys the fact that in England a playwright can go on leading his own life, unaffected by publicity. 'You don't have to live the life of a playwright; I don't think the people in my street think of me as one.'

The one subject which he admits to feeling strongly about is education—'more important than politics, and I very much resent education becoming part of a political wrangle'. He still puts 'teacher' rather than 'writer' in his passport, though he is not sure how long he will be able to find time and energy for both careers. There can be little doubt that if one of them has to be surrendered, it will—most reluctantly—be the teaching.

Nine: Tom Stoppard

Born: Zlin, Czechoslovakia, 1937.
Father: Eugene Straussler, a doctor, emigrated with family to Singapore in 1938 and died there during the Japanese occupation. Stoppard with his mother and brother escaped to India just before Singapore fell to the Japanese, and at the war's end his mother married a British army officer serving in India. Stoppard later took his stepfather's name by deed poll.
Education: Convent school and multi-racial American school in India, followed by preparatory and public school (Pocklington, Yorkshire) in England.
Worked as a staff journalist in Bristol 1954–60 and then as a freelance journalist in London till 1963.
Married (1) in 1965 and (2) in 1972—four children, two by each marriage.
Plays:
A Walk on the Water (Hamburg, 1964; expanded and re-titled *Enter a Free Man*, London 1968; New York 1974). *The Gambler* (Bristol, 1965). *Tango* (adapted from Nicholas Bethell's translation of Slavomir Mrozek; London, 1966). *Rosencrantz and Guildenstern Are Dead* (Edinburgh, 1966; revised for London 1967; New York, 1968). *The Real Inspector Hound* (London, 1968; New York, 1972). *After Magritte* (London, 1970; New York, 1972). *Dogg's Our Pet* (London, 1971). *Jumpers* (London, 1972; New York, 1974). *Travesties* (London, 1974; New York, 1975). *Dirty Linen* and *New-Found-Land* (London, 1976; Washington, D.C., 1976; New York, 1977). *Albert's Bridge* (London, 1976—originally written for radio, 1968). *If You're Glad, I'll be Frank* (London, 1976—originally written for radio, 1965). *Every Good Boy Deserves Favour* (London, 1977).

John Whiting Award 1967; *Evening Standard* Awards 1967,

1972, 1974; *Plays and Players* Awards 1967, 1972; New York Drama Critics Circle Awards 1968, 1976.

TOM STOPPARD is one of the most successful and also one of the most puzzling of the new British playwrights. His work is highly praised by critics in London and New York, and entertains audiences which enjoy being mildly mystified. At one level his best plays are amusing word-games, with wildly implausible and fantastic plots. They also hint at deeper philosophical meanings, and reflect on the state of our society. Learned articles have been written about their deeper significance. When interviewed, Stoppard, who dislikes talking about his work, usually disclaims any deep purpose, and says he is primarily an entertainer.

He made his name in the British theatre with *Rosencrantz and Guildenstern are Dead*, the first of his plays to be staged in London. But *A Walk on the Water* first shown on British television in 1963, had already been staged in Hamburg, Germany. It did not reach London, re-written and retitled *Enter a Free Man*, till a year after *Rosencrantz*. It was more conventional than Stoppard's later plays, with a recognizable family drama as its central plot and with such familiar themes as a husband's boredom with his marriage and the generation gap between parents and children. It also contained clues to Stoppard's later preoccupations with the abuse of logic and language. The family drama showed affinities with writers like Shaffer and Nichols, the linguistic games with Ionesco, N. F. Simpson, and ultimately Lewis Carroll.

The 'free man' of the title is George Riley, a self-styled inventor (also familiar from Lewis Carroll) whose inventions, including a reversible envelope which can be used twice and an arrangement of plumbing to provide 'indoor rain' for plants, are superficially attractive but contain an obvious logical flaw. Riley lives in his fantasy world, leaving home for the pub every Saturday convinced that he is about to market an invention and start a new life. He even gives the people he meets imaginary names; his wife, whom he calls Persephone, supports his illusions with love and understanding. She values him for being 'different'. Their daughter Linda, on the other hand, despises him for living in a dream world and refusing to accept the reality of his failure and unemployment. She also despises her mother for accepting the situation.

The play's principal theme is this conflict between ordinary life and being 'different'. Persephone has the shrewdest understanding of this conflict, and tries to explain it to Linda. At one point she uses logic to answer Linda's complaint.

Linda: Do you ever think of yourself that there's a kind of sameness about your life?
Persephone: It's be a funny life if there wasn't.

But she is capable of defending her life, and her husband, much more explicitly.

Persephone: There's lots of people like your father—different. Some make more money, because they're different. And some make none, because they're different. The difference is the thing, not the money.

When Linda's irritation really explodes, Persephone's love and understanding flare up in anger.

Linda: We're carrying him, you and me, and I don't know about you, but I'm tired. He may be a lovely feller to stand a drink in the pub, great value for money, I'm sure—but as the family joke, he's wearing a bit thin. We're lumbered, and we'll go on being lumbered till he's dead, and that may be *years*—— Oh, God—I didn't mean that—I just meant——
Persephone: You didn't mean anything because you don't know anything and you don't think. You don't ask yourself why—you don't ask yourself what it costs him to keep his belief in himself—to come back each time and start again—and it's worth keeping, it's the last thing he's got—but you don't know and you don't think and you don't ask. It costs him—every time he comes back he loses a little face and he's lost a lot of face—to you he's lost all of it. You treat him like a crank lodger we've got living upstairs who reads fairy tales and probably wishes he lived in one, but he's ours and we're his, and don't you ever talk like that about him again. You can call him the family joke, but it's our family. We're still a family.

When Linda asks the point of keeping the family together, Persephone movingly puts the case for family life, something of the case that Clive's father put to him in Shaffer's *Five Finger Exercise*. It is the typical argument of our time, between the parents who provide material comfort and security, and the children who despise them for it.

> Persephone: I've kept our life tidy—I've looked after you, and him, and got you this far—perhaps it is a waste of time. You never went to sleep on a damp sheet and you never went to school without a cooked breakfast—and what was the point of that? I worked for you—I stood behind a counter so that your school clothes were the same colour as everyone else's. What was the point? You tell me why I worked late for a red blazer. It hasn't all gone your way, but it's a good home—you've never wanted for a kind word and when you looked for a clean hanky or a jumper you found it. What was the point of that?

The ending of the play is mildly sentimental and superficially 'happy'. Linda discovers that the man with whom she is eloping is already married, returns home, and accepts her father's eccentricities. He accepts his failure as an inventor and agrees to register for unemployment pay—a victory for reason but also the destruction of a 'free man'.

Enter a Free Man is fairly conventional in form, as well as in subject, though scenes at home are merged into scenes in the pub (on opposite sides of the stage) in a dream-like way, without any formal break between them. Some dialogue between Riley and his drinking companions in the pub, attacking the symptoms of modern civilization, using a formidable battery of clichés in the process and concluding with some inconsequential, near-nonsense exchanges, is a precursor of things to come in Stoppard's later plays.

> Riley: No wonder the country is going to the dogs. Personal enterprise sacrificed to bureaucracy. No pride, no patriotism. The erosion of standards, the spread of mediocrity, the decline of craftsmanship and the betrayal of the small investor.

Harry: It's terrible really. I blame youth.

Carmen: Education.

Harry: The Church is out of touch.

Carmen: The family is not what it was.

Harry: It's the power of the unions.

Carmen: The betrayal of the navy.

Harry: Ban the bomb.

Carmen: Spare the rod.

Harry: I'm all right, Jack.

Carmen: The little man goes to the wall.

Harry: Supermarkets.

Carmen: Everything's plastic.

Harry: Country's going to the dogs. What happened to our greatness?

Riley: Look at the Japanese!

Harry: Look at the Japanese!

Riley: The Japanese look after the small investor!

Harry: All Japanese investors are small.

Carmen: They're a small people.

Harry: Very small. Short.

Riley: The little man!

Harry: The little people!

Riley: Look at the transistor!

Harry: Very small.

Riley: Japanese!

Carmen: Gurkhas are short.

Harry: But exceedingly brave for their size.

Carmen: Fearless.

Riley (*furiously*): What are you talking about?

Not being sure what the characters are talking about is a hallmark of Stoppard's later work. It is indeed the whole point of *Rosencrantz and Guildenstern are Dead*, his first big hit. The verbal dexterity and quasi-philosophical games in this play are clever and amusing, while the published text shows Stoppard's extreme theatrical professionalism.

He marks optional cuts, explaining that the play will work better at different lengths depending on the style of production and the place where it is being performed. The author's note also stresses that the play, 'whatever else it is, is a comedy. My intention was comic, and if the play has not turned out funny I would have considered that I had failed. Quite a lot of solemn and scholarly stuff has been written about it, which is fine and flattering, but it is worth bearing in mind that among the productions staged all over the world, two were comparative failures, and both of these took the play very seriously indeed.'

The principal characters are obviously those minor characters in Shakespeare's *Hamlet* who are always being confused with each other. In Stoppard's play they are confused about their own identities, and about the nature of the world around them. They engage in quasi-philosophical and zany cross-talk which immediately recalls the dialogues between the tramps in Beckett's *Waiting for Godot*. The play opens with Guildenstern repeatedly tossing a coin, Rosencrantz repeatedly announcing that it is 'heads' and pocketing it, and Guildenstern expressing no surprise at the unnatural run of 'heads'. Instead, he tries to rationalize what is happening.

> Guildenstern: It must be indicative of something, besides the redistribution of wealth. (*He muses*) List of possible explanations. One: I'm willing it. Inside where nothing shows, I am the essence of a man spinning double-headed coins, and betting against himself in private atonement for an unremembered past. (*He spins a coin at Rosencrantz*)
> Rosencrantz: Heads.
> Guildenstern: Two: time has stopped dead, and the single experience of one coin being spun once has been repeated many times . . . (*He flips a coin, looks at it, tosses it to Rosencrantz*) On the whole, doubtful. Three: divine intervention, that is to say, a good turn from above concerning him, cf. children of Israel, or retribution from above concerning me, cf. Lot's wife. Four: a spectacular vindication of the principle that each individual coin spun individually—(*he spins one*) is as likely to come down heads as tails and therefore should cause no surprise each individual time it does. (*It does. He tosses it to Rosencrantz*)
> Rosencrantz: I've never known anything like it!

Guildenstern: And a syllogism: One, he has never known anything like it. Two, he has never known anything to write home about. Three, it is nothing to write home about . . . Home . . . what's the first thing you remember?

Rosencrantz: Oh, let's see—the first thing that comes into my head, you mean?

Guildenstern: No—the first thing you remember.

Rosencrantz: Ah (*Pause*), it's no good, it's gone. It was a long time ago.

Guildenstern: You don't get my meaning. What is the first thing after all the things you've forgotten?

Rosencrantz: Oh I see. (*Pause*) I've forgotten the question.

Sometimes Stoppard adds sexual *double entendre* to his dialogue. When Rosencrantz and Guildenstern meet the travelling players, the players offer a private performance of *The Rape of the Sabine Women*, with audience participation. 'Exhibitions' and 'trade' are part of the prostitute's professional jargon.

Rosencrantz: You're not—ah—exclusively players, then?

Player: We're inclusively players, sir.

Rosencrantz: So you give—exhibitions?

Player: Performances, sir.

Rosencrantz: Yes of course. There's more money in that, is there?

Player: There's more trade, sir.

Rosencrantz: Times being what they are.

Player: Yes.

Rosencrantz: Indifferent.

Player: Completely.

Rosencrantz: You know I'd no idea——

Player: No——

Rosencrantz: I mean, I've *heard* of—but I've never actually——

Player: No.

Rosencrantz: I mean, what exactly do you *do*?

Player: We keep to our usual stuff, more or less, only inside out. We do on stage the things that are supposed to happen off. Which is a kind of integrity, if you look on every exit being an entrance somewhere else.

This is to some extent a description of what Stoppard is

doing in this play (and more precisely of what Ayckbourn did later in *The Norman Conquests*).

When they all meet again in Elsinore, the Player reproaches Rosencrantz and Guildenstern for walking out on the roadside performance and expounds on the strange nature of acting and on the actor's lack of identity. He poses a similar personal challenge to one posed by Challenor in Trevor Griffiths' *Comedians*.

> Player: You don't understand the humiliation of it—to be tricked out of the single assumption which makes our existence viable—that somebody is *watching*. (*Lost*) There we were—demented children mincing about in clothes that no one ever wore, speaking as no man ever spoke, swearing love in wigs and rhymed couplets, killing each other with wooden swords, hollow protestations of faith hurled after empty promises of vengeance—and every gesture, every pose, vanishing into the unpopulated air. We ransomed our dignity to the clouds, and the uncomprehending birds listened. (*He rounds on them*) Don't you see? We're *actors*—we're the opposite of people! (*They recoil nonplussed, his voice calms*) Think, in your head, now, think of the most *private—secret—intimate* thing you have ever done secure in the knowledge of its privacy. (*He gives them, and the audience, a good pause. Rosencrantz takes on a shifty look*) Are you thinking of it? (*He strikes with his voice and his head*) Well, I saw you do it!

Anyone who complains that they don't really understand what is going on in a Stoppard play is to some extent answered by the Player. Just as actors are the opposite of people, but mirror them, so the uncertainty in the plays mirrors life.

> Guildenstern: We have been left so much to our own devices —after a while one welcomes the uncertainty of being left to other people's.
> Player: Uncertainty is the normal state. You're nobody special.
> Guildenstern: But for God's sake what are we supposed to do?
> Player: Relax, respond. That's what people do. You can't go through life questioning your situation at every turn.

Guildenstern: But we don't know what's going on, or what to do with ourselves. We don't know how to *act*.

Player: Act natural. You know why you're here at least.

Guildenstern: We only know what we're told, and that's little enough. And for all we know it isn't even true.

Player: For all anyone knows, nothing is. Everything has to be taken on trust; truth is only that which is taken to be true. It's the currency of living. There may be nothing behind it, but it doesn't make any difference so long as it is honoured. One acts on assumptions. What do you assume?

So the plight of Rosencrantz and Guildenstern is related to the universal human plight, and to some eternal metaphysical puzzles. Yet Stoppard never forgets the structure and plot of his play. A conversation between Rosencrantz and Guildenstern when they have mislaid the King's letter to England about Hamlet is funny in itself, and leads to them finding and reading the letter, discovering that Hamlet is to be murdered. This in turn gives Guildenstern the opportunity to speculate about the nature of death, and to decide by twisted but plausible logic that as death is so mysterious it is best not to interfere to prevent it. When the letters are switched, and Rosencrantz and Guildenstern realize that *they* are to die, this provides the excuse for final speculation about their importance and identity.

As Stoppard says, however, his play is comic, and can be enjoyed without considering philosophical problems. Indeed, many people in the audience are quite unaware of the philosophical problems or only become aware on seeing the play a second or third time. They cannot miss the jokes, or the amusing commentary on Hamlet, including a pointed reminder of the illogicality of Shakespeare's plot: Why did Claudius succeed to the throne, and why didn't Hamlet object more directly? Guildenstern pretends to be Hamlet, and lets Rosencrantz probe his behaviour, with verbal dexterity and sexual innuendo.

Rosencrantz: So—so your uncle is the King of Denmark?!

Guildenstern: And my father before him.

Rosencrantz: His father before him?

Guildenstern: No, my father before him.

Rosencrantz: But surely—

Guildenstern: You might well ask.
Rosencrantz: Let me get it straight. Your father was king. You were his only son. Your father dies. You are of age. Your uncle becomes king.
Guildenstern: Yes.
Rosencrantz: Unorthodox.
Guildenstern: Undid me.
Rosencrantz: Undeniable. Where were you?
Guildenstern: In Germany.
Rosencrantz: Usurpation, then.
Guildenstern: He slipped in.
Rosencrantz: Which reminds me.
Guildenstern: Well, it would.
Rosencrantz: I don't want to be personal.
Guildenstern: It's common knowledge.
Rosencrantz: Your mother's marriage.
Guildenstern: He slipped in.

Literary parody and allusions are constant elements in Stoppard's work. *The Real Inspector Hound* is partly a parody of an old-fashioned stage thriller, and partly a satire on theatre critics. Birdboot and Moon, two critics, are seen watching a play. Moon is a deputy and is obsessed with his status; Birdboot arrives late, disturbing the audience, and is interested in a new young actress in the play they are watching. Ultimately both Birdboot and Moon get involved in the action of the play, which takes place in an isolated country-house, surrounded by foggy marshes. The radio broadcasts police warnings that a dangerous lunatic is hiding in the vicinity. Mrs Drudge, the comic charwoman, constantly gives out detailed information about the people in the house and its isolation, setting up the scene and the characters in the crudest old-fashioned manner. Eventually Moon answers the telephone on the stage, when Mrs Drudge is not there; the call is for Birdboot, who steps into the action, replacing a character who has been murdered. Later Birdboot becomes the detective, while the murdered man and the original detective, Inspector Hound, take the critics' places in the audience. All this is worked out with Stoppard's customary precision and logic, and the audience is inevitably intrigued and amused by its subtlety. A dead body which lies on the stage throughout the play, unobserved by the living characters, even turns out in the end to be the body of Moon's boss. The play is simple to stage; like *Rosencrantz* and *Free Man*, it has been very popular with repertory and amateur companies. But it is emptier than them, not stimulating any particular thought or showing any great psychological insight; its parody, both of stage thrillers and of drama critics, is fairly obvious.

Jumpers is in every way more ambitious, more original and more thought-provoking. Indeed it is so thought-provoking that it is possible to miss some of its sheer humour and entertainment value while trying to follow its philosophical arguments; equally, it is possible to be so diverted by it as to miss its thought. As Stoppard himself said about his plays in an interview with Steve Grant in *Time Out*: 'It's a matter of taste whether one says they're wonderfully frivolous saddened by occasional seriousness, or whether there's a serious play irredeemably ruined by the frivolous side of this man's nature.' The plays which mix these two aspects most astonishingly, *Jumpers* and *Travesties*, need to be seen or read at least twice if there is to be any hope of absorbing them fully.

Once again, in the preface to the published edition of *Jumpers*, Stoppard displays his theatrical professionalism by indicating that the play can be staged in various ways depending on the technical facilities available. He calls the published text 'a basic version'. 'In preparing previous plays for publication, I have tried with some difficulty to arrive at something called a 'definitive text', but I now believe that in the case of plays there is no such animal. Each production will throw up its own problems and very often the solution will lie in some minor change to the text, either in the dialogue or in the author's directions, or both.' Peter Wood's production for the National Theatre at the Old Vic used a revolving stage; some changes were made in the staging and the text for the revival a few months after the premiere and further changes were made when it came to the larger stage of the Lyttelton in 1976.

The cast of the play includes a team of eight gymnasts, the 'Jumpers' of the title, in addition to the principal speaking characters, and the play opens and closes with a spectacular gymnastic display, almost a ballet. These Jumpers are followers of Sir Archibald Jumper, vice-chancellor, philosopher, psychiatrist and philanderer as well as gymnast. The jumping is a physical parallel to the mental gymnastics which occupy a great part of the dialogue, and is symbolic of the jumps in thought, in careless logic or in religious or metaphysical speculation.

The principal character, a professor of philosophy called George Moore (not *the* George Moore, the author of *Principia Ethica*, but another George Moore who is often mistaken for him) is preparing a lecture to counter the prevailing school of linguistic philosophy and to justify his belief in God. He tries to prove that there must be a creator or first cause and he 'jumps' from the existence of the concept of moral goodness in all societies to the conclusion that this goodness is part of what is called God. His principal opponent, Professor McFee, never appears in the play; in fact, he is shot dead in the opening scene, during the gymnastic display. Moore's wife, Dotty, an ex-musical comedy star, is the prime suspect. Stoppard's complex plot also involves the vice-chancellor's constant visits to Dotty, though whether as her psychiatrist or as her lover is never made absolutely clear, a comic police detective who also appears to seduce her, and Moore's pets, a goldfish, a tortoise and a hare, which disappear and die in strange circumstances. One of Stoppard's typical dialogues, in which the speakers are entirely at cross-purposes, occurs when Moore is confessing to an anonymous phone call to the police about noise while Bones, the police inspector, thinks he is confessing to the murder of McFee. Sidelights in the play are man's first landing on the moon, which caused Dorothy to abandon her stage career with its 'moon' songs and which raised doubts in her mind about the universality of our earthly ethical systems, and the vice-chancellor's attempts to hush up the murder of McFee by offering university chairs to those who will accept the death as suicide.

Bones: If McFee shot himself inside a plastic bag, where is the gun?

Archie (*awed*): Very good thinking indeed! On consideration I can give you the Chair of Logic, but that is my last offer.
Bones: This is a British murder enquiry and some degree of justice must be seen to be more or less done.
Archie: I must say I find your attitude lacking in flexibility. What makes you so sure that it *was* Miss Moore who shot McFee?
Bones: I have a nose for these things.
Archie: With the best will in the world I can't give the Chair of Logic to a man who relies on nasal intuition.
Dotty (*off*): Help! (*Bones reacts. Archie restrains him*)
Archie: It's all right—just exhibitionism; what we psychiatrists call 'a cry for help'.
Bones: But it *was* a cry for help.
Archie: Perhaps I'm not making myself clear. *All* exhibitionism is a cry for help, but a cry for help *as such* is only exhibitionism.

In addition to its philosophical arguments and jokes at the expense of philosophers and psychiatrists *Jumpers* also contains some sexually ambiguous dialogue, when George Moore questions Sir Archibald about Dorothy.

George: Well, I don't know what's the matter with her. She's like a cat on hot bricks, and doesn't emerge from her room. All she says is, she's all right in bed.
Archie: Yes, well there's something in that.
George: What exactly do you do in there?
Archie: Therapy takes many forms.
George: I had no idea you were still practising.
Archie: Oh yes . . . a bit of law, a bit of philosophy, a bit of medicine, a bit of gym . . . A bit of one and then a bit of the other.
George: You examine her?
Archie: Oh yes, I like to keep my hand in.

The Jumpers provide the play's splendid visual set-pieces. At the end of the first act they come to remove McFee's body, which has been lying about unseen in Dorothy's bedroom rather like the body on the floor in *Inspector Hound*. They do this in a formal gymastic dance accompanied by a recording of one of Dorothy's songs.

> *Archie moves downstage, facing front, and like a magician about to demonstrate a trick, takes from his pocket a small square of material like a handkerchief, which he unfolds and unfolds and unfolds until it is a large plastic bag. six-feet tall, which he gives to two Jumpers. These two hold the mouth of the bag open at the door; at the climax of the 'dance' the four Jumpers throw the body into the bag: bag closes, bedroom door closes, Jumpers moving smoothly, front door closes, and on the last beat of the song, only Archie and Dotty are left on stage. Blackout. End of Act One.*

The conclusion of the play, a 'coda' which follows the second act, is equally theatrical. It is a philosophical symposium staged like a mock trial or television panel game, with Jumpers acting as jurors and holding up votes for the speakers, and characters like an atheist Archbishop of Canterbury appearing as witnesses. The final witness is Dorothy Moore, who descends on a spangled crescent moon singing a philosophical ditty to an old-fashioned musical comedy tune. The play ends inconclusively, with Archie pointing out cynically that the world is not too bad—'more eat than starve, more are healthy than sick, more curable than dying; not so many dying as dead; and one of the thieves was saved'. Last of all, Dotty sings 'Goodbye spoony Juney Moon'.

At the National Theatre the play's central focus was a magnetic and brilliant performance by Michael Hordern as George Moore, complete with the phoney hesitations, sudden spurts of excitement, and artificial mannerisms which seem to be the stock-in-trade of modern academic philosophers. Similarly, *Travesties*, again directed by Peter Wood but this time for the Royal Shakespeare Company, had a riveting central performance by John Wood as Henry Carr, the narrator and catalyst of an extraordinary piece which brings Lenin, James Joyce and Tristan Tzara together in a comedy which is also a pastiche of Oscar Wilde's *The Importance of Being Earnest* and a discussion of the role of art in society.

Travesties has some slender basis in historical fact: the

characters depicted *were* all in Zürich towards the end of the First World War, though they did not all meet, and there *was* a Henry Carr at the British Consulate, who did act in an amateur performance of *The Importance* organized by Joyce, and did subsequently get involved in arguments and litigation with Joyce about fees and alleged libels. Carr in Stoppard's play appears to be the British Consul, and has a manservant called Bennett; in fact the Consul was Bennett and Carr, who had been invalided out of the British army, had only some modest job at the Consulate. Soon after *Travesties* opened in London, Stoppard received a letter from Carr's second wife giving the biographical facts about her late husband, who died in 1962. In his historical note to the published edition of the play, Stoppard says gracefully that he is indebted to her 'for her benevolence towards me and towards what must seem to her a peculiarly well-named play'.

Nearly everything spoken by Lenin and his wife Nadezhda Krupskaya in the play comes from their writings—and some of it is even spoken in Russian. Henry Carr, as first presented by Stoppard, is entirely fictitious—an ageing man trying to write his memoirs, his memory playing him tricks and his own role in the events embellished and exaggerated. Most of the play shows Carr as he remembers himself or wants to be remembered—a dandified young man, playing a key role in discussions on politics and art with the other, more famous characters. Frequently there are what Stoppard calls 'time-slips'—the same scene is repeated in different versions, representing the older Carr's alternative accounts of the past. At the very end of the play his younger sister Gwendolen provides him, and the audience, with some historical correctives, pointing out that he never met Lenin, that the amateur dramatics organized by Joyce were after Lenin's departure for Russia, and that Carr was not really the consul.

The action of the play alternates between the British Consulate and the public library. where Lenin, Joyce and Tzara all worked. After a brief opening scene in the library, there is a long introductory speech by the ageing Carr, fumbling pompously with his memories and with the clichés of autobiographical reminiscence. Yet even then, Stoppard's characteristic love of alliterative word-play and of sowing mental confusion is fully deployed.

Carr: I well remember the first time I met Lenin, or as he was known on his library ticket, Vladimir Ilyich Ulyanov. To be in his presence was to be aware of a complex personality, enigmatic, magnetic, but not, I think, astigmatic, his piercing brown (if memory serves) eyes giving no hint of it. An essentially simple man, and yet an intellectual theoretician, bent, as I was already aware, on the seemingly impossible task of reshaping the civilized world into a federation of standing committees of workers' deputies. As I shook the hand of this dynamic, gnomic and yet not, I think, anaemic stranger, who with his fine head of blond hair falling over his forehead had the clean-shaven look of a Scandinavian seafaring—hello, hello, got the wrong chap, has he?—take no notice, all come out in the wash, that's the art of it.

The play is full of literary parody. Even before Joyce asks Carr to act Algernon in *The Importance of Being Earnest*, Carr is addressing his manservant in Wildean epigrams.

Carr: I'm not sure that I approve of your taking up this modish novelty of 'free association', Bennett. I realize that it is all the rage in Zürich—even in the most respectable salons to try to follow a conversation nowadays is like reading every other line of a sonnet—but if the servant classes are going to ape the fashion of society, the end can only be ruin and decay.
Bennett: I'm sorry, sir. It is only that Mr Tzara being an artist—
Carr: I will not have you passing moral judgment on my friends. If Mr Tzara is an artist that is his misfortune.

Carr's first meeting with Joyce and Tzara is written in limerick form, and is described by Stoppard as 'obviously an Irish nonsense'. They are introduced by Gwendolen.

Gwen: Mr Tzara writes poetry and sculpts,
     with quite unexpected results.

```
           I'm told he recites
           and on Saturday nights
           does all kinds of things for adults.
Joyce:  I really don't think Mr Carr
        is interested much in da-dah—
Tzara:  We say it like Dah-da.
Joyce:  (to Carr): The fact is I'm rather hard up.
Carr:   Yes, I'm told that you are,
        if it's money you want, I'm afraid . . .
Gwen:   Oh, Henry!—he's mounting a play,
        your official support . . .
        And Mr Joyce thought
Carr:   Ah. . . !
Joyce:  . . . And a couple of pounds till I'm paid.
Carr:   I don't see why not. For my part
        HMG is considered pro-Art.
Tzara:  Consider me anti-.
Gwen:   Consider your auntie?
Joyce:  A pound would do for a start.
Carr:   The Boche put on culture a-plenty
        for Swiss, what's the word?
Joyce:                          Cognoscenti.
Carr:   It's worth fifty tanks.
Joyce:  Or twenty-five francs.
Carr:   Now . . . British culture . . .
Joyce:                       I'll take twenty.
```

The complex plot of *Travesties* develops partly along Wildean lines; not only do the young ladies have the same names as in *The Importance* but at one point Carr impersonates Tzara's imaginary brother to gain the confidence of Cecily, the librarian, about Lenin's plans for getting to Russia. Many lines of dialogue are taken almost verbatim from Wilde. There are also other occasional literary parodies—for example, a conversation between Tzara and Gwendolen starts as a discussion of Shakespeare's eighteenth sonnet, moves into pure pastiche of *Hamlet* and glides imperceptibly into pastiche of *The Importance*, with Tzara asking Gwendolen if she would still love him if he did not admire Joyce.

His line-up of characters also gives Stoppard opportunities for more serious discussion of the role of art in society, and its relation to revolutionary politics. Lenin is depicted as wishing to support the arts, but as being by nature a philistine and also conscious of the need for political censorship. Tzara puts the extreme case for artistic freedom and for 'art' meaning anything an artist cares to do, while Carr puts the 'common sense' view that that is simply to change the meaning of the word Art. In reply, Tzara argues that politicians do the same thing with words like patriotism, duty, love, freedom, king and country. Tzara thinks is contradictory that revolutionaries like Lenin should be hostile to revolutionary art.

Carr: There is nothing contradictory about it . . . Revolution in art is in no way connected with *class* revolution. Artists are members of a privileged class. Art is absurdly overrated by artists, which is understandable, but what is strange is that it is absurdly overrated by everyone else.
Tzara: Because man cannot live by bread alone.
Carr: Yes, he can. It's *art* he can't live on. 'Bread—Peace—Freedom'—that's the slogan of revolution, I believe. What possible connection could there be between *that* and the shrill self-enclosed squabbles of rival egomaniacs—formless painters, senseless poets, hatless sculptors—
Tzara (*coldly*): You are insulting me and my comrades in the Dada Exhibition—
Carr: —and exhibitionists in general. When I was at school, on certain afternoons we all had to do what was called Labour—weeding, sweeping, sawing logs for the boiler-room, that kind of thing; but if you had a chit from Matron you were let off to spend the afternoon messing about in the Art Room. Labour or Art. And you've a chit for *life*? (*Passionately.*) *Where did you get it?* What is an artist? For every thousand people there's nine hundred doing the work, ninety doing well, nine doing good, and one lucky bastard who's the artist.

This attack on the artist's privileged position which often got an enthusiastic burst of applause in the theatre not only expresses a widely held view among the general public but also the guilt felt by many artists today, including at one time, Stoppard himself. Carr goes on to argue that in the old days, hunters and warriors did their own art, and the artist was not a special kind of human being.

Not only does Stoppard here touch on the value of art, including his own; in another dialogue between Carr and Tzara he makes Tzara defend the very exposure of false logic which is his own speciality as a dramatist.

> Tzara: I am sick of cleverness. The clever people try to impose a design on the world and when it goes calamitously wrong they call it fate. In point of fact, everything is Chance, including design.
> Carr: That sounds awfully clever. What does it mean? Not that it has to mean anything, of course.
> Tzara: It means, my dear Henry, that the causes we know everything about depend on causes we know very little about, which depend on causes we know absolutely nothing about. And it is the duty of the artist to jeer and howl and belch at the delusion that infinite generations of real effects can be inferred from the gross expression of apparent cause.
> Carr: It is the duty of the artist to beautify existence.
> Tzara: Dada dada dada dada dada dada dada dada dada dada dada dada . . .
> Carr: Oh what nonsense you talk!
> Tzara: It may be nonsense, but at least it's not clever nonsense.

It is Tzara who provokes Joyce into a passionate defence of the true artist, and an attack on the phoney one, expressing Stoppard's own views.

> Joyce: You are an over-excited little man, with a need for self-expression far beyond the scope of your natural gifts. This is not discreditable. Neither does it make you an artist. An artist is the magician put among men to gratify—capriciously—their urge for immortality. The temples are built and brought down around him, continuously and contiguously, from Troy to the fields of Flanders. If there is any meaning in any of it, it is in what survives as art, yes even

in the celebration of tyrants, yes even in the celebration of nonentities. What now of the Trojan War if it had been passed over by the artist's touch? Dust. A forgotten expedition prompted by Greek merchants looking for new markets. A minor redistribution of broken pots. But it is we who stand enriched, by a tale of heroes, of a golden apple, a wooden horse, a face that launched a thousand ships—and above all, of Ulysses, the wanderer, the most human, the most complete of all heroes—husband, father, son, lover, farmer, soldier, pacifist, politician, inventor and adventurer ... It is a theme so overwhelming that I am almost afraid to treat it. And yet I with my Dublin Odyssey will double that immortality, yes, by God, there's a corpse that will dance for some time yet and *leave the world precisely as it finds it*—and if you hope to shame it into the grave with your fashionable magic, I would strongly advise you to try and acquire some genius and if possible some subtlety before the season is quite over. Top o' the morning, Mr Tzara!

Travesties is the richest and most thought-provoking of Stoppard's plays, though it is possible that the weight of argument is too much for the structure of the play. It is hard for any audience to take in all the arguments *and* enjoy the sheer humour and theatricality of the piece. Even more than *Jumpers*, *Travesties* demands to be seen or read more than once, enjoyable though it is the first time.

With his next play, Stoppard returned to pure entertainment, and indeed *Dirty Linen* is arguably the funniest of all his works. Although it has no philosophical connotations, it does in its purely farcical way embody a plea for sexual freedom and an attack on newspaper hounding of public men for their private lives. Though it is only a short play, originally written for a season of lunch-time plays presented by the Ambiance Theatre Club at their Almost Free Theatre, it is as ingenious in construction as any of Stoppard's works.

Actually *Dirty Linen* failed in two crucial respects to be the play that was commissioned by the Ambiance. Lunch-time plays should run between thirty and forty-five minutes; this one runs for nearly an hour and a half, like one of the plays

Edward Bond wrote for the same season. However *Dirty Linen* was so successful that it was transferred to evening performances at the tiny Arts Theatre Club, and also to a much larger Broadway house, even though it is not long enough for a full evening's entertainment. Secondly, the play was commissioned for a season to mark the American bicentennial and, coincidentally, the British naturalization of the Ambiance's American-born director, Ed Berman. Stoppard says that *Dirty Linen* 'went off in another direction'—in fact it has nothing to do with America at all. So he added a second playlet, *New-Found-Land*, specifically about Berman's naturalization, which is 'buried' in the middle of *Dirty Linen*; the action of both plays takes place in the same committee room of the House of Commons, and is continuous, so that the combination can really be regarded as one play.

Dirty Linen is about a parliamentary committee which is investigating newspaper allegations of immorality and promiscuity among Members of Parliament. Stoppard's treatment is entirely farcical, using the theme as an excuse for every conceivable variety of verbal joke and for a number of visual ones. A repeated and effective visual joke concerns the state of dress, or rather undress, of the committee's secretary, Maddie Gotobed. Her name indicates her character and she is indeed involved sexually with all the members of the committee and is the main subject of the newspaper reports being investigated. She starts the play wearing very little, though this is not obvious when she is sitting at her desk; when she gets up she invariably reveals glimpses of cleavage and buttocks. Each time this happens, the action 'freezes', with a member of the committee staring at her while others gaze at a pin-up photo in a newspaper. When she moves around the stage, further garments drop off her at the merest touch from a member of the committee, and on one occasion she conceals her near-nakedness from them, but not from the audience. There is considerable play with panties and men's Y-fronts. When Miss Gotobed and the only female member of the committee pass each other behind a screen, they linger there and the MP emerges with her hair dishevelled and her suit unbuttoned.

Verbal jokes are launched as soon as the play begins, with a dazzling series of foreign language clichés, starting with 'Toujours la politesse' and 'Noblesse oblige', and working through 'Che sara, sara' to 'De gustibus non est disputandum'. There are a number of sexual *doubles entendres* as well as jokes about Miss Gotobed's secretarial incompetence and ostensible dumbness. Sometimes the two are mixed up together.

> Maddie: I didn't get a wink of sleep all last night . . . It's not every girl who gets advancement from the Home Office typing pool.
> McTeazle, MP: I expect it's not every girl who proves herself as you have done, Miss Gotobed. Do you use Gregg's or do you favour the Pitman method?
> Maddie: I'm on the pill.

Stoppard uses malapropisms, among his favourite verbal jokes, to confuse sexual and political jargon to glorious effect as when McTeazle is staring at Maddie's cleavage.

> Cocklebury-Smythe, MP: McTeazle, why don't you go and see if you can raise those great tits—boobs—those boobies, absolute tits, don't you agree, Malcolm and Douglas—though good men as well, of course, useful chaps, very decent, first rate, two of the best, Malcolm and Douglas, why don't you have a quick poke, peek, in the Members Bra—or the cafeteria, they're probably guzzling coffee and Swedish panties—Danish . . .

Sometimes the members of the committee speak at slow speed to enable Miss Gotobed to take down what they say, and there is a hilarious scene when she tries to learn by heart the names of the restaurants she is supposed to forget—where she had rendezvous with the committee members.

There are also jokes of a more serious nature about bureaucratic procedures, and there is a witty yet biting account of the way life peerages are granted, which seemed particularly topical in 1976 when Sir Harold Wilson's resignation honours list provoked considerable merriment.

> Cocklebury-Smythe: The PM offered me a life peerage, for services which he said he would let me know more about in

due course if I were interested. 'I hear you're a keen gardener, Cockie,' he said, 'we can call it services to conservation.' 'Not me, Rollo,' I said. 'All I use it for is a little topiary in the summer.' 'Services to sport,' he said—ignorant fool. 'No, no, Rollo,' I said, 'I really have no interests of any kind.' 'That will be services to the arts,' he said. 'Stop making such a fuss—do you want a life peerage or don't you?' 'No I don't,' I said to him. 'What with only a couple of bachelor cousins in line ahead, one of whom is an amateur para-chutist and the other a seamstress in the Merchant Navy, I prefer to hang on for a chance of the real thing.' He said to me, 'My dear Cockie, life peers *are* the real thing nowadays.' 'Oh no they're not, Rollo,' I said. 'That's just the kind of confusion you set up in people's minds by calling them Lord This and Lord That, pour encourager hoi polloi. *They* think they're Lords—they skip off home and feed the budgerigar saying to themselves, My golly gorblimey I'm a Lord! They'd be just as happy if you suddenly said they were all sheikhs. They'd put the Desert Song on the gramophone and clap their hands when they wanted cocoa. Now *you'd* know they're not really sheikhs and *I'd* know they're not really sheikhs, and God help them if they ever showed up east of Suez in their appalling pullovers with Sheikh Shuttleworth stencilled on their airline bags—no, my dear Rollo,' I said, 'I'll be a real peer or not at all.' 'Now look here, Cockie,' he said to me. 'If they weren't real peers they wouldn't be in the House of Lords, would they?—that's logic.' 'If that's logic,' I said, 'you can turn a regimental goat into a Lieuten-ant Colonel by electing it to the United Services Club.'

Eventually Miss Gotobed seduces French, the only puri-tanical and priggish member of the committee, who was press-ing for a serious investigation of members' morality, and persuades him to adopt instead a resolution affirming that their private lives are their own business. Maddie Gotobed, for all her apparent naivety and stupidity, is the voice of common-sense, saying people don't care what MPs do in their spare time, so long as they do their jobs, and that Fleet Street should be told to go and take 'a running jump'.

Two-thirds of the way through *Dirty Linen* the committee adjourns temporarily and the room is immediately occupied by two Home Office officials considering an application for British citizenship from an American living in London. *New-Found-Land* has just two characters; one is very ageing and gets laughs by asking 'What's that?' when Big Ben strikes, and who falls asleep while his younger colleague makes a long speech about America which is a parody or pastiche of every corny travelogue, laced with the titles of American popular songs. Humour is also obtained from the description of the applicant, an in-joke for those who know that Ed Berman ran a commune called 'The Fun Art Farm'. A crucial part of this play's success was the performance by Richard Goolden, an octogenarian actor who seemed to be actually falling asleep on stage but who 'awoke' in time to say his lines and to tell a long, rambling anecdote about Lloyd George. Stoppard switches back into *Dirty Linen* after the long apostrophe to America by the simple expedient of having the original committee members return and claim their room.

Stoppard mentally divides his plays into the 'real' ones, which are about something other than what they appear to be about and which take a long time to write, and the mere entertainments, which he can do very quickly. *Dirty Linen*, for example, was written in about three weeks, and the *New-Found-Land* section was done while the main part was being rehearsed. 'It's easy to write about MPs in committee but hard to write about art and society. *Travesties* took about nine months to write, and that's about par for the course. It's full-time writing —I go to bed worried and wake up worried for the whole of that nine months. And for a long time I'm not at all certain that I will ever finish. I've already been writing my latest play in my head for several months.'

This play is *Every Good Boy Deserves Favour*, which had its first performance at London's Royal Festival Hall with actors from the Royal Shakespeare Company and with the London Symphony Orchestra The collaboration was a triumphantly successful experiment, and the play finds Stoppard more explicitly concerned than ever before with human freedom. Written for 'prisoner of conscience' year, it is about a political detainee in a psychiatric hospital in Leningrad. He is kept in a cell with a genuine lunatic of the same name who believes he is running an orchestra; they are treated by a doctor who actually does play in one. This gives Stoppard opportunities for typical confusions of identity and verbal tricks, but also enables him to expose the empty promises in the Soviet constitution and the tortures practised there in so-called 'special' hospitals. The result is an extraordinary but effective mixture— hilarious farce and moving political drama. The original idea for a play with full orchestra came from André Previn, who wrote and conducted the music, but neither he nor Stoppard could have originally envisaged the powerful and novel work which emerged. Indeed Stoppard's first idea was simply to write about a millionaire who owns an orchestra.

Travesties arose because Stoppard had heard that Lenin and Tzara were in Zürich at the same time, because he wanted to write a play for John Wood, and because he wanted to say something about the role of the artist in society. 'James Joyce came into the play at a late stage, after I'd started working, because John Wood didn't look a bit like Lenin and I thought he could play Joyce. But Lenin, Tzara and Joyce had to be roughly equal parts, and I wanted to write a large part for Wood. So I started looking for a seat to hold my three-legged stool together. I came across Henry Carr as a role for Wood— later on I discovered that they even looked alike.

'Once I had this group of people to manipulate, I used them to get various things off my chest. At first there was no narrative line, but then I discovered that Joyce and Carr were mixed up in a production of *The Importance of Being Earnest*. That gave me the linking theme. I couldn't write an inconsequential Dadaist play. Instinctively I'm out of sympathy with Tzara and that kind of art, and I had to think very hard to give Tzara good arguments in the play. My prejudices were all on Joyce's side —I utterly believe in his speech at the end of Act 1 on what an artist is. I used to have a slight guilt feeling about being an artist, but I don't any more. When I tried to visualize a completely technological world without culture, I realized that one does not have to apologize for being an artist. It took me years to reach that understanding.'

Jumpers had its origin in a television play of Stoppard's, *Another Moon Called Earth*, about a woman in bed while her husband is writing a history of the world in the next room. 'I wanted a device enabling me to set out arguments about whether social morality is simply a conditioned response to history and environment or whether moral sanctions obey an absolute intuitive God-given law. I've always felt that whether or not 'God-given' means anything, there has to be an ultimate external reference for our actions. Our view of good behaviour *must* not be relativist. The difference between moral rules and the rules of tennis is that the rules of tennis can be changed. I think it's a dangerous idea that what constitutes 'good behaviour' depends on social conventions—dangerous and unacceptable. That led me to the conclusion, not reached all that willingly, that if our behaviour is open to absolute judgement, there must be an absolute judge. I felt that nobody was saying this and it tended to be assumed that nobody held such a view. So I wanted to write a theist play, to combat the arrogant view that anyone who believes in God is some kind of cripple, using God as a crutch. I wanted to suggest that atheists may be the cripples, lacking the strength to live with the idea of God.

'I never studied philosophy formally, and I like to think that philosophers and logicians operate at a much deeper level than I can. My philosophy is the sort of philosophy that anyone can think out in their bath-tub, but perhaps I can put these speculations into dialogue and epigrams better than most. I read a lot of moral philosophy in preparation for *Jumpers*—some of it is taken straight from modern philosophical works. I'd never read Wittgenstein before, and I read him several times without understanding lots of it—it's like reading poetry.'

Stoppard does not have any interest in word games and puzzles, outside his work as a playwright. 'I don't do crossword puzzles. But the way language and logic can be used or misused amuses me—it's a wonderful garden to enjoy. At one time I thought perhaps I enjoyed playing with the English language because I came to it late; I used to compare myself to Nabokov and say it was like suddenly finding oneself on top of a mountain and looking down, instead of laboriously climbing up as most people do when they learn a language from childhood. But then I discovered that Nabokov had spoken English from childhood and anyway I myself had never been literate in any other language. English was the working language at my schools in India. I think I'd probably have been interested in language just the same, if I'd been a Czechoslovak writer instead of a British one.'

It is tempting to speculate whether Stoppard's Czechoslovak origin is in any way relevant to his concern for human rights behind the Iron Curtain and his recurring interest in problems of identity. If so, it can only be unconscious as he left Czechoslovakia when he was one and does not remember his father.

Stoppard first started writing stories and plays when he began to get bored with journalism. At first his energies were entirely devoted to becoming a first-class journalist; then he started to look for other horizons. He explains his preference for plays, rather than other forms of writing, by saying that everyone was writing for the theatre in Britain in the late 1950s. Also, he thinks plays get more concentrated attention. 'The impact of a novel is dispersed, it's not dangerous enough. Nobody concentrates on a television play in the way they do in the theatre—one is always being distracted. So I'd probably have preferred the theatre even if everyone else hadn't been writing for it. And I don't mind writing for an élitist audience, if that is what the audience turns out to be. I find it crucial to be at rehearsals— there is no notation for writing down what one intends to happen on the stage. You may think that my stage instructions are detailed, but they are a basic minimum to me. I don't say my plays have got to be done the way I want them—I once saw *Rosencrantz and Guildenstern* in Italy, played in perspex boxes and with a woman as Rosencrantz— and I loved it. But if I'm at the rehearsals, the play works according to my prejudices. If I'm not there, it either becomes half of what I want—and that is awful—or it becomes something utterly different. That can either be awful or superb.'

Part 4

Politics, mild and bitter

THESE PLAYWRIGHTS ARE all political, in the sense that they are at least as concerned about the state of British society as they are about individual human relationships. David Hare, Howard Brenton and Howard Barker want to overthrow the present political and economic system; Trevor Griffiths is debating whether such a revolution would be practical and desirable; Stephen Poliakoff does not want a revolution but certainly does not like things the way they are. The political content of the plays is decorated with a great deal of human conflict and visual excitement, and a few of them may not at first sight seem political at all.

Ten: David Hare

Born: St Leonard's-on-Sea, Sussex, England, 1947.
Father: in Merchant Navy.
Education: Lancing College (where he was contemporary with Christopher Hampton) and Jesus College, Cambridge, where he read English. Adapted plays for puppet shows when he was a small boy, directed plays at Cambridge, where he was a keen filmgoer. Was introduced to theatre by his friend Tony Bicât, with whom he formed Portable Theatre, a group touring art colleges, village halls, universities, army camps.
Married, one child.

1968–71 Director of Portable Theatre.
1969–70 Literary manager, Royal Court.
1970–71 Resident Dramatist, Royal Court.
1974   Co-founder of Joint Stock Theatre Group.
Continues to direct plays, including *Teeth 'n' Smiles*.

Plays:
Inside Out (an adaptation of Kafka's diaries, written in collaboration with Tony Bicât), (1968) ⎫
How Brophy Made Good (1969)   ⎬ all written for Portable Theatre.
What Happened to Blake? (1970)   ⎭

Slag (London 1970, New York 1971). *The Rules of the Game* (adaptation of Pirandello, London 1971). *Deathsheads* (Edinburgh 1971). *Lay-By* (with others, Edinburgh and London 1971). *The Great Exhibition* (London 1972). *England's Ireland* (with others, Amsterdam and London 1972). *Knuckle* (Oxford and London 1974, New York 1975). *Fanshen* (adaptation of the book by William Hinton, London 1975). *Teeth 'n' Smiles* (London 1975).
'Plenty' (1978)

NONE OF HARE's plays has yet had a smash-hit success or a very long run; indeed only two of them, *Knuckle* and *Teeth 'n' Smiles*, have had West End runs at all, both of them short. The others have been staged, sometimes to great critical acclaim, in 'fringe' and club theatres. The four considered here have all had considerable impact. Although they are very distinctive, they all reveal Hare's considerable theatrical flair. He mixes comedy, fantasy and realistic drama in disconcerting but exciting ways, and his highly critical, near-revolutionary attitude to our social institutions and conventions is never much concealed. On the other hand his precise attitudes and messages, if any, are hard to discern. He once said, in an interview with Peter Ansorge in *Plays and Players*, that his plays are intended as puzzles—the solution is up to the audience.

In the same interview he said that *Slag* is about all the educational establishments he has known, including Cambridge University. Ostensibly it is not about a reputable establishment at all, but is set in one of the more inefficient and eccentric kinds of private school. It is primarily a zany farce about three bizarre schoolmistresses. It was first produced at the tiny Hampstead Theatre Club in London, and then off-Broadway. At times it seemed like propaganda for Women's Lib, but the characters spoke and behaved in such kinky and absurd ways that it could also be taken as an anti-feminist satire. It was one of the first plays in which women talked crudely and basically about sex, in the manner pioneered by male characters in avant-garde plays. And it revealed a new writer with a sense of grotesque fun, with a revolutionary approach, and with a considerable feeling for dramatic conflict. The author, in a brief introductory note, says it is 'written deliberately with as few stage and acting instructions as possible. Blackouts should be instant, gaps between scenes brief, and scenery minimal.'

The cast of three consists of Ann, the rather masculine headmistress of a private school, Elsie, her sexy deputy who claims to be pregnant without having had a man, and Joanne, a revolutionary whose activity is divided between re-living the great films of the past and teaching her pupils masturbation and female emancipation. Some of the humour borders on slapstick: a bucket falls on Joanne's head from a door, Ann falls from the roof and Joanne digs a tunnel to escape. The characters themselves are humorous, especially Ann marching around with a hypodermic announcing, 'I'm giving everyone flu injections this year to prevent the school grinding to a halt'. In fact it has already ground to a halt, as most of the pupils have been withdrawn. Joanne, who is a virgin, delivers a pompous and inaccurate lecture on female orgasms, Elise makes Ann lick her toes and cut her toenails with her teeth and the first act ends with them making love. Later Joanne suggests that Ann is the father of Elise's baby. There is, of course, no baby, and the play has no real conclusion.

The next of Hare's own plays, as distinct from adaptations or collaborations, to reach London was *The Great Exhibition*. This was also staged at Hampstead and is also a kind of black comedy.

Hare described it as a deliberate parody of all Royal Court-type plays, and explained that it's about people who suffer with a capital S, mainly from lack of self-knowledge. The hero is a Labour Member of Parliament, called Hammett, who employs a private detective to trail his wife. The 'exhibition' of the title refers to Hammett's rather ludicrous attempts to expose himself on Clapham Common. There are shades of Shaffer—the private detective might be out of *Public Eye*, Hare's two acts are called *Public Life* and *Private Life*, and Hammett is constantly concerned with role-playing.

> Hammett: I sat down at the age of twenty-one and I thought, 'I'm going to need some enthusiasms to get me to the grave.' And I chose three. Food, sex and socialism.

When he goes to Clapham Common, he is wearing the obligatory raincoat and rehearsing his 'flash'. He meets his match in Catriona, to whom he flashes. She turns out to be amused and quite willing to 'flash' back; she also turns out to be a friend of his wife's, to be employing the same private detective, and to be deliberately chasing Hammett. Indeed the detective is working for all three of them.

In addition to the complexities of this plot, which ends with Hammett's wife taking over his constituency, there is some slapstick humour. The detective demonstrates orgasm with a bottle of beer, and Hammett stops his phone ringing by squirting soda water over it. There are also bitter jokes about

socialists who despise the people, the Campaign for Nuclear
Disarmament and the English educational system. These
ingredients do not weld into a very coherent whole.

Knuckle is much better organized with a plot akin to that of a
conventional thriller. When it was produced in the West End
at the Comedy Theatre Michael Blakemore directed as if it
was a thriller, so that its appeal was partly as a parody of a
familiar form of entertainment and partly in keeping the audience guessing how much of the action was real and how much
was fantasy. This was not Hare's intention, though he admits
the play can be read in that way. It is a play about a man who
sees himself as a detective—role-playing again; ostensibly he
is investigating the disappearance of his sister Sarah, but in the
process he finds himself investigating the morals and life-styles
of supposedly respectable middle-class Guildford. Curly, the
central character, sometimes addresses the audience directly
and acts as link between the numerous short scenes. He delivers
Osborne-like diatribes and gets involved in Shaffer-like tension
with his father. Hare himself says that it is a very difficult play
to stage; he admits that he deliberately set problems he did not
know how to solve and, although he is an experienced director,
he would hate to have to direct it himself.

Because of its thriller aspect, *Knuckle* is held together by suspense. In best detective story tradition, nearly all the characters
are suspects. Curly's father Patrick is a self-righteous and
successful businessman. Sarah was an unconventional and
promiscuous girl, uncompromising in her search for truth.
Patrick explains the difference between their philosophies.

> Patrick: I think people may choose to build their lives on a
> series of misunderstandings, or wrong ideas, or maybe
> deliberate deceits: that's their business. Everyone's entitled to
> their own illusions. Sarah thought not. Sarah thought every-
> one should know everything. She told the Bishop of Guildford
> that his son was known as Mabel and the toast of the Earl's
> Court Road.

It gradually emerges through various twists of the plot that
Sarah discovered too much about one of her father's unsavoury
business deals, involving the dispossession and committal to

a mental hospital of an elderly woman, to make way for the demolition of her home and a property development. Patrick tried to explain the commercial necessities of life but she was unconvinced. He left her threatening suicide on a beach.

The central conflict of the play, between the moral standards of Guildford and the critical searchlight in which Curly exposes them, is neatly summarized in his brief exchange with the 'housekeeper' who is living with his father.

Mrs Dunning: I wonder why all the words my generation believed in—words like honour and loyalty—are now just a joke.
Curly: I guess it's because of some of the characters they've knocked around with.

Curly makes his money by arms trafficking, which he defends in paradoxical Shavian fashion, pointing out that deaths in wars have decreased as trade in arms has increased. His choice of occupation is partly a reaction and deliberate snub to his father's more 'respectable' form of money-making.

Curly: Have you seen inside the City of London? Inside the banks and the counting houses? It's perfect. Men with silver hair and suits with velvet pockets. Oiling down padded corridors. All their worries papered over with ten pound notes and brilliantine. I first went there when I was seven. The crystal city. You could just hear the money being raked in like autumn leaves. My father moved as silkily as anyone . . . When he got home at night, out with the cello and the Thackeray. He made his money with silent indolence. Part of a club. In theory a speculator. But whoever heard of an English speculator who actually speculated and lost? Once you were in you had it sewn up from paddock to post . . . So I chose guns. The noisiest profession I could find.

Curly's attack on the values of the acquisitive society, on the age of John Bloom, Jack Cotton and Emil Savundra, hits home rather more accurately when he explains why he returned home after a long period abroad.

Curly: When I got back I found this country was a jampot for swindlers and cons and racketeers. Not just property. Boarding houses and bordellos and nightclubs and crooked charter flights, private clinics, horse-hair wigs and tin-can motor cars, venereal cafés with ice-cream made from whale blubber and sausages full of sawdust . . . Money can be harvested like rotten fruit. People are aching to be fleeced. But those of us who do it must learn the quality of self-control. . . . Wherever I've travelled, wherever I've been, there's been a tiny echo in my mind. The noise in my father's office. The soft pulping of money. The slight squelch of Dad's hands in the meat . . . I came back because I'm ready. I've grown up.

Curly explains all this to Jenny, a friend of Sarah's who helps him with his investigations and with whom he falls in love. She makes her own attack on 'respectable' local society.

Jenny: Young women in Guildford must expect to be threatened. Men here lead ugly lives and girls are the only touchstones left. Cars cruise beside you as you walk down the pavement. I have twice been attacked at the country club, the man in the house opposite has a telescopic lens, my breasts are often touched on commuter trains, my body is covered with random thumbprints, the doctor says he needs to undress me completely to vaccinate my arm, men often spill drinks in my lap, or brush cigarettes against my bottom, very old men bump into me and clutch at my legs as they fall. I have been offered drinks, money, social advancement and once an editorial position on the *Financial Times*. I expect this to go on. I expect to be bumped, bruised, followed, assaulted, stared at and propositioned for the rest of my life, while at the same time offering sanctuary, purity, reassurance, prestige—the only point of loveliness in men's ever-darkening lives.

It is no surprise, in view of Curly's cynicism, that he finally decides not to expose his father. In pretending to Jenny that his father is innocent, he loses her, as she knows the truth. Sarah

is in fact alive, abroad, and has told her everything. *Knuckle*
ends with Curly's final address to the audience:

> Curly: Why should I feel ashamed of myself? Why should I
> feel inferior? Why should I feel anything? Jenny would go
> to the newspapers. They didn't believe her. And anyway
> Sarah was alive. It was autumn again. In the mean square
> mile of the City of London they were making money. (*Smiles*)
> Back to my guns.

Fanshen, a documentary play about the Chinese revolution,
is explicitly political. With about nine actors playing about
thirty roles and with a Brechtian production on a small bare
stage, Hare is remarkably successful in re-creating the life of a
Chinese village. The play starts with the principal characters
introducing themselves directly to the audience, and announcing
how much land they each possess. It is explained that
'fanshen' means 'to turn over', and during the revolution came
to mean both the turning over of property and the change in
men's attitudes. We see the villagers being led into organizing
a trial of someone suspected of collaborating with the Japanese,
then refusing to pay rent, seizing the landlord's possessions, and
redistributing wealth among themselves according to a points
system based on need and on the extent of their political participation. A work team comes to the village, condemns the local
leaders for taking too much wealth for themselves, and orders
a new redistribution entirely according to need. Then the work
team itself is condemned for 'Left extremism'. Democratic
meetings are very convincingly shown, with extremely natural
dialogue; some peasants prove too nervous or too inarticulate
to participate, and some attack each other on quite irrational
grounds. The impression is given that the whole revolution
was conducted with sweet reasonableness and endless discussion, as an exercise in education and democracy; in the end
even the erring leaders are to be re-educated rather than
punished. The play is dogmatic about opponents of the revolution; the Kuomintang is denied any role in fighting the
Japanese and the landlords are depicted as invariably selfish
and dishonest.

Even people who object to the propaganda content of the

play, or regard is as naïve and misleading, have to admire
Hare's skill in dramatizing such seemingly intractable material.
The trial scenes and the public discussion meetings are par-
ticularly gripping.

Similarly, people who do not get the 'message' of *Teeth 'n'
Smiles*, or who are irritated by it, can still enjoy the play's
theatricality and its lively dialogue. Set in Cambridge University
during a college ball in 1969, it is more concerned with the
fortunes of a visiting pop group than with the members of the
university, though both are unflatteringly portrayed. Maggie,
the group's singer, is permanently drunk, and is finally arrested
because Peyote, the bass guitarist, has hidden his drugs in her
bag. Arthur, who writes her songs and was for a long time her
lover, is re-visiting the college where he was educated and airs
his anti-establishment, anti-university views. The only present
members of the University represented are Anson, a nervous
medical student who engaged the group, and Sneed, an apparently subservient college porter, despised by the group, who
fetches the police and gets them 'busted'. The play's remaining
characters are Saraffian, the seedy but shrewd manager who
has come to sack Maggie and wind up the group, and Ran-
dolph, a moronic and ageing but still good-looking pop singer
who is Saraffian's latest protegé but whose function in the plot
of *Teeth 'n' Smiles* is not clear. In the second half of the play,
Saraffian gives a long, intense account of the bombing of the
Café de Paris in London during the Second World War, carefully pointing out that the restaurant was decorated to look like
the ballroom of the *Titanic*. And the play ends with the cast
singing a melancholy song called 'Last Orders on the *Titanic*',
underlining that Britain, like the pop group and Cambridge
University, is a doomed ship.

The earlier parts of *Teeth 'n' Smiles* are quite cheerful, with
frank badinage about sex and drugs, which shocked the West
End audience when the play transferred there, and with several
musical numbers. These pose some of the same problems as
Trevor Griffiths' *Comedians*—we are never quite sure whether
the jokes or the music are meant to be so bad that we should
feel guilty at being mildly entertained by them. There is always
a temptation for the performers to put them over more skilfully

than the author intended. Griffiths and Hare also face a similar problem to that which Osborne faced in his much earlier play *The Entertainer*—persuading the audience to see a slight backstage story as an allegory for our society.

Hare has been no more successful in solving this problem than the other writers. *Teeth 'n' Smiles* is at its best in the quick verbal exchanges at the beginning. One of the pop group, explaining why they don't set up their own equipment, says, 'You don't ask Oistrakh to go out and strangle the cat'. Arthur's description of undergraduates is: 'Rich complacent self-loving self-regarding self-righteous phoney half-baked politically immature neurotic evil-minded little shits'. Then he goes on to attack college discipline and, by somewhat arbitrary extension, our whole social system.

> Arthur: They invent a few rules that don't mean anything so that you can ruin your health trying to change them. Then overnight they re-draft them because they didn't really matter in the first place. One day it's a revolution to say 'fuck' on the bus. Next day it's the only way to get a ticket. That's how the system works. An obstacle course. Unimportant. Well, perhaps.

Perhaps the most crucial exchange is between Arthur and Maggie.

> Arthur: Leonardo da Vinci drew submarines. Five hundred years ago. They looked pretty silly. Today we are drawing a new man. He may look pretty silly.
> Maggie: You still want it to mean something, don't you? You can't get over that, can you? It's all gotta mean something . . . that's childish, Arthur. It don't mean anything.

David Hare shares Arthur's curiosity about the 'new man' and also wants 'it' all to mean something. So do many of us in the audience. Hare's uncertainty about the meaning makes his play almost as disconcerting as life. But *Teeth 'n' Smiles* is not altogether convincing as a slice of life, despite the use of documentary technique at the end. Just before the final song, Arthur asks significantly, 'Why's everyone frightened?' and then news reports are flashed on to a screen, purporting to tell us the fate of the characters, as if they were real people.

'ANDREW SMITH NICKNAME PEYOTE INHALED HIS OWN VOMIT DIED IN A HOTEL ROOM IN SAN ANTONIO TEXAS APRIL 17TH 1973 MAGGIE ARTHUR SARAFFIAN THE BAND ALFIE WELL LIVING IN ENGLAND.'

One trouble is that we have never been made to care for any of these people, or to believe in them. And it's not clear why a seedy pop group should be taken as symbolic of Britain, or what is the relevance of Saraffian's long and moving account of the destruction of the Café de Paris. His description ends with a taxi-driver refusing to drive away one of the wounded, saying, 'I don't want blood all over my fucking taxi.' This is scarcely typical of London behaviour during the blitz. Saraffian tells the story as an example of the class war which he claims is always going on, 'a war of attrition'. Maggie does not believe in that either.

Maggie: Well, I'm sure it gives you comfort, your nice little class war. It ties things up very nicely, of course, from the outside you look like any other clapped-out business man, but inside, oh, inside you got it all worked out. (*Pause*) This man has believed the same thing for thirty years. And it does not show. Is that going to happen to us? Fucking hell, somebody's got to keep on the move.

Like Maggie, Hare is impatient with the state of things and the pace of progress. He regards this impatience as typical of his generation, with which he constantly identifies himself. He started Portable Theatre because he regarded conventional theatre as decadent. 'We thought good theatre should be simple and economical. We started with a free typewriter given us by Olympia, and we performed at Jim Haynes' 'Arts Laboratory', where anyone could appear without vetting or having to win advance approval. I started by directing plays; then a play we were planning to do failed to turn up and I wrote *How Brophy Made Good* to fill the gap. Michael Codron, the impresario, read it and asked me to write another. Originally

I didn't want to be a writer because like most of my generation I despised artists and writers—I thought they were useless, self-indulgent people. I didn't really feel committed to writing till after *Knuckle*, when the intensity of the audience reaction convinced me that writing could be worthwhile. I believe in what used to be called socialist realism, that you should try to show how things are and how things could be. Plays have tension if you do both; if you only show how things are it's boring and if you only show how they could be, it's strident and hollow.

'Most of us try to be very hard-headed, with no illusions but not disillusioned either. It's unarguable that there's got to be change and most of us find the delay painful. Political change is overdue. Socialism would be a beginning—by socialism, I mean people feeling that they have some control over their own lives, with much greater public accountability for political leaders and officials. This isn't unattainable, though it's not attained anywhere yet. My plays argue that the main reform needed is moral; at present people know that they are damaging themselves by their behaviour, and need to change. This is especially obvious in *Knuckle*, which is my favourite among my plays. Curly's behaviour is partly a reaction against his father— I've noticed that the desire to impress or shock parents often provides people with very strong motivation. That's not my case—I don't have that sort of relationship with my parents at all. Similarly there are people in my plays who think sexual reform is the key to the new society. I myself have doubts about that, though I think it's admirable and exciting that people should try to change the sexual patterns of their lives. But I think our relationships fall into patterns largely determined by what we think other people expect of us. People are unsure of themselves and do things to be liked, or to impress. I tried to bring this out particularly in *The Great Exhibition*.

'I try to make all my plays different, so that nobody can say they know what a David Hare play is going to be like. This is because of my dislike of the self-indulgent, self-pitying writer, always writing about his own problems. I deliberately avoid writing about myself, my world, and my experiences. What attracted me to adapt William Hinton's book, *Fanshen*, was the chance of writing about a society where things have unarguably got better, where six hundred million lives have been improved materially and spiritually by revolution. Historically it's obvious that things don't look too bright for Europe, and I wanted to get away from the gloom of our society. And I chose to concentrate on aspects of the Chinese revolution which would seem recognizable and relevant to a European audience. The audience actually leans forward when the wealth is redistributed, to see how it's done, as they know one day it might happen here. When the politicians come to explain themselves to the people, the audience wishes our politicians here would do the same. The book was more objective, and to some extent I deliberately vulgarized it.

'*Teeth 'n' Smiles*, which I was writing about the same time as *Fanshen*, was the exact opposite, about people who feel themselves to be in decline and the present state of our society to be unreal. I also decided to break my rule about not writing about my own world. People were asking me why I always wrote about other people's lives; so I decided to set the play in the Cambridge I remembered, with the sort of rock group I knew when I was there. This is *absolutely* my only autobiographical play; I will certainly not do another.'

Hare says he usually starts a play with a few ideas, maybe a few arresting images. He started *Fanshen* with the idea that it should be mainly about the need for justice if people were to feel happy, though this idea evaporated in the writing.

'With *Knuckle* I knew from the beginning that there would be a scene on the beach. At first *Teeth 'n' Smiles* was to be all about Maggie, but actually she is only on the stage for about forty-five minutes. You start with an idea or a character but you don't always know exactly what it is or how it will work out. Bits of dialogue come later, and as you write you learn to develop a clear sense of the weight an idea or a character can bear.'

Having had his plays produced at the Royal Court and in the commercial theatre, Hare is emphatic that the subsidized theatre should be kept for plays that the commercial theatre will not handle. 'If you can survive in the commercial theatre you should, so that public money is saved for the plays that really need it. Pinter, for example, should not be at the National. I only did *Teeth 'n' Smiles* for the Royal Court because *Knuckle* had lost so much money in the West End that no commercial management would risk another of my plays.'

Eleven: Trevor Griffiths

Born: Manchester, England, 1935.
Father: a chemical process worker, mother did various jobs, including bus conductress.
Education: St Bede's College, Manchester (one of the first generation of working-class children to benefit from 1944 Education Act), Manchester University, where he read English.
1955–57: National Service in the army: 'I hated it, especially doing nothing. I tried every kind of sport. I was always very physical, and good at football, cricket and basketball; in the army I also did tennis, athletics and rifle-shooting. I got very interested in how my body worked, and I came out of the army a perfect fascist. I had been fairly unpleasant at school, but I was deeply unpleasant by this time, with so much to learn.' Then worked as a schoolteacher, lecturer and BBC education officer for eight years. 'I went into teaching by accident, like most things in my life. I had no job, and no desire for a job. All I wanted to do was put ideas down on paper. I'd wanted to do this since I was 13, but in the working-class kids don't write anything much except notes to the milkman. Between the ages of 10–13 I read about ten American western novels a week, obtained from the public library—I can still remember their authors' names. When I was 13 I wrote a derivative novella in this form. When I was 16–17 I started writing poems, and continued till I was 25–26. Several were published in the university poetry magazine. When I got into teaching, that took up a lot of my creative fat. I did a lot of political journalism in Manchester, for Left-wing magazines—writing about anything I felt angry about. I was deeply involved in the various Left movements of the late 1950s and early '60s. I joined the Labour Party for eighteen months—the only

political party I've ever joined—but left in disillusion
when they went on selling arms to South Africa, etc. I've
very ambivalent feelings about the Labour Party, which
I've worked out in various plays.'

Plays:
The Wages of Thin (Manchester 1969, London 1970). *Occupa-
tions* (Manchester 1970, London 1971). *Apricots* (London 1971).
Thermidor (Edinburgh 1971). *Lay-By* (part author—*see* Brenton,
Edinburgh and London 1971). *Sam Sam* (London 1972). *The
Party* (London 1973). *All Good Men* (London 1975). *Comedians*
(Nottingham and London 1975; New York 1976). *The Cherry
Orchard* (adapt. from Tchekhov, 'but more of a new play than
you would think; it's mine as well as Tchekhov's'; Nottingham
1977). (*The Wages of Thin, Apricots* and *Thermidor* are short
plays, produced in fringe and club theatres. *Thermidor* was
written to go with *Apricots* and a play by John McGrath in a
tour by his mobile company.)

GRIFFITHS IS GENERALLY described as a political writer,
and his plays *are* concerned with socialism. But they are equally
concerned with human beings, and with the problems they
face in reconciling their ideals with the realities of the world
they live in, and with the need for a satisfying private life.
The ideals are always radical and usually political. The plays
often include long didactic speeches, but they are not didactic
plays. Their success is due mainly to the skill with which
Griffiths balances political, practical and emotional problems
and presents his characters in depth. His presumptions are
that reform or revolution are worth striving for, and that this
is hard, perhaps impossible, to attain.

Sam Sam was the first stage play Griffiths started writing,
though it was not produced till after *Occupations*. It was directed
by Charles Marowitz at his tiny Open Space theatre club,
where it seemed extremely entertaining but rather derivative.
The first act is a series of revue-style sketches of working-class
life, earthy, crude, funny and true, and reminiscent of a lot of
Peter Terson's work. The second act is a fairly naturalistic
family drama, with a number of deliberate references to
Osborne's *Look Back In Anger*, such as Sam's description of a

dying father who had slaved away all his life in industry for very little reward, his violent quarrel with middle-class parents-in-law, and his passionate love-making with his wife immediately after a row reducing her to tears.

The two Sams of the title are brothers, both played by the same actor. The first act Sam remains in the working-class environment of his birth, and also talks directly to the audience with critical detachment, in music-hall manner, about the squalid personal habits of his wife and mother. His brother is brighter, has become a schoolteacher and married into the bourgeoisie. He is active in his local Labour Party. His wife patronizes his mother on a visit, and he gets his revenge, in the highlight scene of the play, by calmly calling her parents drunkards, asking them how often they still get sex, and spitting his drink all over his father-in-law's face. After they have gone, his wife bursts out saying she hates him and hits him till he bleeds. They 'they begin a frenzied session. Their love-making is hyenal'. They act out a fantasy in which she is the bossy mistress telling him to get cleaned up, and he is servile calling her 'madam'. They are interrupted by her lover on the telephone. Sam interrupts the ensuing conversation, calling the lover 'a right burk' and asking, 'Why don't you just hang that thing of yours up and retire? At all events keep it out of my wife.' The play ends with Sam trying, and failing, to flirt with the *au pair* girl, making a polite phone call to his wife's parents, and settling down to his record player. His marriage and his life will continue as before.

Occupations was first performed at the small Stables Theatre Club in Manchester, and then by the Royal Shakespeare Company in one of their experimental seasons at an equally intimate theatre club in London, The Place. It aroused immediate interest and critical praise, despite its unlikely and superficially remote content, and it was recognized as revealing a new writer with a distinctive voice of his own.

It is set in Turin in 1920, a time of industrial strikes and lock-outs and the threat of revolution. Griffiths only reveals the place and the relationship of the characters gradually, during the dialogue. The play starts with the voice of a speaker at the Communist Third International, and then shows two

women in an hotel bedroom. One of the women is an exiled
Russian aristocrat, now the mistress of Kabak, a Communist
revolutionary organizer. She is dying of cancer and wants him
to be with her. He neglects her for his duty to travel around
Europe on behalf of the Soviet Union. In the very bedroom
where she lies drugged and dying, he interviews a local Communist leader, a corrupt municipal official and, finally, a boss
of the Fiat company. Both Kabak and Gramsci, the local
Communist leader, are excellent theatrical roles, loosely
modelled on real historical figures. Kabak is dynamic, confident and volatile, Gramsci is a hunchback and almost a
dwarf, anxious and burningly sincere. The minor parts—the
devoted maid, the ingratiating hotel manager, and the other
officials—are rewarding too. The play's occasional dryness
and Gramsci's lengthy political speeches require convincing
and gripping acting to hold the audience.

The first question discussed between Kabak and Gramsci is
whether the workers of Turin should take a lead in industrial
action, regardless of the rest of Italy, or agree to a compromise
with the employers. Kabak counsels insurrection, without
which there can be no revolution, and sneers at caution.
Gramsci counters that if they lead an insurrection which is not
followed up there will be no organized working class left in
Turin, to fight another day. Their argument develops from
this practical basis into a dispute between Kabak's cold calcu-
lations and Gramsci's warmer feelings for the working class.

Gramsci: We have risked too much already. I will not allow
that class to be wiped out. I could not survive it.
Kabak: No sentimentalisms, please. You mustn't confuse
revolutionary duty with bourgeois conscience.
Gramsci: Nor shall I, comrade.
Kabak: You cannot say you fear to put your working class
at risk and then imagine you say something profoundly revolutionary.
Gramsci: That isn't what I'm saying. I am saying that they
are too important to the world revolutionary movement to
squander on a dubious adventure that could well have been
concocted precisely to produce their annihilation.

Kabak: And you . . . could not survive it? Do you mean . . . you love them?

Gramsci: Yes I do. That's exactly what I mean.

Kabak: I see.

Gramsci: What?

Kabak: You cannot *love* an army, comrade. An army is a machine. This one makes revolutions. If it breaks down, you get another one. Love has nothing to do with it.

Gramsci: Oh, comrade. Oh, comrade. Listen. There is nothing more relevant than love. There is nothing in the world more relevant than love. When I was a child—inside this . . . body—I imagined I could never be loved. For many years, the thought that I could be loved seemed an absolute, almost fatal, impossibility. So perhaps I came to the masses with the same mechanical views of them, and my own relation to them, as you have just propounded. Use them. Tool them up. Keep them greased. Discard when they wear out. But then I thought, how can a man bind himself to the masses, if he has never loved anyone himself, not even his mother or his father. I thought, how can a man love a collectivity, when he has not profoundly loved single human creatures. And it was then I began to see masses as people and it was only then that I began to love them, in their particular, detailed, local, individual character. You would be wrong to see this . . . love . . . as the product of petit-bourgeois idealism. It is the correct, the only true dialectical relationship between leaders and led, vanguard and masses, that can ensure the political health of the new order the revolution seeks to create. Treat masses as expendable, as fodder, *during* the revolution, you will always treat them thus. I'll tell you this, Comrade Kabak, if you see masses that way, there can be no revolution worth the blood it spills.

Gramsci's speech touches on the crux of a problem which constantly concerns Griffiths—that power is needed to better the world but the pursuit of power itself tends to destroy the real urge to betterment. In *Occupations*, Gramsci is deeply unhappy when the workers have to give up their struggle, for the time being, though that is what he himself recommended.

Kabak is playing a double game. He bribes the supposedly anti-Communist municipal official and, when it becomes clear that Italian labour will compromise and go on working for its capitalist employers, he does a deal with the Fiat boss to ensure supplies for the Soviet Union. Maybe his mission was simply to test out the strength of the Italian revolutionary will, before committing Soviet gold to the Italian bosses. Maybe he even wanted the militant workers to be destroyed in a doomed uprising. It is not clear. It is clear only that he is entirely un-scrupulous, and unscrupulous too in his private life, seducing the maid while his mistress lies dying and refusing to take the women with him when he leaves Italy. The play ends with the dying woman committing suicide and with a photo-projection of Molotov and Ribbentrop signing the Nazi-Soviet pact. Kabak was a forerunner of Stalin.

John Tagg, in some ways the central character of *The Party*, is Trotskyite and theoretically anti-Stalinist, but he is as ruth-less and unscrupulous an organizer as Kabak or any Stalinist. Like Kabak he is willing to abandon his allies for the time being, in pursuit of a long-term aim; like Gramsci he is afraid of destroying the hard core of militant workers by encouraging them to start an insurrection too soon. Like Gramsci too, he is an invalid, dying of a tumour.

By contrast with Griffiths' earlier plays, *The Party* was given a big prestige National Theatre production at the Old Vic, with a cast headed by Laurence Olivier. He gave Tagg the powerful brooding presence specified by the author and made his long revolutionary speech seem sincere and persuasive. The other principal characters were played by some of the National's best-known actors—Frank Finlay, Ronald Pickup, Denis Quilley and John Shrapnel. The play was directed by John Dexter.

The Party can be taken as referring to the Revolutionary Socialist Party, Tagg's Trotskyite group, and to the party which forms the main body of the play: a gathering of left-wing intellectuals at the smart, trendy home of Joe Shawcross, a television drama director. It is hinted that his unsatisfactory private life is linked with his desire to immerse himself in politics and there is some suggestion that guilt about the

materialism of his home-life may be one of the causes of his
failure to satisfy Angie, his wife, sexually. His ex-wife shares his
political interests which bore Angie, who wants him sexually
but may be seeking satisfaction elsewhere.

The Party, mainly a political debate, takes place at the time
of the student rebellion in Paris, which forms a background of
reality, in photo projections and news bulletins, to stress the
theoretical nature of most of the talk. The original version, as
written and published, starts unrealistically, with a music-hall
style prologue. First there is a monologue parodying a stand-
up comedian, commenting laconically on photo projections of
Trotsky, Marx and Lenin, and joking about de Gaulle and
Cohn-Bendit, the student leader. Then comes a mimed scene,
described by Griffiths as 'a sort of abstracted fuck-ballet' for
Joe and Angie. 'The fuck is bad. Joe is frozen; Angie goes down
with her lips. He kneels for a while, inert, takes it: then imperceptibly draws away from her.' But none of this was performed
at the National Theatre, where the play began with a bickering
dialogue for Joe and Angie in their bedroom.

At the end of this brief scene, there are more photo projections and a song about sperm, while the stage direction says:
'Joe kneels on the bed to face the wall-length mirror, takes out
his penis, fists it, begins to beckon it to life.' There are further
touches of 'total theatre' later in the play, and occasional
stretches of extremely frank dialogue, to make the characters
more human and to sugar the pill of abstract political debate.
Malcolm Sloman, a drunken playwright, says he has told a
newspaper that 'they can stick their best-play award up their
managing editor's capacious and much-lipped rectum'. When
Joe is preparing food for the party, Sloman says, 'You don't
need a wife, Joe, you need a husband'; later Joe describes to
Sloman in considerable detail the occasion of his first fuck, in
the back of a car.

The main antagonists in the political debate are Andrew
Ford, a sociologist, Tagg and Sloman. Ford gives a long academic lecture analysing Marxism and attempting to bring it
up to date. Tagg sneers at this theoretical approach and says
what is needed is an efficient, truly revolutionary party, instead
of the Stalinist Communist one. Touching on one of the central

themes of Griffiths's plays, he says supporters of his Revolutionary Party must cut themselves off from 'personal relationships, career, advancement, reputation and prestige'.

Tagg: From my limited acquaintance with the intellectual stratum in Britain, I'd say that was the greatest hurdle of all to cross. Imagine a life without the approval of your peers. Imagine a life without *success*. The intellectual's problem is not vision, it's commitment. You enjoy biting the hand that feeds you, but you'll never bite it off. So those brave and foolish youths in Paris now will hold their heads out for the baton and shout their crazy slogans for the night. But it won't stop them from graduating and taking up their positions in the centres of ruling class power and privilege later on.

Tagg's speech ends the first act. Sloman, who spends most of the time wandering around drunk and dropping casual insults, makes his big speech in the second, saying that one political party is much like another and that Tagg's is as autocratic and harmful as any. He believes the revolution will happen spontaneously.

Sloman: There won't be a revolution because John Tagg forms a tiny Bolshevik party in South London. There'll be a revolution, and another, and another, because the capacity for 'adjustment' and 'adaptation' within capitalism is not, contrary to popular belief, infinite. And when *masses* of people, masses mind, decide to take on the state and the ruling class, they won't wait for the word from the 'authentic voice of Trotsky' or anyone else. They'll be too busy 'practising the revolution'. And the class will throw up its own leaders and its own structures of leadership and responsibility. And they'll find the 'germ' from inside the class, not from 'outwith'. Because the germ's there, the virus is there, and however many generations of workers are pumped full of antibiotics or the pink placebos of late capitalism, it will persist, the virus, under the skin, waiting.

The debate is inconclusive. Tagg makes a telephone call to Paris and calmly reveals that his cadres there are not joining the rebellious students, because it is not a real workers' revolt and has not been properly organized. Even if the revolt succeeded, it would only help the Stalinist Communists, who would eventually sell out the workers in a 'realistic' power agreement with de Gaulle. This cynicism shocks Joe and seems to resolve one of his problems. Until now he has been undecided whether to give financial backing to his younger brother's business efforts. He was reluctant to support a capitalist venture; now he decides to do so. *The Party* ends with an inconclusive scene, similar to the opening one, in which Joe and Angie seem to be deliberately avoiding direct communication with each other.

All Good Men was originally written for television, but later produced by the National Theatre as a lunch-time attraction. It is another study of the relationship between political principles, practical politics and private life. Edward Waite is an elderly retired Labour politician, of working-class origins, now living in bourgeois comfort in a Surrey mansion. He has written his autobiography and Richard Massingham, a trendy and supercilious young television producer, has come to his home to do a programme about him. Waite's second wife has left him, and the other characters are William and Maria, his son and daughter. Both think their father has abandoned or betrayed his principles, but the son is much more aggressive and hostile in saying so. He is a sociologist whose researches have uncovered the fact that his father secretly voted against the General Strike and, as a miners' leader, took a leading part in reaching a settlement with the employers. In the crucial scene of the play, William first asks his father why successive Labour governments have only made modest changes in our society and then accuses him of wanting to be respectable and accepted, of betraying his class.

Griffiths gives Waite a long speech, defending and justifying the records of the various Labour governments, emphasising what enormous social reforms were achieved, and pointing out that you cannot have total change in a night. William accuses him of being much the same as a Conservative.

William: Did it ever occur to you that Edward Heath might give exactly the same definition as the one you've just

propounded? Is a socialist reality the same as a Tory one
then?

Waite: We live in the same world. It doesn't change because
we shut our eyes and dream.

William: It doesn't change *unless* we shut our eyes and dream.

Waite reveals that he has accepted a life peerage and wants
Maria to accompany him to the Palace; she refuses, gently,
saying that he must do what he thinks right but for her it would
be an 'obscene pantomime' and a betrayal of the poor kids she
teaches at school. William encourages the television producer
to ask Waite a leading question about his attitude to the General
Strike, and the play ends with the producer doing just that.

The implication of this open ending—we never see Waite
answer the question or the rest of the television interview—is
that British Labour leaders have betrayed their trust by selling
out to the establishment. This implication is strengthened by
the fact that Waite has a heart attack during the play, another
symbolic sign of his failure, like Tagg's tumour in *The Party*.
However, Griffiths is careful to balance matters a bit in the
other direction by making Waite a sympathetic and humane
figure, as well as an invalid, whilst Massingham and William
are arrogant and aggressive. There is some suggestion that
Massingham is motivated by class antagonism and William by
Oedipal jealousy. Maria is the most sympathetic of the younger
generation, making her point of view clear without being offensive to her father. All the characters are roundly drawn as
credible human beings.

In *Comedians*, Griffiths pursues his study of the way worldly
ambition forces compromise and retreat from idealism, and his
view of the conflict between age and youth. But he transfers
the scene from politics to the stage. Superficially, at any rate,
this is a play about how to make a success as a professional
entertainer, about the ethics of getting laughs through vulgarity
and racialism, and about the art of the 'true' comedian. Like
Griffiths' other plays, it also explores the relationship between
its characters' private and professional lives: Eddie Waters,
once a successful music-hall comedian, lost his talent for getting
laughs when he saw the remnants of Buchenwald concentration

camp, and Gethin Price, his star pupil, stages a bitter and angry act which may be partly the result of being deserted by his wife. Griffiths regards *Comedians* as a political play, a play about the possibility and desirability of revolution, though this is only hinted at obliquely.

Because it can be taken at so many levels, *Comedians* is more ambitious and more controversial than Griffiths' earlier plays; because in the end it is not clear how it is meant to be taken, it is in some ways the least satisfactory. But that is not to deny its evident theatricality. It was an immediate success when it was first staged at the Nottingham Playhouse. That production, with the original cast, came to the Old Vic for a guest season, and later, with one change of cast, transferred to Wyndhams Theatre for a short West End run. It was also enthusiastically received by the critics when it was staged, in a slightly rewritten form, on Broadway.

Comedians was more popular than Griffiths' earlier plays, partly because of its unusual setting and theme, and partly because a play about comedians, including a number of would-be comics telling jokes, obviously has a wider appeal than a sustained political debate. The first act takes place in a dingy secondary school in Manchester, being used for adult evening classes. The class we are shown is taught by Eddie Waters, a role first taken by Jimmy Jewel, himself formerly very well-known as half of the comedy team of Jewel and Warriss. His class is a mixed assortment of working men who want to be professional comedians but he has much higher ideals than simply helping them to become famous or to make money.

Waters: A real comedian—that's a daring man. He *dares* to see what his listeners shy away from, fear to express. And what he sees is a sort of truth, about people, about their situation, about what hurts or terrifies them, about what's hard, above all, about what they *want*. A joke releases the tension, says the unsayable, any joke pretty well. But a true joke, a comedian's joke, has to do more than release tension, it has to *liberate* the will and the desire, it has to *change the situation*. There's very little won't take a joke. But when a joke bases itself upon a distortion—a 'stereotype' perhaps—

and gives the lie to the truth so as to win a laugh and stay in favour, we've moved away from the comic art and into the world of 'entertainment' and slick success.

This outburst is precipitated by a conventional dirty limerick recited by Price. And it is Price, in the end, who produces the most revolutionary and angry performance, too angry and revolutionary for Waters. Here in allegory are Griffiths' favourite conflicts, between the theoretical reformer who fights shy of action and the practical revolutionary, and between age and youth. *Comedians*, however, is explicitly concerned with the immediate fortunes of the stage aspirants. Bert Challenor, an agent from London, comes to audition Waters' pupils in a working men's club. He tells them he is looking for comics who give the public what it wants, escapism, without any missionary zeal. He suggests that they should all try to be Max Bygraves. This builds up considerable suspense. What will Waters' pupils, trained to have higher ideals than that, actually do in the audition which occupies the whole of the second act?

The audition is presented as an unwelcome interruption of the club's habitual bingo. Griffiths shows considerable technical skill and great love and knowledge of music-hall techniques in his handling of this show within a show. Some of the comedians alter their acts in attempts to please Challenor, but Price alters his the other way. He does an angry mime, based on Grock, playing the 'Red Flag' on a miniature violin and pouring scathing abuse on two cardboard cut-outs representing the bourgeoisie. His act is embarrassing and, in my view, boring; the real audience in the theatre is left uncertain whether he is meant to be admired and, if so, why. That is one trouble with the whole audition: it is not sufficiently clear which comedians are living up to Waters' ideals. It is also unclear whether some of them are meant to be funnier, or less funny, than they actually are. The distinction between 'liberating' jokes, based on truth, which Waters admires, and cheap 'stereotype' jokes making fun of minority groups, is extremely imprecise. The 'commercial' comedians, despised by Waters and eventually booked by Challenor, tend to appeal to the audience more than the ones it feels it is supposed to admire. So the total effect is unsettling: perhaps deliberately unsettling but still distracting, detracting from the point Griffiths is trying to make.

The third act of *Comedians*, a classroom post-mortem on the audition, is the least satisfactory section of the play. Challenor makes brief comments on the audition, but there is no analysis of what went wrong, for example with the two brothers who quarrelled and got lost in their act. When everyone else has gone, Waters and Price stay behind. Waters tells Price he was brilliant but terrifying; Price tells Waters that at least he did not sell him out, as the others did. Finally, Waters tries to explain why he did not like Price's act, despite the sincerity and brilliance he found in it.

> Waters: It was ugly. It was drowning in hate. You can't change today into tomorrow on that basis. You forget a thing called . . . the truth.
> Price: The truth. Can I say . . . look, I wanna say something. What do you know about *the truth*, Mr Waters? You think the truth is *beautiful*? You've forgotten what it's *like*. You knew it when you started off, Oldham Empire, People's Music Hall, Colne Hippodrome, Bolton Grand . . . Because you were still in touch with what made you . . . hunger, diphtheria, filth, unemployment, penny clubs, means tests, bed bugs, head lice . . . Was all *that* truth beautiful? . . . When I stand upright—like tonight at that club—I bang my head on the ceiling. Just like you fifty years ago. We're still caged, exploited, prodded and pulled at, milked, fattened, slaughtered, cut up, fed out. We still don't belong to ourselves. Nothing's changed. You've just forgotton, that's all.

This is the cue for Waters to tell Price the story of his visit to Buchenwald, since when he cannot laugh at jokes about Jews or make jokes at other people's expense. He confesses that the experience was not only repulsive; he also got an erection. Something in him actually loved it. He seems to be saying that our inmost gut feelings are too dangerous, too uncontrollable, to be fit for humour. And this does not seem consistent with what he was teaching earlier. (The Buchenwald anecdote was omitted from the New York production, for which Griffiths wrote some new dialogue.)

Price decides to go his own way, without further help from
Waters. A Pakistani student wanders in and tells Waters a joke
from his country, which Waters recognises as a variant of an
old Jewish joke. He enrols the Pakistani for his next course.
The play ends as it began, with the school caretaker cleaning
the empty room, surveying some foul language on the black-
board, and muttering 'dirty buggers'. Nothing is resolved.

Griffiths' plays are deliberately open-ended. He does not
want to use them to preach his own views, but to stimulate
debate on what he regards as the vital issues of our day. 'My
own views are not necessarily any more valid or realistic than
anyone else's. And I'm sure one must keep bearing in mind that
one's own view may be wrong, otherwise one can't grow as a
thinker. As I was born in the working-class at a time of misery
and unemployment, and as I've taught working-class children,
I've seen immense proletarian talent wasted daily, or led into
violence and senseless activity. Of course I want all this changed
as quickly as possible, but the process of rapid change carries
certain costs. We have to go on offering accounts of the costs
of revolutionary struggle and the costs of non-struggle. The
good life for some of us is propped up by the terrible lives of
those who are suffering in Asia or Latin America, and those in
this country who risk, for example, dying of hypothermia. We
must keep insisting on moral accountancy. My plays try to do
this but I don't deliver the tablets. I want to leave the audience
arguing and debating—I suppose it's something to do with the
methods I used when I was a teacher. And I'm absolutely
delighted by the very heavy mail I receive, discussing points
raised in my plays.' In a television interview with Benedict
Nightingale, however, he said that if he thought he could do
more to change Britain 'on the streets or in the political
parties', rather than in the theatre, he would go there.

Griffiths says he has never had any great urge to submit his
plays for production or to get recognition as a dramatist. He
lost the first three plays he ever wrote, which were intended for
television but never submitted. 'I'm writing more for therapeutic reasons, working things out for myself and for a close
circle of friends. I'd tried writing stories and poems, and there
always seemed to be something missing. When I started writing

plays, it was all suddenly there. My thinking tends to be by way of question and answer, with never less than two voices at work in my mind, so writing dialogue and structuring scenes came very naturally. It was a dizzying effect. And I've never been interested in writing anything but plays since the mid '60s. I'm not at all a devotee of the theatre—I knew very little about it when I started writing plays, just childhood experience of circus, pantomime, music-hall and Blackpool summer shows. The first real play I discovered was Strindberg's *Easter* on the radio—a shattering experience. I still feel uneasy in theatres, trapped, and I don't usually have a good time there. I prefer films. I don't 'attend' rehearsals of my plays—I work at them, shoulder to shoulder with the director and the actors, and I seek out directors who will work like this, not trying to protect the actors from me or me from the actors. You have to learn how to talk to actors—I used to be much too abstract. Once Jack Shepherd gave me the key, when he said 'that's terrific, Trevor, but I can't act it'. I learnt to use my teaching technique of posing questions again, like asking an actor why he is standing at a certain point. Actors often come up with good ideas in rehearsal—the author has no exclusive key to the best ideas. Some actors enrich the meaning of one's lines—those are usually the actors who are most faithful to the text. If the lines don't work, they don't suggest changing them till they've tried every possible interpretation. I don't get on well with actors who always want to change lines to suit themselves, though some of those are very good actors.

'Of course I go to the first nights of my plays, as a practitioner in working dress, to see how they go. But it's often a weird experience, being mixed up with all the special people having special drinks in the interval—I couldn't feel remoter if I'd just been dropped in Kuwait.'

The French student riots of 1968 had a deep effect on Griffiths, as they did on Christopher Hampton. Not only do they figure as background to *The Party*, but they also led, indirectly, to *Occupations*. 'I wanted to write a play about my response to the events in Paris, but I couldn't find a play there and I looked for a historical equivalent. I came across Gramsci's essays under the title *The Soviets in Italy* and this led me to do

research in Turin during a two weeks holiday. I talked to a lot
of people who knew Gramsci and based my character on the
historical one. He *was* crippled, did chain smoke, was extremely
untidy and cleaned his shoes with his hat. Kabak is an amalgam
of about three historical Comintern agents working in Italy at
the time. He is a practitioner of *realpolitik*—he does really want
revolution in Italy but when he sees that it is impracticable he
does a deal with Fiat instead. This reflects the Comintern's
dual aims at the time—to foment revolution and to consolidate
the economic power of the Soviet Union. British actors aren't
always good at capturing that degree of cynicism, and British
audiences don't readily accept it, which is why so many people
think perhaps Kabak never really wanted the revolution at all.'

   Sam Sam, on the other hand, is largely autobiographical.
Griffiths says he will never forget the time when his father
retired and was given a souvenir gold watch by the firm. 'He
was so bloody proud of it, it made me sick, and very sad.' This
incident re-occurs in several of Griffiths' plays, and the description of Sam's father's death from cancer, is also based on his
own father. In addition, Griffiths has an elder brother. 'In most
respects he is my equal, yet his life is very different because he
was born two years too soon to benefit from the 1944 Education
Act. So our lives have diverged—he remains a factory worker.
In some ways the brother who is educated and moves into the
middle-class is not really liberated, but finds his role pre-empted
for him by social conventions. I know this is an unfashionable
view, but it's similar to Jimmy Porter's problem in *Look Back in
Anger*. The echoes of Osborne in *Sam Sam* are quite deliberate;
not that I wanted to write a pastiche of Osborne's play, but to
comment on it.

   'The music-hall section of *Sam Sam* and of some of my other
plays was influenced by my visits to northern music-halls when
I was young. I saw a lot of famous stand-up comics like Albert
Modley and Jimmy James. The first Sam is one of them, a
ring-master defining his experience in circus or music-hall
terms.'

   I asked Griffiths why he made Tagg in *The Party* an invalid,
dying of a tumour. 'Not consciously, but unconsciously, I may
have wanted to make some statement that there are very few

of those dedicated, fanatical people around any longer, and that we die when we fail to take root in those around us. I was very anxious that Tagg should not be played sentimentally. Olivier eschewed sentimentality very well, though even he sometimes felt he must clutch at his stomach to indicate pain and prepare the audience. I didn't want that at all, but I understood an actor's need to do it. I want to present real people, not stereotypes. That's why I've tried to make all the characters in *The Party* reasonably sympathetic—you meet very few people who actually think of themselves as shits. It would be easy to depict a character as a shit, but that would be to miss something about him. I like to give my characters the dignity of their own space—I try to put myself in the space they inhabit. And I try to understand the relationship between people and the causes they adopt. That's something I've explored in a lot of my television plays, and in *All Good Men*.

Griffiths is emphatic that *Comedians* is a political play. 'It covers more effectively some of the same ground as *Sam Sam*, the cost of escaping from one's class or from what is socially expected. It was my first three-act play, and it's very dense; I think it needs to be seen more than once, or read as well as seen. This is probably true of most of my plays. As well as being a political play, it's also a moral play, about how one can be good. The question why we laugh at certain things becomes a metaphor for the question why we live the way we do. Originally I saw the play as a conflict between Waters and Challenor, between integrity and commercialism. But after six or eight pages of the first draft, Gethin Price came through and superseded that confrontation, making it a conflict between liberal humanism and proletarian revolution. Gethin bursts the category of comedy, he is an artist, and his art is finer than it usually seems on the stage. His whole act is based on Grock, and should have grace, inventiveness, daring and an obscure singleness of purpose, almost like Lenin. Waters is the typical English social reformer, often found in adult education. He is full of integrity and absolutely incorruptible. I carried all these ideas around in my head for about two years, before the play took its final shape.'

Referring to the frequent correlation of sex and politics in his plays, and the constant use of basic four-letter words, Griffiths said with some pride that Olivier had told him he was the first writer to have the word 'cunt' spoken on the stage of the National Theatre, though, Olivier added, 'the actors have said it under their breaths often enough'. 'I absolutely insist on using the language that would actually be spoken by my characters,' Griffiths says, 'though television is always trying to stop me. I'm influenced by Reich on the connection between political and sexual states. We aren't always in touch with our sexuality or aware of it as much as we should be, but yes, certainly, there is sexual insistence in my plays.'

Griffiths finds it impossible to say how he would have managed before the abolition of the Lord Chamberlain and theatre censorship. He feels that traditional suppression of direct sexual references led to a kind of pornography, similar to the sort of thing still carried on in mass circulation newspapers with their supposedly titillating photographs. 'That sort of thing is not about genital potency, it's masturbatory fantasy. Similarly the old-style music hall comedians dealt in innuendo and inverted prudishness, and they have a vested interest in preserving censorship and attacking the new "permissiveness".'

Twelve: Howard Brenton

Born: Portsmouth, England, 1942.
Father: a policeman for many years, then became a Methodist Minister.
Education: Chichester Grammar School and Cambridge University, where he read English.
Married in 1970—two children.

'My father was an amateur actor and director, and very keen on theatre—he did a bit of everything, including scenery painting. I have vivid memories of being taken to my first theatre, Arthur Askey in *Mother Goose*, when I was about six—there was an amazing shadow play. I acted in plays at school and wrote them, along with poems and novels, at Cambridge. I always took it for granted I would work in the theatre'.

On leaving Cambridge, worked as Assistant Stage Manager in various repertory theatres. Got Arts Council bursaries for two years after production of *Revenge*, and has been full-time professional writer since then, helped by numerous Continental productions and two film scripts, and by the John Whiting Award in 1970.

1972–73: Resident Dramatist, Royal Court Theatre.

Plays:
Ladder of Fools (A.D.C. (amateur), Cambridge 1965). *Winder, Daddykins* (Dublin 1965). *It's My Criminal* (London 1966). *A Sky-Blue Life* (adapted from Gorky) (London 1966 and revised 1972). *Gargantua* (Brighton 1969). *Gum and Goo* (Brighton 1969, London 1971). *Revenge* (London 1969). *Christie in Love* (London 1969). *Heads* and *The Education of Skinny Spew* (Bradford 1969, London 1970). *Fruit* (London 1970). *Wesley* (Bradford 1970). *Scott of the Antarctic* (Bradford 1971). *Lay-By* (with others, Edinburgh and London 1971). *Hitler Dances* (Edinburgh and London 1972). *How Beautiful With Badges* (London 1972). *Measure for Measure* (adapted from Shakespeare, Exeter 1972). *England's Ireland* (with others, Amsterdam and London 1972).

A Fart for Europe (with David Edgar, London 1972). *The Screens* (adapted from Genet, Bristol 1973). *Magnificence* (London 1973). *Brassneck* (with David Hare, Nottingham 1973). *The Churchill Play* (Nottingham 1974). *The Saliva Milk-shake* (London 1975). *Weapons of Happiness* (London 1976). *Government Property* (Aarhus, Denmark, 1976). *Epsom Downs* (London 1977). *Evening Standard* Award 1976.

BRENTON IS AS political as Trevor Griffiths, and perhaps even further to the Left. Like Griffiths, he expresses strong dissatisfaction with present-day Britain but, instead of being naturalistic and relying largely on rational argument, Brenton's plays are fantasies, full of bizarre and theatrical visual effects. The dialogue is often artificial and surrealistic, attempting to show people as they really are, beneath the veneer of conventional behaviour and polite talk. Brenton is obsessed with the violence lurking beneath the surface of apparently respectable upholders of law and order, and with the way this suppressed violence brings the oppressed and the oppressor, the worker and the criminal, the politician and the policeman, closer together than is generally realized. The result is often extremely amusing, as well as frightening.

Brenton's theatrical career is almost as unusual as the content of his plays. Early experience writing for fringe companies like the Brighton Combination, the Portable Theatre, the Bradford University Drama Group and the Traverse Theatre Workshop, Edinburgh, was followed by London productions at the Royal Court's Theatre Upstairs and then in the same theatre's main auditorium. Two of his most important full-length plays, *Brassneck* (written jointly with David Hare) and *The Churchill Play*, failed to transfer to London, despite praise from the critics who saw them at Nottingham Playhouse. On the strength of them, however, and without any previous production in a large London theatre, Brenton became the first writer to have a play commissioned and staged by the National Theatre in its new prestigious Lyttelton auditorium. He had suddenly 'arrived'.

Brenton's first full-length play to be staged in London was *Revenge*, produced at the Royal Court's Theatre Upstairs. Its characters and language are highly original, but soon became familiar as typical of Brenton's work. As in his later plays, there are criminals, prostitutes and policemen involved with each other in bizarre situations and using artificial language which is often very funny in its outspoken and exaggerated expression of thoughts which normally remain unspoken. Also, like Brenton's later work, *Revenge* is very theatrical. One actor has several very quick changes to 'double' the roles of Adam Hepple, a notorious ageing criminal, and Assistant Commissioner Archibald MacLeish, the detective who has always hounded him. This doubling, apart from giving the actor a chance to impress the audience with his virtuosity, also underlines the parallel between policeman and criminal. The love-hate relationship between Hepple and MacLeish, and their obsession with each other, is remarkably similar to the criminal-detective relationship in Simon Gray's *Dutch Uncle*, produced in London in the same year—another example of the mysterious *Zeitgeist* which causes contemporary writers to pick similar or even identical themes.

The play starts with Hepple being released from Brixton Gaol after serving an eight-year sentence for robbery. An earthy, vigorous tone is set straight away. The Voice of Brixton Gaol advises Hepple to mend his ways and he obscenely vows to be a big criminal again and to get his revenge on MacLeish. Hepple meets two of his former criminal buddies, who tell him most of the others are now dead or in the House of Lords! They are reluctant to work for him, but Hepple forces them. Other characters are Hepple's daughters, both prostitutes, and two policemen who flirt with them. Albert, the younger one, who is fancied by the girls, is machine-gunned by Hepple during his raid on MacLeish's house; Hepple writes his name on the ground in Albert's blood, claiming to be putting his name on England and on MacLeish.

MacLeish is a figure of farce, a religious fanatic who believes he is one of the Elect and that God is helping his hunt for Hepple. His great scheme is to keep Hepple on the run till he collapses from heart failure, and he vows not to shave till Hepple is caught because 'Al Capone never shaved when he was after a man'. When George, a junior policeman, points out that this is England, not Chicago, MacLeish disdainfully replies that they are 'both foreign parts to a Scot'.

In the end, all the characters die, each in turn spectacularly biting a sack of stage blood and spitting out the contents. So *Revenge* ends like the Jacobean or Victorian melodrama which Brenton is parodying. The deaths also symbolize a dying Britain, or at least the passing of an age. Before Hepple and MacLeish die, they confront each other in a mutual nightmare, and have identical visions of the Britain of the 1980's.

MacLeish: It's the 1980's now. Rapes every night. No citizen abroad after dark. The coppers armed. Gangs roaming at will, burning down police stations. The country's gone to the devil. You lived before your time, Adam.
Hepple: Funny. My dream of a criminal England, it's all come true with the 1980's. The casino towns, the brothel villages, the cities red with blood and pleasure. Public life the turn of a card, the fall of a dice. The whole country on the fiddle, the gamble, the open snatch, the bit on the side. From Land's End to John O'Groats the whole of England's one giant pinball table. The ball running wild, Glasgow, Birmingham, Leeds, Coventry, London, Brighton. Wonderful.

The social criticism implicit in *Revenge* is overshadowed in the theatre by the play's violence, humour and explicit amorality, so that it's doubtful if many members of the audience are stimulated to question the social system. The same is true of *Christie in Love*, also presented at the Theatre Upstairs (after a try-out at the Oval House in South London). Once again Brenton is concerned with criminals and police, this time with the notorious real-life murderer, John Reginald Halliday Christie, who killed and buried numerous women in and around his house in Notting Hill Gate. Brenton lived near there, and was fascinated by Christie and by the area. It's a one-act play, written in a mixture of naturalistic and surrealistic styles. In a detailed production note, Brenton explains that it could be quite funny if played fast as a black sketch, 'but I categorically forbid anyone to do so. I want it to last nearly an hour. It is written to be played very slowly'. The original productions were directed by David Hare, who, Brenton says, 'got it right'.

The play starts with a very slow scene in which two clownish policemen are digging in Christie's house, and Christie comes to life from beneath a pile of newspapers. The policemen talk directly to the audience and also exchange dirty stories and limericks—

> Inspector: There was this faith healer. The most famous in the land. Anything he touched, he . . . (*pause*)
> Constable: I see, sir.
> Inspector: Cured. He had what you'd call a wonderful touch. (*A pause*)
> Constable: Cured, sir.
> Inspector: Anyway, this faith healer, he got married. And the first time in bed with his wife he ran his hands all over her, and sealed her up.

Brenton's production note explains his use of the policemen. 'They are stage coppers. But they have "sudden lights", unpredictable speeches beyond the confines of pastiche. As if a cardboard black and white cut-out suddenly reaches out a fully fleshed, real hand. It's a bathos technique. It's very cruel.'

With Christie, on the other hand, 'I tried to write a fully fledged naturalistic part', though Christie's first appearance is far from naturalistic. It is 'in the Dracula tradition. Happy horror, creeps and treats. He rises from the grave luridly, in a frightening mask. It looks as if a juicy evening's underway, all laughs, nice shivers, easy oohs and aahs. But that's smashed up. The lights are slammed on, and the mask is seen as only a tatty bit of papier mâché. Off it comes and what's left is a feeble, ordinary man blinking through his pebble glasses.'

Before the lights and the exposure of the mask, Christie is heard on a tape recording, in a long soliloquy of hate against women. The actor playing Christie gets increasingly excited during this speech, panting and finally miming orgasm. He lies exhausted just before the lights brighten and he is interrogated by the police. Similar alternations of mood and style recur throughout the play. Brenton says this is the play's basic device: 'a kind of dislocation, tearing one style up for another, so the proceedings lurch and all interpretations are blocked, and the spectator hunting for an easy meaning wearies, and is left only with Christie and his act of love'.

The act of love is, of course, necrophiliac, as is made crystal clear to the audience in a series of bizarre and extremely crude interviews between Christie and the Inspector. Finally, the two policemen lose their tempers and all self-control, and hang Christie. They are shaken, but soon calm down.

Inspector: That's that then.
Constable: Yes, sir.
Inspector: Another crime solved.
Constable: A blow struck for married life.
Inspector: Yes.
Constable: Yes.
Inspector: Just . . . Clean up a bit. Someone else's garden now.
Constable: Sir.
Inspector: Get on with it then.
Constable: Sir.
(*The Constable covers the body of Christie with the spade, slowly, smooths the surface of the paper down, then looks around the audience, shamefacedly, and slips away. End play.*)

Christie in Love certainly ends without any 'easy meaning'; it struck many people as a mere exercise in bad taste. But it does try to show that even a perverted mass murderer is also a human being, and it again underlines parallels between the criminal and the police, one of Brenton's favourite themes, using typical verbal and visual shock tactics. *Lay-By* is very similar. It too was first produced by Portable Theatre, in association with the Traverse Theatre in Edinburgh, and then was brought to London for Sunday night performances at the Royal Court followed by a short season at the Open Space. It is an experiment in collaboration between seven writers, including David Hare, (who originally suggested the collaboration), Trevor Griffiths and Stephen Poliakoff and, like *Christie in Love*, it is based on an actual crime, this time a case of rape and indecent assault.

Lay-By starts with a ventriloquist and his dummy telling the story of the rape and then presents Lesley, the alleged victim, as a girl who is willingly making pornographic films. The actor who played the ventriloquist becomes a private detective, interrogates Lesley and finds that she thinks being beaten with a cane constitutes rape! She also claims to have been forced to commit fellatio, but the detective points out that in fellatio the man is actually at the woman's mercy. He tells her that neither flagellation nor fellatio are rape. But Jack, the man she accused, and Marge, who sat in the car watching Jack with Lesley, are both gaoled, Lesley is subjected to a slapstick parody of a medical inspection, her naked body being manhandled and roughly dropped, until eventually she dies. Her body is then washed in red 'bloody' water, hoisted up on a pulley and deposited in an enormous refuse bin. It is followed by the bodies of Jack and Marge, while the two attendants disposing of the bodies discuss over-population ('too many fucking people') and world starvation. One of them digs his hand into the refuse bin and brings it out covered with jam (blood?). The two of them sit down and share it, one of them finishing the play: 'You could have stirred it up a bit more.' In a *Plays and Players* interview, Brenton described this scene as 'a great outburst of nihilism . . . one of the most beautiful and positive things you can see on a stage'.

Physical details of torture, death and decomposition are again bluntly described in *Hitler Dances*, and there is also a resurrected corpse, as in *Christie in Love*. But *Hitler Dances* is much more of a fantasy, with the actors swapping roles, speaking directly to the audience and occasionally breaking into song. It's a two-act play, originally written for the Traverse Workshop in Edinburgh and then presented at two London studio theatres—the Young Vic and the Theatre Upstairs. The actors appear as children playing games connected with the Second World War. Sometimes these are simply games, as when they compete to describe new ways of killing enemies. But most of the time they get caught up in a tale, and carry the audience with them, of a German soldier killed on his way home at the end of the war. He comes to life and chats with one of the girls, who in her turn imagines herself to be Violette Szabo, the French resistance heroine.

The resurrection scene is presented like a TV play, with the other actors watching, commenting in mildly blasphemous terms, eating chocolates and discussing television commercials. Brenton's stage directions are very specific, not just about what the actors should do, but about what effect they should have on the audience: 'The soldier coming out of the ground's written here as a horror/holy theatre piece; with Carole and Kevin's dialogue, I want to destroy the image's holiness for a time by cheap laughs, but still hold the power, to lodge the corpse in the play as *hard* as possible'.

In some ways *Hitler Dances*, in its style and technique, anticipated the hit musical *Godspell*, though its content is much harsher and its 'message' is, of course, anti-war rather than pro-God. Whatever Brenton's intention, however, the theatrical effectiveness of the piece is stronger than its somewhat confused moral.

Magnificence was Brenton's first play to be staged in a full-size London theatre as distinct from an attic or basement. Even so, it only had a short run at the comparatively small Royal Court. Described by Brenton as 'a kind of tragedy', it's about a group of illegal squatters who eventually decide to assassinate a Cabinet Minister. The first of the play's two acts deals with the squatters, a callous bailiff, and the efforts of the squatters to get their message over to the public, undistorted by the media. Their slogans are not very specific:—'We are the writing on your wall' and 'Weapons of Happiness', later used by Brenton as the title of a play. Veronica, one of the squatters, is very conscious of their failure to communicate.

Veronica: I loathe us. I loathe all the talks we had. That we'd really do it. Come down to the people whom it really hits. . . . And do it for them. I loathe us, I loathe our stupid, puerile view of the World. That we have only to do it, that we have only to go puff, and the monster buildings will go splat . . . I loathe us, I loathe what we've descended to do here . . . Our domesticity . . . Ten days with the fleas and the tin opener lost, never for once questioning . . . That we are in any way changing the bloody, bleeding ugly world . . . Direct action! For us it's come down to sitting on a stinking lavatory for ten days . . . Why didn't we get the local people on our side? Oh we bawled a few slogans at passers-by. Got the odd turd back from the street, and philosophized there upon. But 'Mobilize the People'? We can't mobilize a tin opener. . . .

This act also contains a visual set-piece, when the squatters sort their supplies and transform the room 'into an orderly, indoor camp'.

The second act opens in a Cambridge college, with two politicians walking in the garden. They are called Babs and Alice, an easy but rather cheap method of making them seem amusing and worthless. Babs tells Alice he is dying and indulges in a fantasy speculation about his obituary in *The Times* ('corrupter of youth', 'outrageous old queen, happily no longer with us') and about the ensuing ceremonies.

Babs: What do they do with Ex-Cabinet Ministers who are queer and dead? There should be some . . . splendid event, should there not? Some massive ceremonial. A number of masturbatory images rise up. Ten thousand working men, jeering sweetly. . . . The mind wanders. . . . But the Ministry of Works would foul it up. Terribly butch lot. Commit some grave error of taste. Nude Guardsmen riding bareback. . . .

Fantasy then spreads to the squatters. Jed has a visitation from Lenin, who tells him to hate the bourgeois 'class politician' and aim for a 'violent collision'. Will describes going on hallucinatory drug 'trips' with his girl friend and day-dreams aloud about wearing black leather on a black motor-bike, with Jean Genet on his pillion. Back in the country, Alice describes how Babs died in his arms. The squatter-conspirators surround him, and attempt to kill him with a gelignite mask which fails to explode. Alice discovers that they are so inefficient that they are even misinformed about his post in the Government. He asks why they are after him.

Alice: I know you . . . Hold me, in some way personally responsible. For what I don't know. The World's ills? Some particular event? Or just, perhaps, for being in public life? Having dirty hands? No. . . . Purity of Intent. Is that what you see yourselves as having? Purity of Intent? No doubt you do. How dreadfully unfair. (*Pause*) For being myself? For being me? The terrorist's vendetta, there's no answer to it then. It may come from anywhere. Perhaps you've had a bad life. Have you had a bad life? I would like to know. Because you may yet decide to assault me, and it is very easy to injure. . . . It would be a mild comfort, Jed, if the balance is going to tip. . . . And you are going to come at me and kick me. . . . Why?

Jed: Oh, Mr Public Man. (*Jed stands up. Alice flinches, but Jed releases Alice from the handcuffs*)

Alice: Thank you. You couldn't . . . Give my shoulder-blade a rub could you?

(*Jed ignores that and picks up the gelignite mask*)

Jed: Dunno, I dunno. Can't get rid. Can't shake it off. Magnificence, that it would be magnificent to have you bleeding on the lawn.

That is the only explicit clue to the title of the play. Jed wishes the gelignite mask were real, throws it to the ground, and its explodes, killing him and Alice. Cliff, another of the gang, closes the play.

Cliff: Jed. The waste. I can't forgive you that. The waste of your anger. Not the murder, murder is common enough. Not the violence, violence is everyday. What I can't forgive you, Jed, my dear, dead friend, is the waste.

What the audience may find hard to forgive is the play's obscurity, not much clarified by this closing speech. Brenton says he deliberately gave Cliff the last speech, because Cliff is the most vigorous and sensible of the gang, even though he says very little during the course of the play. He wants the audience to think about Cliff, and maybe to re-read or re-visit the play, to discover Cliff's point of view. In the penultimate scene, Cliff attacks Jed for being 'A nothing. Zero. A crank with a tin box of bangs'. He says the explosion is just a 'fucking stupid gesture' and that the label 'revolutionary' will be a mockery. The alternative Cliff offers is 'work, corny work, with and for the people. Politicizing them and learning from them, everyone of them'. But Brenton himself admits that this little

speech is likely to have been forgotten by the end of the play,
and that audiences tend to pay more attention to the principal
characters, to the ones who talk the most. It is a fault in the
construction of *Magnificence* that it fails to make its point, holding the audience's attention while it is in progress but leaving
it irritated and dissatisfied.

Many of the same themes—half-baked working-class revolutionaries, a tired reformist politician and even an apparition
of a dead Soviet leader—recur, along with the title-slogan, in
Weapons of Happiness.

In between, however, Brenton produced *Brassneck* and *The
Churchill Play*, both ambitious political works staged at the
Nottingham Playhouse but not transferred to London. They
were probably too large-scale for the commercial theatre,
while the National preferred to commission a new play,
Weapons of Happiness. *Brassneck* was written with David Hare.
Sometimes they sat at separate typewriters and sometimes one
hovered while the other typed. The authors' note says 'every
scene, every word was jointly worked; there is nothing which
is more one of us than the other. The work is indivisible'. The
note also explains that 'brassneck' is a Midlands dialect word
meaning 'cheek' or 'nerve', and has criminal connotations.

Brassneck was extremely topical, dealing with nepotism and
corruption in local government and in the awarding of building
contracts. It was produced when big scandals of this sort were
just becoming common knowledge and reaching the courts;
as in real life, the officials and building contractors in the play
are closely associated with the Labour Party. The action begins
in 1945, with photo projections of Churchill and the Royal
Family at the Victory parade and then of Churchill, Attlee
and other Labour leaders at the General Election. Alfred Bagley, an old man, hitch-hikes a lift to his home-town of Stanton,
where he buys a few slum houses and sets himself up as a
builder and property developer. The first act of *Brassneck*
traces his progress—making himself pleasant to the local big-
wigs on the golf course, getting elected to the Masonic Lodge
and even, as a compromise candidate, to be Master of the
Lodge, and sitting in a train dreaming that he has been
elected Pope! He sends his nephew, Roderick, a telegram

announcing that he is dying; Roderick and his family arrive at
the station with flowers, and are looking for a taxi to take them
to the hospital, when they are greeted by the perfectly fit
Alfred. He sets Roderick up as an architect, though unqualified,
and uses bribery and blackmail to get him the contract for the
new hospital, in preference to Clive Avon, an established architect and a member of the local squirearchy. The first act ends
with a wedding party for Roderick's daughter, Lucy, held
simultaneously with the Queen's Coronation. The bridegroom
never appears—he is being sick in the lavatory; Clive Avon
calls Lucy a prostitute and describes the wedding as pus, and
Alfred makes a rambling, drunken, autobiographical speech.
Then, as a tap dancer steps out of the huge wedding cake,
Alfred cuts the table in two with a huge knife, and drops dead.
Lucy, the bride, is left screaming, 'I wanna divorce, I wanna
divorce'.

By the second act Roderick has become prosperous and
arrogant and his spoilt children are middle-aged. The action
takes place at a hunting-party picnic. Roderick is entertaining
a Tory ex-Minister as a means to getting new overseas contracts, but Clive Avon calls the politician a vaseline man
('Vaseline—the stuff buggers use') and drops horse dung down
his back. In revenge, the Bagleys deprive Clive of a drainage
contract. The act ends with the news that Roderick has over-
extended his business and gone bankrupt. In the last act,
Roderick's buildings turn out to be shoddy, he admits giving
bribes, and is told not to use the Labour Club premises any
more. He is tried and sent to prison. When he comes out, in
1973, he is mad, heavily sedated, and exiled to the country.
One of his sons has changed his name and become a Eurocrat
in Brussels, while another is running the local strip-club. A
family conference in the club decides to go into heroin traffic;
they plan to use the club's call girls as distributors and sell the
stuff to schoolchildren. As they look forward to worldwide
expansion and vast profits, a dancer wearing mayor's robes
strips to reveal Masonic aprons, and then a bowler hat and a
rubber tube which she uses for a hypodermic 'fix'. Sidney
Bagley toasts the last days of capitalism as the floor gives way
and the family sinks out of sight.

The Churchill Play was produced at Nottingham eight months after *Brassneck*, with many of the same actors and with the same director, Richard Eyre. An italicized note under the title of the play adds: *As it will be performed in the winter of 1984 by the internees of Churchill Camp somewhere in England.* We are in a near-Fascist Orwellian Britain. A group of political prisoners takes the opportunity of a visiting delegation of M.P.s to make their protest through a theatrical performance and to use it as a cover for an escape attempt. Captain Thompson, the liberal-minded medical officer, encourages them with their subversive play, to the annoyance of Colonel Ball, the commanding officer, and of tough, discipline-conscious Sergeant Baxter, who despises Thompson and is openly insubordinate to him. The soldiers guarding the camp have been brutalized by shooting down terrorists in Northern Ireland and strikers at home. In the play performed by the prisoners, Churchill rises from his coffin and is depicted in an unfavourable light. He is ridiculed, having a bath with Stalin, with another actor as a shared piece of soap! When he visits a bombed-out family in the blitz, he is told, 'We can take it. But we just might give it back to you one day', translated in his memoirs as, 'We can take it. Give it 'em back'.

After the play within the play, there is an attempt at an armed breakout by the more militant prisoners. They are encircled by troops and Mike, one of the leaders, calls off the attempt.

Mike: We turn the guns in.
Jimmy: No. . . .
Jack: . . . No! That's not human!
Mike: What's human? Here we find ourselves. And we go out the door, and they cut us down, and Joby, Ted, Furry, Jimmy, Jack, Peter, Mike are shredded meat. Hanging on the wire for the birds. . . . That 'Human'? (*A pause*) Nowhere to break out to, is there. They'll concrete the whole world over any moment now. And what do we do? (*A slight pause. Smiles*) Survive. In the cracks. Either side of the wire. Be alive.

All this makes a theatrical and frightening vision of the

future. The horror, as prisoners are occasionally removed and 'dumped' (murdered) by the guards, is convincing. The tensions between officers, N.C.O.s and various prisoners, and their rough attempts at humour to make life bearable, are well depicted, and so are the three members of the inspecting delegation. But the attempt to belittle Churchill, and the simplistic message that people rather than great men win wars, detract from, rather than add to, the effectiveness of the play. Similar political uncertainty and naivety mar *Weapons of Happiness*.

This play, specially written for the National Theatre, presents an interesting situation, not previously treated in the theatre, and touches an important problem. But the situation is not explored, the problem not tackled. Josef Frank, a historical Czechoslovak Communist leader who was hanged in the Stalinist purges of 1952, is shown as alive and well and living in London. He is working in a potato crisp factory and arousing the curiosity of the young British workers. His experience of real revolution, and of the horrors of torture and Stalinist interrogation, makes him quite alien to them and to their romantic view of revolution and Communism. But the workers are depicted as so stupid and so ignorant of history and revolutionary theory that he is forced to dismiss them as 'children'. There is no real debate about the best way of changing Britain. Although he warns them that their attempt to run the factory themselves, without any expertise, is doomed, there is no serious discussion of how and when workers' control can be practical. Nor is there any exploration of the consequences of violent revolution, and whether it must inevitably breed further violence, political despotism and economic inefficiency, as it has done in the Soviet countries. The workers never learn the truth about Soviet Communism, because Brenton's Frank cannot be bothered to try teaching them. As depicted in this play, they are unteachable. The play ends, after Frank's death, with an exchange between two of them.

Billy: 'Ere Jan, that old man. Old Joey. You really got funny for him, didn't you? (*Janice shrugs. She and Billy begin to walk off, their arms round each other*)
Janice: So?

Billy: What was he?
Janice: He was a Communist.

Quite apart from the artificiality of Billy's question, Janice's answer is presumably intended to send the audience out of the theatre with the idea that being a Communist is enough, or is like being a Man with a capital M, or being a saint. The implication is that, despite all the faults of their system, Communists are the only people who really care about working people. This gives the play a lamentably weak conclusion; if it is a point of view that Brenton seriously wants to propound, he needs to provide much more argument in support of it.

Weapons of Happiness is further diluted and made less convincing by the introduction of some unlikely and almost incredible sex. Janice, a young half-educated revolutionary, seduces the veteran Frank on the floor of the London Planetarium. This provided David Hare, the director, with an excuse to exploit the National Theatre's elaborate lighting system, but it seems implausible and irrelevant to the play's political theme. The wife of the factory owner is presented as a tiresome bitch, taunting her husband in public about his mistress and Frank for being a foreigner, and suddenly telling the police inspector and the trade union official that her husband does not like her to touch her own breasts.

The play is of course partly fantasy, and unites several of Brenton's favourite themes. As in *The Churchill Play*, the subservient police middle-ranks upholding the establishment are irritated by genteel upper-class posing. The factory owner wants to be 'nice' and to be liked by 'his' workers, while at the same time selling the factory behind their backs. Brenton's interest in the police finds a natural outlet. Trivial incidents in Britain, like police questioning about hooliganism in the street, trigger off Frank's memories of brutal police interrogations in Czechoslovakia. In a series of flash-backs, British policemen and bosses become Communist torturers, with a suggestion that the two really have got something in common. After Hitler, Lenin and Churchill in earlier plays, Stalin is gently satirized in this one. He appears in a blaze of light, accompanied by a huge banner-portrait and a hidden Russian choir, to greet Frank and Clementis in Red Square, only to invite them to toast the Soviet ice-hockey team! Later, in prison, Frank and Clementis discuss whether Stalin knows how they are being treated.

Just as Frank is reluctant to hear Stalin criticized, when he gets to Britain he is equally reluctant to take any part in political action. He feels his mind is partly destroyed, his humanity diminished, and he just wants to rest, without worries or responsibilities.

Frank: Now, I do not even want revenge on all that I once believed in. I wish only to lie in the sludge of the debris, of what was once a fine building. Miles deep, stirring only for a little warmth.

Characterization like this is graphic and convincing. The factory owner and the hack trade union official are also very credible; the revolutionary workers are less so and are barely distinguishable, one from another. But Brenton sometimes expresses the revolutionary and anti-revolutionary points of view extremely succinctly, as in this dialogue between Hicks (the trade union official), Stanley (the factory foreman) and some of the workers.

Hicks: Now you want to unionize yourselves. And before we all go up in the air 'bout strikes that means discipline. That means all agreements you have evolved over the years with the Makepeace family, with the management, not only rates of pay but conditions, over-time practice, safety, sickness. . . . All that will have to be put down. On paper.
Billy: We don't want any of that shit. . . .
Hicks: Everything. Think about it. Because you may not like it. . . . See, the best you can hope for in this world is to nudge. Give it a bit of a nudge. Industrial relations, that's a mighty animal. Bit of a dinosaur. Or, to look at it another way, bit of a giant oil tanker. . . .
Billy: What the fuck is he talking about?
Stanley: Billy Mason.
Billy: I can't help it. He hurts my brain.
Stanley: Why won't you listen, why won't you learn? Mr

Hicks is a respected man. Spent many years keeping the
wolf from the door of working men and women.
Hicks: 'Nough said, Ted.
Stanley: And you do not know it, but Mr Hicks may one day
be your union-sponsored M.P.
Billy: Wow. Let's all have a good wank.
Stanley: Right. That's it. That's the remark I been waiting
for. All go home now. Strike? You're wet behind the ears, or
gaga. Yes, I'm talking about you, Alfred Mallings.
Alf: Nice.
Stanley: Silly old man. Go and warm your hand up 'front a
your telly set, 'fore you catch your death. Weed your window
box. And the rest a you. Go on. Get home to your Mums
and Dads.
(*A pause. No one moves*)
Alf: If I kick the telly set in and pour Harpic over the win-
dow box, will things get any better? On the whole I'd say
. . . Yes.

It would be wrong to give the impression that *Weapons of
Happiness* is purely verbal. The love-scene in the Planetarium
is immediately followed by a spectacular visual set-piece when
the workers, staging a sit-in at the factory, shower the stage
with potatoes and bags of crisps, which burst all over the floor,
making a rousing ending to the first act. Towards the end of the
play there is an equally spectacular effect when the workers,
escaping from the factory via the drainage pipes, suddenly
emerge into brightly lit countryside. But this only seems incidental, and does not really succeed in putting over the political
message intended.

Brenton slightly demurs from the 'political' label attached
to his plays, not denying that they are political and socialist,
but claiming that all plays are political. 'When they are right-
wing, like William Douglas-Home's or Noël Coward's, nobody
bothers to call them political'. Brenton's socialism could loosely
be called 'Trotskyite'; he describes *Weapons of Happiness* as
'anti-Stalinist and pro-Communist'. A lot of the factual background about Stalinism in Czechoslovakia came from an
official document published by the short-lived Dubček regime;

Brenton is full of admiration for the way it exposed its pre-decessor's guilt. 'No British Government has ever published a complete exposé of what happened at Suez, or is ever likely to do so'.

Like the other Left-wing writers of his generation, Brenton has little time for the gradual social reforms achieved by Labour Governments. 'We're getting an illusion of progress, a sort of sleight of hand, but the oppression remains. The ratio of rich to poor is the same as it was twenty years ago. But we may suddenly move towards socialism unexpectedly'. He does not claim to know how this will happen, but he thinks the only good advice comes from 'the nightmare of European history, the old battleground, the Communist tradition. Some people look to China as an example, as it seems very pure from a distance, but we are Europeans and must learn from Europe'.

In *Weapons of Happiness*, Brenton's intention is to show good advice being given to the inexperienced British workers by Frank, the veteran Czechoslovak Communist. 'He tells them not to waste themselves, but to pursue their basic interests. He tells them to forget about trying to own or run their factory, but to go away and start a new life somewhere else. One of them will learn to read, another how to look after an old man. It's more revolutionary to disappear and start again than to stand around being heroic and waiting to be arrested. There is a huge play still to be written about what happens to these young people when they start again in Manchester, or wherever, but I don't think I could write it yet'.

Discussing the controversial love-scene, Brenton says there is a lot of class snobbery in the criticism of it—'people don't think a working-class girl has complicated sexual needs. But I want to show that she has, just as Frank is attracted to her by her passion, which reminds him of his own youth'.

The title, *Weapons of Happiness*, is meant to indicate what all the characters, in their various ways, are seeking. 'Similarly, every character in *Magnificence* has his own idea of what would be truly magnificent.'

Most of Brenton's plays refer, explicitly or implicitly, to well-known personalities in the news or to topical items from the newspapers. 'It's important to make connections with what the audience already knows. I don't think of myself as writing plays to last, but to be performed at the time I write them. It sometimes seems quite bizarre to see one of my old plays on a bookshelf or to hear that it's being revived somewhere, or staged abroad. With every line I write, I'm thinking about how it will work in the theatre—what sort of actor could speak it, and how, and in what setting. So, of course, I'm concerned with design and lighting, and casting and rehearsals.

'I start a lot of plays which I never finish—I have a continuous convoy of possible plays, crashing against each other, and sometimes one will really take off, begin to gell. I do a lot of rewriting, and it takes about a year to be finally ready. When I had an Arts Council grant, I wrote a play a month, but they were short plays, which are much quicker and easier.

'I'm more of a story-teller than some present-day playwrights—people like Snoo Wilson, Heathcote Williams and the American, Sam Shepherd, do a kind of kaleidoscopic writing, a radical rearrangement of a play, often crammed with so much incident, so much story, that it ceases to be a story. I don't do that, but I don't try to be naturalistic either. A song in a play is artificial, but it can connect in a truly vivid way with people's lives, which is what the theatre must do. And my characters—my policemen for example—are often more realistic than is thought. The trouble is that the audience's expectations are pallid—they want to admire and respect the characters on the stage and if they are presented with ordinary people as they really are, they often think they are being presented with caricatures. But of course I do have a strong comic bent in my writing.

'The theatre could be something really fantastic, incredibly powerful. At present it's full of dead classics and meretricious rubbish. New plays by writers of my generation are much more interesting and enjoyable—much better—than the classics. The more good writing there is, the more it helps to change the theatre. We've got to change how the theatres are run, how the actors act. But the pressures to get a radical new sort of theatre can only come from the writers. The desire to do that is what our generation have in common. We don't exchange ideas for plays, and we certainly don't steal each other's ideas, but there is a curious way in which several of us may seize on the same theme or image at the same time. When I wrote a play about Wesley, I found that two or three other writers had had the same idea.'

Describing himself as a populist, Brenton says he has no scruples about wanting his plays staged in the largest possible theatres, before the largest possible audiences. That is why he wanted *Weapons of Happiness* produced at the National. 'I'd rather have my plays presented to 900 people who may hate what I'm saying than to fifty of the converted. In the '6os, there was a feeling that you could build an alternative society within our society, like a beneficent cancer, with its own institutions, schools, shops and theatres, and that all you had to do was to service it and it would grow and take over our culture. But all you get that way is an artistic ghetto; by the early '70s, I came to feel that there is only one society, one culture, and that the 'alternative' was becoming part of it. The Conservative Party and the Special Branch of the police absorbed the 'alternative culture', needed it and grew stronger on it. So I began to move towards revolutionary politics, and now I try to write about the struggle that is involved.'

Thirteen: Howard Barker

Born: London, England, 1946.

Parents: Father a factory worker and mother a housewife and part-time cashier. 'My parents were ambitious for me and encouraged me to read and pursue literary interests.'

Education: Battersea Grammar School and Sussex University (two degrees in history). 'I wrote poetry, short stories and novels while at school and college, but had nothing to do with the theatre at Sussex University—it seemed to be dominated by middle-class public-school boys.'

'I saw Edward Bond's *Saved* when I was 22 and thought I might do better; I was disappointed by its artificial imitation of working-class speech, but it gave me the idea that one could write naturally about one's own background, using authentic dialogue. After university, somebody suggested I should write a radio play, as that was the easiest medium in which to make a start. I also did a lot of odd jobs—labouring, van-driving, etc. Then I went to York to live with my girl-friend (now my wife) and settled down to writing. I've been a full-time professional writer since 1970, making my living mainly from radio plays and two or three film scripts.'

Married in 1971.

Writer in Residence, Open Space, London 1974–75.

Plays:

Cheek (London 1970). *No One Was Saved* (London 1970). *Face-ache* (London 1972). *Edward, The Final Days* (London 1972). *Private Parts* (Edinburgh 1972). *Alpha Alpha* (London 1972). *Rule Britannia* (London 1973). *My Sister and I* & *Skipper* (London 1973). *Bang* (London 1973). *Claw* (London 1975, New York 1976). *Stripwell* (London 1975). *Wax* (Edinburgh & London 1976). *Fair Slaughter* (London 1977). *That Good Between Us* (London 1977).

BARKER'S FIRST STAGE PLAYS all had their first productions

in London, in small theatre clubs. The first two were at the Royal Court's Theatre Upstairs, after which he was regularly attached to the Open Space. *Stripwell*, his first play to be presented outside a club attic or basement, was in the Royal Court's main auditorium. All his plays have a lot in common with each other and with the political-sexual fantasies of David Hare and Howard Brenton. Indeed they are as similar to Brenton's as are the two writers' names and reviewers and commentators are constantly confusing the two of them. A recurring Barker theme is the equal guilt of the criminal and the ruling classes, and the easy transition between them. Murder and rape figure constantly, nearly always treated in a light-hearted, almost surrealist way. There seems to be a strong influence of Joe Orton. Barker's establishment figures also relate to Trevor Griffiths's tired, disillusioned Labour politicians; they tend to be suspected, and to suspect themselves, of moral hypocrisy. Barker's plots are often more credible, despeit their fantasy content, than those of the other writers mentioned, and his dialogue is amusing and distinctive.

Cheek is a three-act play, played straight through without an interval and lasting just over an hour. Most of Barker's favourite themes and techniques are already apparent, at least in embryo. The 'cheek' of the title is displayed by Laurie and Bill, two unemployed young men, who compete with each other in outrageous behaviour designed to shock society. Their revolt is carried to such lengths that the play becomes a caricature of the so-called permissive society. Laurie's cheek is conscious and deliberate, as he explains when Bill complains that people younger than them are making more money in steady jobs.

Laurie: They're the failures, not us! They're the berks! They sit in their bloody offices, they stand at their fucking benches, working their lives away. That's not living, is it? Is that what you want? That's life to them, the poor sods, they don't know any different, but you and me, we've got the precious gift of insight, haven't we? We've got ideas, haven't we? We've got the cheek to go out there and make it out of berks like them, so we never have to lift a sodding finger, so we can screw till the bloody cows come home!

Laurie despises his father for being stupid, and for having worked long and hard in his humdrum life, and he thinks his father was jealous of him for being more intelligent.

Laurie: He got the Most Retarded Employee Award for ten years running at London Transport. That was before the immigrants of course. Even then he was runner-up.

But this hatred and contempt does not prevent Laurie sitting around waiting to inherit his father's money so that he'd live happily with his mother. While waiting, he tells her his father was not good enough for her, has fantasies of beating school-girls and seducing middle-aged women, and starts an affair with Shirley, a neighbour, persuading her he is in the property business. She is married, with a child, but pretends to be prepared to live with him, in the hope of getting a house. Of course she is not really willing to sacrifice her comfort and her respectability for him (a theme which recurs regularly in Barker's plays). When she discovers she has been cheated about the property, she turns on him in a fury, calling him dirt, hoping he gets killed in an accident, and adding that he is 'bloody hopeless' in bed.

When Bill succumbs to a steady job, Laurie feels betrayed again and rounds on him contemptuously.

Laurie: You never had it in you to be anything out of the ordinary. I could see that from the start. You haven't got the cheek to make it big. Never will have.

But Bill has his own form of cheek. He flirts with Laurie's mother while Laurie is upstairs attending to his dying father. In a grotesque black comedy finale, Laurie carries his father down to the living-room, interrupting his mother and Bill, puts him down on the floor and addresses him as a baby. At first the couple are amused but then Laurie props his father up and tells him to watch while they get on with it. They are shocked and angry, and leave together. Laurie puts his mother's knickers on his father's head and again pretends that he is a baby.

Laurie: You saw all that, did you? Out of the corner of your

eye? Of course, you wouldn't know what it meant. I mean,
you're just a baba. If you saw his hand up her skirt, you
wouldn't know what he was doing, would you? You wouldn't
think he had his fingers up her fanny, would you? It's funny,
but I came out of here. In the afternoon, it was. Out I came,
sliding onto the table—bump! Wheeee-bump! Funny that.
Funny fanny. Fannies are funny! Fun in the funny fanny! I
bet she had to squeeze through. She's got such little hips.
I expect those officers put their finger up her fanny. What a
history her fanny's got. Not that you care, eh? I can see you
don't care. I'm the only one who's actually lived in there,
actually been in all the way, head and shoulders. I expect
you wish you could. But you're too big. She messed us about,
didn't she, baba? I had it all planned, what we were going
to do. And then she did that to us. Poor baba. Now it's just
me and you, eh? Just baba and Dada, eh? Look at that sun.
It's sunny now. Shall I take you in the yard? You want to?
You like that, eh? I wish you were a bit more talkative, you
don't say much. Here, say something, any old thing, even
if it's only boo! You are difficult. You haven't died, have
you? Have you? You wouldn't admit it if you had, you poor
bugger. Come on, let's go. (*Laurie picks Dad up and carries
him out. His voice is heard outside the empty room from the yard*)
Is that all right? See the sunsa shining? And all the little
birdies? Say boo to the birdies, go on, say boo. Say boo! Say
boo!

Alpha Alpha is much more inventive, but contains many of
the same basic ingredients. Once again there are two Oedipal
young men determined to defy society, and an insanely doting
mother. This time the young men are twin brothers, Morrie
and Mickey Scrubbs, obviously if loosely modelled on two
notorious real-life gangsters, the Kray brothers. This time, the
father, instead of being made fun of as he dies, is already dead.
Two other principal characters are Lord Gadsby, a Conservative peer who is friendly with the brothers, and Bernadette,
an Irish nationalist agitator whom the brothers kidnap and
murder.
There are also five subsidiary characters, played by the same

actor, who are caricatures of typical contemporary types: Cyril, a detective who arrests the twins and has an affair with their mother, the fawning photographer and the dim-witted policeman they murder, a trendy 'underground' journalist who comes to interview them, and their schoolteacher, who is so busy campaigning as a Labour politician that he has no time to discuss the 'individual problems' of his pupils.

These characters appear in a series of sketches, in music-hall or revue form, making jokes about obscene language and about violent and outrageous behaviour.

The tone is set right at the beginning, when Mrs Scrubbs claims to be a normal mother taking a pride in her sons, while they open their jackets to reveal guns in shoulder-holsters.

The twins discuss having sex together; later they feel relaxed as a result of doing so, after beating up Bernadette.

When they quarrel, they use almost every imaginable obscenity.

> Morrie: You disgusting bugger . . . you filthy sod.
> Mickey: You piss-bucket! You shit-house turd!
> Morrie: You filthy, low-down stinking—
> Mickey: You bum-licker, you fat-arsed, shitting—
> Morrie: rotten, twisted, farting—
> Mickey: pissing, nauseating, fucking—
> Morrie and Mickey (*together*): Cunt!

The photographer comes to take publicity pictures of Mrs Kersh ('a humble mother in her home, the most persuasive symbol of self-sacrifice').

The twins shoot him, then laugh and throw their arms round each other.

> Mrs Scrubbs: You wicked things! You sinful, evil little maniacs!
> Mickey: You can overdo publicity.
> Morrie: What goes on in our house is nobody's business, Mum.
> Mrs Scrubbs: He said he wished I was his mum . . .
> Mickey: What a pleasant thing to say.

(*They go simultaneously to their armchairs, and putting their hands behind their heads, cross their legs and sit still and relaxed*)

Mrs Scrubbs: They're only kids. It's just a game to them. They don't mean anything, really, it's just a prank. They're immature, considering they're thirty-three . . .

In a flash-back to the day when their father was killed, the brothers put on shorts, as boys of twelve. Just as their mother is telling them the news, a policeman arrives to question them about violence on the school playground. One of them stabs the policeman, who sinks to his knees.

P.C.: You silly bugger . . . you stupid little sod . . .
Mrs Scrubbs: Where did you get that knife?
PC: Somebody get an ambulance . . .
Mrs Scrubbs: Mickey! Where did you get that knife?
Mickey: Found it.
Mrs Scrubbs: Liar!
PC: Will someone get an ambulance please . . .
Mrs S: You tell me where you got that knife!
Mickey: None of your business!
Mrs Scrubbs: Oh, isn't it? Who have you two been mixing with? If I get down that school I'll make a stink!
PC: Oh dear, oh dear, oh dear, oh dear . . .
Mrs Scrubbs: Teachers let you do exactly what you like these days, the kids are running about half wild!
PC (*on the floor*): My lung's punctured, I'm dying, Christ, what a waste! I bequeath your little bastards . . . to the CID . . .
(*He dies, folding his hands across his chest*)
Mrs Scrubbs: You silly, stupid little boys! Look what you've done! And me without a husband. Oh, you're going to be a trial to me . . . (*She looks at them longingly with an expression of resignation and love*)

Like all black comedy, this scene exaggerates a horrific event to the point of making it ludicrous, while still reminding us of its reality. Just as the mother speaks out loud the secret thought that neither she nor her sons are really to blame, so

the schoolteacher openly admits that he is using politics as a
road to social advancement. Barker's cynicism about Labour
politicians is much more bitter than that shown by Trevor
Griffiths.

> Teacher: Bugger the twins. I hate this place. I hate this area.
> I hate the kids. I hate the school. If I get into parliament, and
> I will, because when you want something as badly as I do,
> you get there in the end, you won't see me for dust. It's
> Hampstead for me, then . . . Hampstead, Blackheath, Green-
> wich, Chelsea, Knightsbridge, Richmond, Harrow, Sheen,
> oh fucking hell!

Similarly Gadsby has a frank outburst in which he tells the
audience that he hates all women and is 'a slave to rough trade'.
He bends down on all fours, and the twins ride him. Having
used them, he gets them to shoot Bernadette, who dies uttering
praise of Ché, Ireland, Chairman Mao, the Queen and Hitler.
Mrs Scrubbs announces that she is leaving to live with Cyril
and the twins react like spoilt children.

> Mickey: A woman who goes whoring when she's got children
> isn't better than a bloody rat! A fucking, stinking sewer
> rat!
> Mrs Scrubbs: I never thought I'd see the day . . .
> Mickey: You've seen the day!
> Morrie: Mum . . . how could you be so deceitful? How
> could you be so horribly two-faced?
> Gadsby: Oh, God . . . Oh, God.
> Mrs Scrubbs: I need somebody too . . . I can't go on all by
> myself!
> Mickey: All by herself . . . all by herself . . . You fucking cow,
> what do you think we are! A pair of garden gnomes?
> Gadsby (*facing the audience*): I am experiencing the ultimate
> destructive act! I am a witness to the most outrageous
> crime! A *crime de la crime* committed by these heartless, soul-
> less, brutal, beautiful, exquisite savages! I am erect with
> horror, my veins are rigid with anticipation! God help
> me!

Gadsby tells the twins to shoot her, they do so, and he throws

himself down beside her, looking up with a smile and saying,
'Look . . . blood on my hands.'

Gadsby in his turn then announces that he is walking out on
the twins; they are incredulous, first offering him their bodies
and then threatening to report him to the Queen. But he walks
out, leaving them sitting beside their dead mother, smoking
cigarettes, in a tableau identical with that which opened the
play.

The moral of *Alpha Alpha* is that there is nothing to choose,
morally, between the supposedly respectable Gadsby and the
two gangsters, or rather that there is more excuse for them,
because of their deprived upbringing and because they perform
the acts that Gadsby is too squeamish to do himself. Mickey
puts the social division between them into words when Gadsby,
having used them, is trying to wash his hands.

> Gadsby: When I listen to you talking, the whole world seems
> polluted, acid, like the armpit of a dirty shirt.
> Mickey: I'm sorry for you. It must be terrible, having the
> likes of us squirming and clawing to get a bit of what they
> gave you on a plate.

Barker returns to this theme, even more explicitly, in *Claw*,
possibly his best play. It deals with exactly the kind of 'clawing'
Mickey described, and Noël Biledew, the equally deprived
principal character, gives himself 'Claw' as a nickname. Once
again, Barker uses the technique of short scenes or sketches, to
cover a period of over thirty years. He shows 'Claw's' development from illegitimate baby in 1945 to successful ponce for 'top'
people. Once again there is a large cast but provision is made
for several of the roles to be doubled. The settings are indicated
by slide projections, and there are appropriate popular songs
for each period.

Mrs Biledew is the usual careless, happy-go-lucky Barker
mother, whose son almost inevitably grows up to be a criminal.
He is named after the Noël Coward of *In Which We Serve*, as
Mrs Biledew explains to her husband when he returns from
prisoner-of-war camp. Mr Biledew passively accepts the baby
Noël, but never speaks to him. The boy soon shows the path
he will take, when he comes home from school with thirty

souvenir coronation mugs which he swapped for letting other
boys look at one of the girls behind the lavatories. Mrs Biledew
tells him to take them back, but then speedily acquiesces in
keeping them and tells her husband not to bother where they
came from.

Noël is expelled from school for being deceitful and for taking
and selling photos of girls in the showers. This stimulates
Mr Biledew to speak to him for the first time, confessing his
dislike for him but urging him to use his resentment against
society to help the working class. He joins the Young Communists and claims that his later criminal career is a deliberate
campaign to discredit and destroy the ruling class. He starts by
persuading Nora, a fellow Young Communist, that she would
be doing more effective political action, and be better off, if
she became a prostitute. This leads Noël to an encounter with
a typical Barker policeman, who gives him a pound, takes
Nora behind the hedge, then beats Noël up and takes back
the money. This is the decisive turning point in Noël's life.

Noël: He hit me! I was struck. I won't be struck! Never
again will I be struck, I vow that! (*He sobs with anger, clench-
ing his fists, then raises an arm to the sky.*) I'll tear their skin off
first, I'll rip their faces off their skulls, I'll be a great claw
ripping them, slitting their bellies like ripe fruits! Hear me,
formerly Trotsky of the YCL, declare it on this night, note it
in your calendars, I'll claw them first!

From then onwards Noël calls himself 'Claw' and insists on
everyone else doing so. He wears a leather jacket with a huge
red claw on it to Fortnum and Mason's tea-room, where his
mother is gorging herself on cream pastries paid for with his
money, while Mr Biledew's voice is heard on a tape recording
saying the money is the profits of crime. Like the criminal twins
in *Alpha Alpha*, Noël tells his mother that he is moving on into
higher spheres. He then offers the waitress a job as a prostitute,
asking her if she can simulate an orgasm and telling her to show
him her thighs there and then. Mr Biledew turns up, carrying
a portrait of Karl Marx, on a mission 'to destroy degeneracy'.
Noël tells him he has misunderstood Marx.

Noël: I have had acquaintance with his works. It seems to me the point of old weirdbeard's diagnosis was to hasten the corruption, not run after it with a dustpan and broom. Which confers on me the status of a hero, so sit down and shut your gob.

Mr Biledew crashes the portrait down on Noël's head, and gets seven years in gaol for assault, the magistrate saying the offence was worse for being committed in such a respectable place, 'in the furtherance of some misguided notion of class conflict'. Two hired assassins burst into the Biledew home to get Noël for trespassing on a Mafia gang's territory, and in the fracas Mrs Biledew gets shot in the hand. Noël refuses to allow an ambulance, but gets Nora to put on a rough bandage, using bleach as antiseptic. Then Noël sees a vision of Mr Biledew in prison, telling him to align himself with the prevailing flow of history, and the first act ends with him changing into a posh suit.

The second act introduces Clapcott, the Home Secretary, who is using Noël as a procurer of women, and Angie, his wife, who has affairs with rough leather boys and ultimately, of course, with Noël. Noël's visit to Clapcott's house precipitates disaster, but first provides the opportunity for some gentle satire at the expense, this time, of a Conservative politician.

Clapcott: After the war, looked for a place to conquer, some field where the competition wasn't fierce, and there was the Conservative Party, flat on its back. I got myself a reputation for reliability. Not brilliance, but reliability. They go for that. (*Pause*) And they bought me. I had smooth cheeks. And this way of looking at people in the eyes. Always. Right in the eyes. I suppose you noticed that? (*Pause*) And the handshake. Like a vice, Not too prolonged, but very firm. You can read a handshake. Mine says—reliability. They never liked Rab Butler in this party. His handshake was like a dying fish. Heath's was the same, but he forced himself.
Noël: I've never been in a politician's house before. Been in managing directors' houses, and lawyers' houses. They have a smell. Of endless squirming. (*Pause*) Mind you, my nose is very sensitive, because my eyes are so weak.

Nature's generous like that. My mother's house smelt of panic.

Clapcott: And what does this place smell of?

Noël: Contempt.

Clapcott: My wife's perfume lingering on the air.

Noël: No, it comes from you.

Angie goes off to the country with Noël on his motor-bike and is caught by a policeman having sex with him. The policeman overhears them jocularly discussing Clapcott's murder and notes that Noël is too shortsighted to be driving. He tries to arrest them, and in the struggle Noël knocks out the policeman. Angie confesses to Clapcott and asks him to use his inflence to get proceedings against Noël stopped.

Clapcott has a final interview with Noël. In a biblical parody which is also an indictment of political hypocrisy, he tells him he has committed the cardinal sin.

Clapcott: There is a certain thing known as discretion. In the Tory party, as in life, discretion is the difference between success and abject failure. If you have integrity, but no discretion, then you are nothing. If you have brilliance, but no discretion, then you are nothing. But if you have nothing else, but you have discretion . . . then you are like unto a God.

He arranges for Noël to be kidnapped by security forces and detained in a mental institution. Noël does not know where he is, and learns that nobody else knows or cares. He is guarded by two camp ex-convict male nurses, Lily and Lusby (shades of the politicians in Brenton's *Magnificence*) who pass the time exchanging scandals about famous stars, and naming many of them as prostitutes, homosexuals or drug addicts. Noël has a vision of Mr Biledew, in a geriatric ward, telling him to find a way of dying as a working-class hero. Noël then makes a long speech, in which he explains how he tried to be somebody, and how he came to know the ways of the ruling class. The speech gradually develops into a statement of the philosophy that the rulers are the real criminals and there there must be class solidarity against them.

Noël: . . . our little squabbles and our playground fights and
little murders in the entrances of flats are hardly crimes compared to that crime they are working on us, all of us driven
mad by their brutality and no coppers to protect us against
their claws! Their great claw, slashing us, splitting our people
up, their great claw ripping our faces and tearing up our
streets, their jaguars feeding on our lazy herds. And we have
nothing except each other. Our common nothingness. And
our caring for each other. And our refusal to do each other
down. Like a class of schoolboys who won't tell who is the
thief. (*Pause*) Defend me. Don't murder me.

But Lily and Lusby produce a bath, Noël slowly undresses,
and they drown him in it. The play ends with Clapcott assuring
the House of Commons that an enquiry shows the death was
accidental, 'though there may appear to be a high accidental
death rate at Spencer Park'. The chilling mental institution
where public enemies are secretly liquidated suggests the Soviet
Union, though in fact, like the detention camp in Brenton's
Churchill Play and the lunatic asylum in Bond's libretto for the
Henze opera *We Come To the River*, it is intended as an indictment of our own society.

Like most Barker plays, *Stripwell* is again about a high public
figure in contact with low, near-criminal elements. This time,
he is a judge, with a mistress who is an intellectual strip-tease
dancer, a wife who is complaisant and invites the mistress to
dinner, and a son who is importing heroin in the vagina of an
elephant. The play starts with Stripwell sentencing a criminal
who acted out of a sense of social injustice and being threatened
with death as a reprisal. He decides to give up the law and
start a new life with his mistress, only to discover that she prefers his criminal son. In the end he reports his son's drug
trafficking to the police, but is about to cancel his denunciation
when he is shot by the criminal he sentenced at the beginning
of the play.

Graham Stripwell is bored with his work and yearns for
excitement. When he is about to pass sentence, right at the
beginning of the play, he adjourns the court because 'I have
some shopping to do'. When he sees his son's motor-bike, he
9

puts his yearnings into a soliloquy, expressing the regrets of many a respectable middle-aged man.

> Stripwell: Ah . . . if only I were twenty . . . Well, of course I was twenty . . . And I never did. Live rough with the Amerindians. Work my passage to Goa. Catch youthful gonorrhoea in Kowloon. I have been a carte blanche, smoother than blancmange . . . In a sense, that's been my trouble all along. Not having the confidence to be utterly vulgar. I have been a perfect miniature of modern decorum, and I shall have come and gone with about as much impact as a daddy-longlegs on the lawn.

He also has a line in brutal frankness, telling Jarrow, his father-in-law and a retired Labour politician, that he is senile, and his son that he is 'asphyxiatingly conceited'. When Jarrow retaliates with some home truths, Stripwell simply seizes his wheelchair and pushes it violently out into the garden.

Dodie, his wife, and Tim, his son, take his action with the unnatural coolness which Barker's characters inherit from Orton, while Stripwell only repents in the last minute.

> Dodie (*coolly*): It's getting chilly. You shouldn't have done that.
> Tim (*starting to move*): I'll get him in.
> (*Tim cannot pass Stripwell, who is standing in front of the door*)
> Stripwell: That awful man. (*Pause. He is shaking*) That little blob of rotted ideals and disgusting, shameful memories . . . (*Pause*) He offends me. (*Pause*) Even through my apathy and cynicism . . . he twists my balls. (*He appears to be about to go on, but falters. He goes to his chair and sits. Tim and Dodie look at him. Pause*) Get him in before he dies.

Barker's dislike of the ageing Labour politician who has failed to implement his ideals is as intense as ever, though not fully explained. Babs, Stripwell's mistress, does explain her reasons for pessimistic fatalism.

> Babs: I don't love life. I can take it or leave it. If I got cancer tomorrow and they said, 'Babs, in six months you'll be rose tree fertilizer,' I'd say right on, 'Life's a bugger.' I've got no

illusions, so don't come chanting, 'Where have all the flowers gone' in my earhole. I'm here because I'm here ad infinitum one more time and give us all a big hand! If you expect to get your teeth kicked down your throat you won't be staggered when it happens, will you, just happy that it never happened earlier.

She also explains why she does not want to settle down, when Stripwell presses her to say she loves him.

Babs: You have to keep reducing this to language! When you say 'love' you have this great baggage of associations tied to it. When I say 'love' it's clean and hard and shiny—clunk! (*She clicks her fingers*) Like a brand-new decimal coin.
Stripwell: And with about the same purchasing power, I see . . .
Babs: Oh dear, he's getting bitter, all because we can't have our toothbrushes hanging up together by the sink, and our knickers tangled in the airing cupboard . . .
    Ever since I first allowed an alien tongue into my mouth I've been pestered by people wanting to ravage my privacy. I honestly don't think I care for intimacy. I can take it or leave it. I'm very *Übermensch* in that respect. Everybody seems to be rushing around sniffing one another's bums. Like a pack of strays on Tooting Common. Let me get into your knickers, let me get into your mind.

The second act of *Stripwell* introduces Tim, who explains to the audience that his drug traffic is a great capitalist business enterprise, thus making explicit Barker's view of the link between criminality and supposedly respectable activities, and his contempt for capitalist society.

Tim: Anybody who's wondering what happened to the business talent of the British can stop looking. I'm here. When we invented capitalism it was looked down on as a dirty trick. But it made us very rich. When we kicked in the doors of China and made 'em buy our products it was sneered on as a dirty trick. But we got even richer. When we sold Indian cotton to the Indians people said it wasn't right.

But we were much too rich to worry. That talent is not burned out yet. As with all great enterprises we go hand in hand with crime. Today's criminal is tomorrow's pioneer. I sense a knighthood in the offing, when the import of narcotics is legitimized. In the meantime, let me inform you that an elephant's vagina is six feet long. Its womb can carry several hundredweight. A pair of female elephants can consequently carry in these cavities one ton of heroin, in two-pound plastic packets, very neat. Now ask me why I'm not a trainee manager for ICI.

Tim has come home just in time to meet and fall for Babs, who has arrived for dinner to meet Dodie. On seeing him, Babs freezes and mentally writes the next chapter of her auto-biographical erotic novel, speaking it out loud to the audience.

Babs: And I came in, and he was there, looking at me with those eyes that seemed to consume me, melting my defences like twin laser beams, as I was to write later. Chapter 14.

The dinner party duly takes place, with much acid comment and much misunderstanding between Dodie and Babs. Finally Dodie is provoked into telling Stripwell he is 'a highly subtle form of fascist pig', and 'the kind of person who ends up running concentration camps'. She accuses him of giving up law out of panic because a criminal has threatened him with revenge. Babs then pushes him into stating his deeper reasons.

Babs: Don't let her piss all over you. Tell her!

(*Stripwell hesitates. Tim, with a sarcastic inspiration, jumps up and pours a glass of water, as if for a public speaker. He holds it a little towards Stripwell, keeping a rigid posture. Stripwell ignores him. Long pause*)
Stripwell: I've spent my whole life at a distance. I've always been above it all. And now I think there is an awful immorality in being so detached. Only by being that detached have I been able to do this ghastly job of shifting people from one custody into another, because I always told myself it was no more grotesque than any other job, and only by

being that detached have I been able to live here, because
although it seemed grotesque it didn't seem any more so than
living with other people in another place. I always thought
I had no illusions, but I never had any hope either, and I
haven't any now, only I'm sick of sarcasm, and cynicism and
belittling. I'm sick of everything that made it possible for me
to stick here for so long. And I'm going to be moral. as far as
it is in me to be moral. (*He falters*) Even if it's hopeless to be
moral . . . and it sounds stupid to you. (*Pause*) And no one
else is . . . I want to be . . . to try . . .

Stripwell's statement identifies him to some extent with the
'detached' heroes of plays like Simon Gray's *Otherwise Engaged*
and Christopher Hampton's *The Philanthropist*. His determination to come out of detachment and to 'live' is destined to be
shortlived. When he tries to elope with Babs, she informs him
that she has chosen someone else, someone she doesn't respect,
whom she knows is a shit and a dope-smuggler, but who offers
her more life-enhancing possibilities. Stripwell gets on to a
moral high-horse about all this, provoking Babs into telling
him that the man she is going off with is Tim, his son. He goes
home to Dodie.

In a brief jungle scene, we see an exhausted Babs and Tim
quarrelling. She admits that 'experience is a false concept',
throws her biographical notes away, and shrieks that she is
going to die. Tim slaps her, and she goes into her old go-go
dance routine. Back at home, Stripwell rings the police to
denounce Tim, in what he thinks is a great moral gesture, but
then is told by Dodie that he is only doing it because Tim went
off with his mistress. As he is about to phone the police again,
the criminal from the beginning of the play appears in the
window. Stripwell tries to persuade him that society would be
impossible if individuals pursued their own vengeance and
justice. The criminal leaves, Stripwell takes a drink in relief,
and is just raising it to his lips when the criminal returns,
shouts a defiant 'No', and shoots him.

This surprise ending, similar to the failed murder which
suddenly succeeds at the end of Brenton's *Magnificence*, is a
magnificent theatrical coup. It is also intended to express

9*

Barker's own final 'no' to society, its conventions and com- promises. But it happens too suddenly. The audience finds itself stunned by surprise, and then applauding the cast, without having time to consider the message. Perhaps this is just as well, as few of them would be sympathetic to it.

Barker sees our society as a criminal conspiracy, dominated by a rampant materialist individualism rather than any social ideal, such as he thinks may exist in a country like Cuba. 'The working-class criminals in my plays are victims of a phoney individualism, seduced into aping the ideals and goals of the ruling class and squandering their real talents in the process. I'm more concerned about the corrupting effects of the estab- lishment ethos than its historic failure. The working class is the only potentially progressive force in society, progressive in the sense that it is able to recognize its alienation from the authoritarian corporate state. But it first has to liberate itself from its own reactionary organizations—the Labour Party and the TUC—which have sapped its energy. Until then, it is trapped.

'One can't write stage plays specifically *for* the working class simply because they don't go to the theatre. One writes what one has to write, and my plays tend to be *about* the working class. The theatre is a middle-class institution, and likely to stay that way, though I don't think there is a necessary dynamic there. As the state becomes more authoritarian, the free theatre becomes more vital, but I remain sceptical that it will ever attract a convincing working-class audience.

'I think I'm a popular writer, in the sense that my plays are easily understood, not obscure at all. They're not naturalis- tic because I think naturalism has run its course, become ex- hausted and corrupted. Seeking meticulous reproduction of reality is a blind alley. In any case, as I like my plays to cover a wide range of social types, to describe a whole society, naturalism isn't an appropriate tool. This is a generation thing too. Most writers of my generation have rejected it. I think we have an instinctive agreement on that.'

Although television brings plays more directly to a working- class audience, Barker prefers live theatre. 'It's more satisfying because you can see your plays develop, and the actual physical confrontation of a live audience and the stage is dynamic, not passive. People shout and laugh in a public manner; it's a socially abrasive occasion.' Like most of the new generation of dramatists, he takes an active part in casting and rehearsals, and feels great loyalty to his regular directors, William Gaskill and Chris Parr. He is less concerned about *where* his plays are staged than about *how* they are staged, but nevertheless feels the need for a wider audience. 'If the National Theatre succeeds in attracting a wider, larger public, then that's the place you'd want to go.'

Barker cannot explain why his plays contain so much sexual ambiguity, so many references to homosexuality, nor why his young men are so Oedipal. 'It just happens that way. But male and female roles are also dictated by bourgeois individualism, even to the point of comic distortion. Women's sexual and economic exploitation are intimately related. The mother figures in my plays are working-class archetypes. They prefer their sons to their husbands because the sons offer a form of social mobility, and everything is sacrificed to that end, not least marriage itself. I've tried to do a comic catalogue of male sexual mythology in *Wax*. These myths are actually very dangerous, but they are fundamentally comic. Male sexual egocentricity is a comic manifestation. People have found this rather difficult to take, and the play aroused a lot of hostility. But the victimization of the woman isn't for a moment disguised.'

Many of Barker's plays contain fantasy parodies of well-known living people. In addition to those in *Alpha Alpha*, he admits basing the Home Secretary in *Claw* on a living politician (though this was not apparent). *Skipper* was about Sir Francis Chichester and *Edward, The Final Days* about the fall of Tory Prime Minister Edward Heath. *That Good Between Us*, the first new play in the Royal Shakespeare Company's new studio theatre in London, 'concerns a Home Secretary who might be Mrs Shirley Williams (who was not Home Secretary at the time the play was written) but it's a sympathetic study rather than a caricature. The play is set in the near future with a Labour Government taking repressive measures against a restless working class, initiating an era of spying and informing.

The Home Secretary sees the contradiction between her principles and the economic necessities of the corporate state. I'm gradually moving away from satire and caricature—I think I've done as much as I can with it.'

Fourteen: Stephen Poliakoff

Born: London, England, December 1952.

Father, came from a Russian Jewish family which fled the Soviet Union in 1924, trained as a physicist and went into business. Mother, English, an occasional actress in the 1930s. Maternal grandmother (Firenza Montagu) wrote two plays which were produced in the West-End. 'Despite my Russian-Jewish background, I don't speak Hebrew or Russian, and I've never got very involved in Jewish causes.'

Education: Westminster School ('which was good when I was there—they gave me a lot of freedom and never told me to work instead of writing plays. I wanted to be an actor when I first went there, and was very hurt at being left out of a school play. That started me writing instead, and I've been writing seriously ever since. I had written some plays before, one at my prep school, but they were very imitative —I've only seen pantomimes and Agatha Christies at that time. Once I got to Westminster I saw a lot more theatre, and eventually I started a school magazine giving critical views on the arts in London'.)

Left Westminster early and spent a year writing and gaining experience.

King's College, Cambridge: 'We were treated less like adults than I had been at Westminster. My college was one of the better ones, and I was lucky in my tutor and my supervisor; at most other colleges I'd have been chucked out after my second term. But the idea of becoming a playwright was not taken seriously by the authorities. I was reading history and we were supposed to learn and regurgitate other people's ideas. I really hated what Cambridge was—the lifelessness and the lack of imaginative spark. University theatre was terrible—the most modern play while I was there was Bolt's *A Man For All Seasons*. They were always thinking of how to make money.

Disliking it all so much had a good effect on me; it made me write a great deal, including the first versions of *Heroes* and *Clever Soldiers*, and stories which I'm still using as ideas for plays. I formed a group called 'Feast' to encourage playwriting and public playreadings. I left Cambridge at the end of my second year and I've never regretted it for a single moment'.

Plays:

Granny (Westminster School and amateur performances in London, 1969)

Bambi Ram (written between school and Cambridge, London 1970)

Day With My Sister (Edinburgh 1971—Poliakoff's first professional production)

Lay-By (with others, Edinburgh and London 1971; *see* Brenton)

Pretty Boy (London Sunday night try-out, 1972)

Sad Beat-Up (London 1974)

Carnation Gang (London 1974)

Clever Soldiers (London 1974)

Heroes (London 1975)

Hitting Town (London 1975)

City Sugar (London 1975 and, in 1976—Poliakoff's first non-club, West-End production)

Strawberry Fields (London 1977)

1976: *Evening Standard* Award.

1976-77: Writer in Residence, National Theatre.

STEPHEN POLIAKOFF is the youngest playwright in this book and the youngest for many years to achieve so much success. I confess to a certain almost proprietorial interest in him as I 'discovered' him when he was still at school and was the first critic to review his work. In *The Times* I noted that *Granny* was 'more dramatic, with greater command of dialogue and psychological insight than many plays by older authors' and in *The Stage* I looked forward to his later work. These reviews led Christopher Hampton, then at the Royal Court, to see the play and eventually resulted in Poliakoff's early involvement at the Royal Court.

Granny was the second play Poliakoff wrote at Westminster (the first was in collaboration with a friend), but the first to be given public performances, organized by the 16-year-old author, in two small halls in central London. It seemed to show the influence of Pinter and Orton; Poliakoff himself describes it as 'a heterosexual equivalent of Hampton's *When Did You Last See My Mother?*'. It at once demonstrated his strong dramatic sense and command of vivid and often humorous dialogue. At that time he was naturally interested in the bizarre and often aggressive behaviour of teenagers. The plot concerns two teenage couples who are supposed to be giving the last performance of a satirical revue in a Salvation Army hall. Their leader persuades them to stay at home instead, keeping the audience in the hall waiting indefinitely. He also tricks a pathetic German housekeeper into thinking that her boy-friend has arrived to visit her, and a man who has been Granny's devoted companion for thirty years into thinking that she has died. This study of sadism and mental sickness provides a foretaste of Poliakoff's next plays; so does the comparatively weak development of the plot, and the failure to provide a strong conclusion.

Poliakoff was one of the seven collaborators in *Lay-By*. 'I was only 18 and I got a bit lost in the discussions; I didn't know what all the sexual terms meant! Howard Brenton and David Hare were very much against any sort of naturalism; and I was inclined to be naturalistic. I was determined to keep my end up and I was quite obnoxious, piping up all the time. There was very little of me in the final play.'

The first play of his own to be professionally staged in London was *Pretty Boy*, completed in his first term at Cambridge, and given a Sunday night try-out at the Royal Court. A mood reminiscent of Pinter's *The Caretaker* is established straightaway with the arrival of William and Benny in a deserted but posh-looking apartment. William is old and untidy, Benny is around 20. They are re-occupying the home where Benny was brought up, and where William evidently helped to bring him up. Benny is aggressive and ruthless, William is epileptic and has strange phobias. They are soon joined by a well-meaning spinster who looks after William, an old school friend of Benny's who is gay and revolutionary, an ex-Borstal kid whom he has picked up, and Benny's girl friend. They set out to shake and shock the inhabitants of the rich district around them, smashing windows, removing parking meters and plotting to wreck a literary party, only to find it has been cancelled because of the death of the hostess. All their activities turn out to be equally futile and unsatisfying, but there is constant suspense about their plans and their moods, generating considerable theatrical excitement. Benny is extremely volatile, rounding on his companions in turn. He bullies and then dismisses the weak spinster, neglects and ill-treats the epileptic, teases his devoted schoolfriend and finally chucks him out of the house, and even threatens and assaults his girl with a razor-blade, only to regret it immediately. The play ends inconclusively, with everyone gone except a very disturbed Benny, being nursed and encouraged to think of a new life by his girl.

The Carnation Gang, which had a short run at the small Bush Theatre club and got very good notices, again combines suspense with teenage violence and excitement, and again leaves its dramatic situations unresolved. But the characterizations are stronger than in *Pretty Boy* and the air of menace is better sustained. Alec and Daniel are twin brothers, in their mid-twenties (modelled on the Kray Brothers, inspired by Howard Barker's *Alpha Alpha*?) who share a fairly smart flat, making their living by selling dope to a select circle of clients. The opening dialogue between them, in which they recall their schooldays, establishes that Alec is the cold, calculating one, who used to listen outside the door while Daniel was beaten by the headmaster. Alec was never caught. When their flat is invaded by three teenage hoodlums, seeking dope, it is Daniel who gives in, and eventually flirts with Sharon, their leader. Alec remains apparently detached, getting his kicks out of eavesdropping and spying on them, and out of taunting the two teenage boys to see how far they will go. Alec and Daniel know how to cope with life, and in particular with their drug trade, while the teenagers can only turn to abuse and violence when they are thwarted, a contrast caused by class and educational differences. This contrast is made explicit towards the end of the play. Alec, getting tired of threats and the invasion of his privacy, refuses to sell the teenagers any more drugs. One of them, Steve, turns on him.

Steve: Then we'll just have to try other methods won't we?
Alec (*smiles*): Are you threatening me boy?
Steve: You could say that. (*Pause*). I am. Yeh (*Smiles*) I'm threatening you.
Alec: Because I suggest you don't go through with it. (*Pause*) Because we're probably a little better at it than you are.
Steve: We'll see about that.
Alec: Yes.
Steve: You think that you can get away with anything, do anything, don't you?
Alec: Do we ? (*Steve moves forward*)
Steve: I'm warning you.
Alec (*slight, provocative smile*): Are you?
Steve: You're really asking for it, aren't you?
Alec: Yes. I am.
Steve: Right. (*Steve moving around the room*)
Alec: Going to turn violent now are we? (*Smiles*) That was bound to happen, wasn't it? From the first moment I saw you. Inevitable!
Steve: Yeh. (*He picks up record, takes it out of cover, slashes it with a knife, a quick fllick*)
Alec: (*watching quietly*): Yes. That's all you can do with it. Your only answer, to let your whole violence flood straight out.

Alec continues taunting and challenging Steve, egging him on to attack him. All Steve does is damage the furniture and make a mess of the room. Calling Alec 'fucking crazy', he leaves. Daniel emerges from an inner room, and gently accuses Alec of provoking Steve. They are arguing when Sharon comes in and appeals to Daniel to give her the drugs Alec has refused. The brothers quickly resume their alliance, Sharon messes up the food on the table, drops her hypodermic needle in, and leaves, calling them 'two fucking stupid creeps'. They start to clear up the mess, and discuss what sort of music to play, as the lights fade and the play ends.

The drug-taking scenes in *The Carnation Gang* are so realistic
and compelling that many people took the play as a plea for
greater tolerance or as an attack on the drug culture. But
rather it shows how intelligent, well-educated, rich people can
easily find safe, if illegal, outlets for their instincts and aggres-
sions, while the poorer and less educated fail to do so. The
moral is similar to that constantly being pressed by Hare,
Brenton and Barker. Like their plays, *The Carnation Gang*
succeeds mainly as entertaining and gripping theatre, rather
than as any sort of tract. It comes to no real conclusion.

Class and educational inequalities and their effects on
people's ability to cope with their lives, are recurring themes
in Poliakoff's plays. So is the threat to comfortable existence
posed by outside people or events. In *Clever Soldiers*, Poliakoff
went back in time to a period outside his personal experience.
the First World War. Again a safe, peaceful way of life is
threatened, this time at Oxford University. The conflict is
between officers and gentlemen on the one hand, and soldiers
and a working-class don on the other. Produced at the small but
influential Hampstead Theatre Club, and reviewed by most of
the critics, *Clever Soldiers* divided opinions. It impressed a number of important critics and theatre people, some of whom
found the trench scenes as convincing as those in *Journey's End*.
But others complained that Poliakoff did not succeed in
capturing the feeling of the First World War. Once again the
play was theatrical and gripping; once again too, the message
was less clear.

Clever Soldiers starts with a brief prologue in a public-school
changing room, introducing Teddy and Arnold, at the end of
their last term, and a certain amount of conventional public-
school badinage about fagging and sex. The play proper opens
in Oxford, where Teddy is sharing a room with Harold, a very
affected gay aesthete. A persuasive but fairly stereotyped
Oxford scene is depicted:—Harold is a practical joker, a witty
speaker at the Union, and a narcissist. Teddy is very irritated
by him, and forms an intimate though slightly ambiguous
relationship with David, his young tutor. David comes from a
working-class background and has chips on his shoulder about
the Oxford establishment. Their introductory conversation sets

the slightly unusual nature of their relationship; the dialogue
is not exactly realistic—tutors at Oxford don't generally call
their students 'boy' or treat them so intimately on first meeting,
but it is intriguing in its artificiality.

David: What's your Christian name?
Teddy: Teddy . . . sir.
David: And I'm David.
Teddy: Yes . . . sir.
David: You needn't call me sir.
Teddy: All right.
David: Do you think you're going to like it here?
Teddy: Yes.
David: How can you tell? Have you got a pleasant room?
Teddy: Yes.
David: With a good view I hope.
Teddy: It's very beautiful.
David: It's a beautiful day.
Teddy: (Quiet) It's very wonderful here.
David: So you're not disappointed.
Teddy: No. (Pause) Are you?
David: What do you mean by that?
Teddy: I don't know.
David: Why are you looking at me like that?
Teddy: Why are you staring at me?
David: There's no need to become impudent, boy—that's
one thing I won't tolerate.
Teddy: I'm sorry—Sir.
David: I told you, you're not to call me . . .
Teddy: I know, I'm sorry. (Pause, staring at him). If you don't
mind me saying so.
David: Go on.
Teddy: You're not what I expected.
David: Aren't I? What did you expect?
Teddy: I don't know . . . now.
David: You're not what I expected either, not really. (He
stared at him) So we're both surprised apparently. . . .

Later David tells Teddy about his lowly Welsh background,
and how he read twenty books a week when he first came to

Oxford, then burnt them all in a bonfire in his room. He also tells him of his belief that it's a special time, that there are 'murmurings in the air', and that he has 'a magnificent hatred' for the place. He speaks of 'a complacency that is totally savage' and of the coming cataclysm which will change everything. Eventually they have what is almost a love scene, with David tending a cut on Teddy's arm, but there is a tactful blackout before we discover whether their love is consummated or not.

Meanwhile Teddy also has an affair with Arnold's sister, who is a precursor of women's lib, likes the idea of free love and of being taken for a tart. Arnold hates the Oxford 'bloods' who are constantly out on drunken sprees, and frequently gets his room raided because of his attitude. When war is declared, both Arnold and Teddy enlist, and David, who is medically unfit for service, arms Teddy with a Dostoievsky novel for the occasion. The first act ends enigmatically with a parting scene between Teddy and Harold, who have established a kind of love-hate relationship.

Harold: You've hardly spoken to me for weeks. Have you? Are you happy?
Teddy: Just a little, yes.
Harold: And this rain is so savagely melancholic, it makes one even happier, doesn't it?
Teddy (*smiles*): Yes—you're right.
Harold: Do you like me, do you?
Teddy: Like you? (*Pause*). I don't think that matters very much now. (*Quiet, slight smile*) Look at it, I don't expect it'll ever stop raining, the whole building will probably drown in this rain and we'll wake up, . . . and there'll be nothing but water round our beds.
Harold (*quiet*): At least it's warm here. (*Looks at him*) You're really very excited, aren't you?
Teddy (*quiet*): Yes.
Harold: Why Teddy?
Teddy (*looks up*): Why?
Harold (*staring at him*): Yes.
Teddy (*quiet*): Come here . . . (*Pause*) Come on. (*Harold moves*

slightly) Don't you realise what this means then . . . this . . .
don't you?
Harold: No, tell me. (*Pause*) Go on.
Teddy (*quiet small smile*) I shall . . . When it's started.
Fade—end of Act 1.

The second act opens with Sarah, Arnold's sister, seeing
Teddy off at the station. She is campaigning against the war,
makes fun of his uniform, and starts undoing his buttons and
trying to make love to him on the platform. He describes
himself as 'a correspondent really, sent by David to see the full
explosion'. At the front, he and the other officers treat raids on
the enemy lines like public-school sporting events ('let's get to
their touchline'). Teddy is intrigued by the way the soldiers
follow him like sheep and confesses to one of them that he only
made the raid because he felt like it. The soldier says he knew
that all the time, and adds laconically: 'All officers do it.'
While Teddy approaches the war in a detached, observing
spirit, waiting for the revolution and trying to prod his soldiers
into starting it, Arnold is the conventional. loyal officer, who
finally feels so guilty over ordering a premature release of gas
that he shoots himself.

On home leave, Teddy has a row with David, accusing him of
enjoying the war, living it vicariously through his students,
while having a cushy time and awaiting promotion at the
university. David is furious, and predicts a socialist revolution.

David: Look me in the eyes. I'm selfish yes and rather arrogant too, and apart from that deep down there's also a
crust of madness that makes me see very clearly.
Teddy (*quiet*): I see.
David: Very soon there's going to be such a holocaust you
know. The World's biggest battle, bigger than anything ever
before, and whatever the outcome, this revulsion is going to
start working. This wave of revulsion—and revenge, that is
building all the time, is going to reach explosive proportions,
and will sweep the country, see, and it'll be of such intensity,
such sheer colossal size, that it's going to penetrate the minds
of every little bastard in this country. Each one . . . even the
most sluggish—the most deceived, even the totally passive.

It's going to completely slash through this stupor we're in—do you hear, boy, and everything will go down before it. This government, this place, and all its assorted barbarizing, the whole hierarchy will collapse. Smashed clean open, stunned out of existence. Nobody . . . that was responsible for all this can possibly survive it. It can't .That's certain and inevitable. The war has only lasted as long as it has, because of the strength of what it's removing. But you can feel it already—the force of what's coming, for the natural thing is going to happen, boy.

Teddy: A revolution.

David: Yes. Socialism—it has to happen.

Sarah tries to persuade Teddy to let her friends wound him, so that he will be unfit for further service. But he wants to go back; he can't bear the idea of missing 'the most interesting show'. Back at the front, he is persuaded by the soldiers' blind obedience that nothing is going to change. He decides that England is untouched, that everything will survive, that there'll be no real change.

Then, like Alec in *The Carnation Gang*, he taunts a soldier into attacking him. They fight, and then Teddy rounds on the soldier.

Teddy: You've made me bleed. You've broken my lip soldier, see, blood. I could have you court martialled for that.

Private (*quiet*): What you trying to make me do then? (*Staring at him*) What you want?

Teddy (*quiet*): You're going to finish us. Get rid of us, aren't you soldier? You have to, don't you realise what you're really fighting? (*Staring at him*). You can do it . . . Come on, soldier. You can!

Private: But you're here, sir.

Teddy: You're going to shoot me, Private, aren't you? Pick it up—go on.

Private: What you trying to do? . . . What you want?

Teddy: Up! Your rifle—that's an order (*gun between them, both kneeling*). Now, fire, soldier. Come on, straight through . . . fire.

(Silence, gun between them, both kneeling)
Private *(slight smile)*: I can't kill you, can I sir? They'd kill me twice for it. Wouldn't they—straight away? Burn me in hell too, if they could, wouldn't they? *(Leans forward, smiles).* But you could do it. Yeh . . . You're mad, aren't you—sick inside you are. You could do it easily. You could mate. . .
Teddy *(Hits him across the face)*: You struck an officer. You threatened him with a rifle. Drew blood. I will have you shot for that, Private, and you know it Your life's on a knife edge, isn't it? Completely *(Pause)* What's the matter with you? *(Pause)* You've got it, have you?
Private: Yes. I've got it mate. I have, got it—sir. Right in the middle.
Teddy: In the chest, haven't you? Bleeding very fast. Really you should have stopped me. Like I told you to. Come here. My chest's full quite full of splinters too.

They lie down together, and both presumably die, though that is not shown or made explicit. In a brief final scene back at Oxford, David notes that everything is back in its place, only the paint is a little scabby. 'The holiday's over', he says, as he and Harold get ready to face another term.

Heroes, which was staged at the Theatre Upstairs the following year, was less enthusiastically received, mainly because it took place in some nameless city, which sometimes seemed to be in present-day Britain and sometimes in pre-Hitler Germany. The irony is that this very uncertainty, much condemned by the critics, only occurred because Poliakoff listened to the critics who complained that *Clever Soldiers* betrayed ignorance of the First World War. He had originally written *Heroes* while still a student; then he had called it *Berlin Days* and it was unequivocally about the appeal of fascism to young Germans. Poliakoff was fascinated by the fascist strand in everyone, especially the young and ambitious. The play had been staged by students at Cambridge and brought to the Little Theatre in London for a few performances. At first it was Poliakoff's intention to revive it in something close to its original form; he rewrote it, preserving its German setting, and it was accepted by the Royal Court in that form. Then,

Poliakoff says, 'I got frightened by half the critics saying I couldn't write about a period before I was born, and I should stick to what I know about, and so I rewrote again. I broke a cardinal rule which you can't break, in England anyway, that a play must be set in a specific place. I decided to link present-day Britain with early fascist Berlin, so that the play could be then, could be now. I kept rewriting it till the very last minute —writing five nights running. And then most of the critics attacked me for it.'

Perhaps *Heroes* was ahead of its time. If it had been produced a year later its picture of rapid inflation, rising unemployment, extremist political agitation and gratuitous violence might have seemed more obviously relevant to Britain and there could have been less argument about how far it related to pre-Nazi Germany. The parallel between the two situations might have seemed more appropriate at a time when even the Prime Minister was warning of the danger of riots in the streets or of extremist dictatorship. Despite its vagueness about place and time, *Heroes* conveys a strong sense of doom and of political, economic and moral collapse. It contains some of Poliakoff's best dialogue, stylized and ambiguous, and several of his favourite themes and characters are brought together.

Once again, a comfortable bourgeois existence is threatened by a rough outsider and by feelings of guilt. Julius, a would-be artist living on an allowance from his mother, wakes up one morning in his lodgings to find Rainer, a total stranger, claiming the room as his own. Rainer, a strong working-class figure, attacks Julius for not doing any real work. Eventually, however, he leaves, only to follow Julius to a café and to join the conversation between Julius and Albert, an older man who has evidently known better days and whom Julius now partly supports. During the course of the play, Julius moves from his close relationship with Albert to a fascination and involvement with Rainer. Albert represents the past (he helped to bring Julius up), and Julius eventually 'dismisses' him, explaining that he still hopes for the future. He goes off with Rainer on a stolen motor-bike to join the fascists and 'clean up' the country. During Julius's transition to Rainer, a series of short scenes shows them trying drugs, going to a cinema where a sadistic gangster film breaks down, and just missing some ugly riots. Julius is both repelled and fascinated by the rising violence around them, and works himself into a state of excitement when discussing it.

The relationship between Julius and Albert recalls Benny and William in *Pretty Boy*, the precocious children who demand cigarettes and go out on the streets looking for punch-ups remind us of the teenagers in *Carnation Gang* and the diatribe against synthetic cream and general slovenliness in the café anticipates the café scenes in *Hitting Town* and *Strawberry Fields*.

Hitting Town and *City Sugar* are companion plays, with two characters in common. They won Poliakoff the 1975 *Evening Standard* 'most promising playwright' award. Both are set in a small provincial city, not anonymous as in *Heroes* but named as Leicester. *Hitting Town* is only a one-act play. Ralph, a practical joker, has come from Birmingham to visit his sister Clare. He takes her out on the town, setting out to shock her and everyone else, and eventually goes to bed with her. Just as drugs struck many people as the main theme of *Carnation Gang*, so incest dominated a lot of the publicity aroused by *Hitting Town*, but the play is mainly about the emptiness of urban life and how some people deliberately flout conventions to relieve their boredom.

Ralph tells Clare about a couple making love in the lavatory on the train he arrived on, announces that a solitary lady somewhere is responsible for the muzak piped into all the restaurants and airports in the country and puts on an assumed voice to ring the local commercial radio station and tell the DJ that he is an eleven-year old boy having sexual intercourse with his sister of the same age. Ralph and Clare visit a sleazy café where service is non-existent. Ralph mixes together various highly coloured artificial foods and carves open a plastic tomato to reveal chewing gum, half a sardine, cigarette butts and a tooth among its contents. This very funny scene epitomises the characters' disgust with their environment. After Ralph and Clare have made love, she tells him to go home and gets ready to go to work. That is all—nothing has changed.

Leonard Brazil, the disc jockey, and Nicola Davies, the idle waitress in the café—very minor characters in *Hitting Town*—

are the protagonists of *City Sugar*. This two-act play followed *Hitting Town* at the Bush Theatre Club (a small upstairs room in a pub) and the following year was transferred to the Comedy Theatre, becoming Poliakoff's first work to reach the West End. Adam Faith, formerly a well-known pop singer, took over the role of Brazil. Unfortunately at the early performances he seemed unable to dominate the stage or to differentiate between Brazil's phoney enthusiasm on the air and his cynicism off. (Poliakoff says he improved enormously during the run), His performance did not get the ecstatic notices needed for a West End run and the play attracted only a small audience. The transfer had probably been left too long after the favourable publicity and reviews obtained at the Bush.

Brazil, a former schoolmaster, is intended to be portrayed as a cynical DJ shamelessly exploiting his audience on Radio Leicester and aiming for a transfer to Capital Radio in London. He gets intrigued by Nicola Davies's voice on a phone-in, and fixes her to be one of the finalists in a big publicity-stunt 'Competition of the Century', in which the prize is a visit to London with a pop group. The other principal characters are Rex, Brazil's ambitious young technical assistant, and Susan, who works with Nicola in a supermarket. The play is partly a very amusing satire on commercial radio and audience participation shows, partly an exposure of the empty lives shared by the clever but disillusioned DJ and the stupid but naïve shop assistants who are exploited by his commercial stunts. Brazil also exploits Rex, stealing his ideas and giving him very little credit. When he clinches his London job, however, he calmly allows Rex to take his place at the Radio Leicester microphone.

During the final round of the competition, in the studio, Brazil bullies Nicola and Jane, the other contestant, bombarding them with questions, not allowing them to say 'don't know'. and making them rush around playing a humiliating game of musical chairs. Nicola has put everything she has got into the competition—quite literally, as she used all her possessions to stuff a model of one of the pop singers for an earlier round of the contest. But she loses to Jane. Leonard Brazil, like Alec in *The Carnation Gang* and Teddy in *Clever Soldiers*, asks her why she does not resist.

Leonard: This competition has been a great puller, you'll be
pleased to know—the most successful of all, you're the only
lucrative corner of the market left, that never fails, do you
know that—
Nicola (*staring straight at him*): Yes.
Leonard: All you have to do is just stop buying, don't you,
as simple as that, just stop, refuse to lap it up any more. Spit
it out. *I mean that.*
(*Suddenly loud*). Do you—understand a word I'm saying?
Nicola: Yes . . . I do.
Leonard: I don't often meet any of my audience this close. I
picked you out, do you know that, homed in on you. . . I
picked out that voice, that slightly dead, empty sort of voice.
Picked it out as Miss Average—which in fact you probably
are not, and I followed that flat voice, each announcement
was aimed at it.
Nicole: Oh, I see—
Leonard: I let it get through each stage, let you clamber up
here, because I wanted to see it . . . *meet you*, face you. (*Loud*)
And now you're here.
Nicola (*quiet*): Yes.
Leonard (*louder*): Is monosyllables all I'm going to get?
Nicola: Yes.
Leonard: What did you think of the Competition, then?
(*Pause*) Come on . . .
Nicola: I don't know, (*She looks straight at him, cold*) I don't
know what I thought of it.
Leonard (*abrasive*): Got a little out of hand—though it'll
have sounded all right down there. Is that how you'd put
it?
Nicola: I don't know.
Leonard: There was a touch of revenge, don't you think? I
must want a little revenge . . . I glanced at you before the
last question and saw that stare, that blank, infuriatingly
vacant gaze, and then it just happened. I wanted to see just
how far I *could push you*, how much you'd take—I was hoping
you'd come back—that something would come shooting back,
that you'd put up a fight, Nicola. That you'd explode,
Nicola, you'd explode. Do you see, why didn't why don't

you? What's the matter with all you kids now, what is
it?

Nicola cannot answer. She goes back to her shop, considers
wrecking it but decides it's not worth it. 'Maybe next time'.
Discouraged by Nicola's feebleness, Brazil, who has been
hesitating about committing himself to mindless pap on a
bigger scale announces on the air that he has accepted the DJ
job in London. He signs off Radio Leicester and *City Sugar*
with a long, artificially cheerful farewell.

> Leonard: . . . I hear it'll need four people to fill my job here,
> which is nice, but I'm going to London where all the action
> is—where I'll be giving a few jokes and all the hits and more,
> all the sounds and more, all the luck and more, where I'll
> be seeing us through our present troubles, obliterating the
> bad times—that's a Big Word—and remembering the good
> times, oh yes, and letting people remember and letting them
> forget. Drowning all our sorrows, yes I said drowning, till
> we're emerging out of the clouds, of course . . .
> We're going to lick it, of course we will. No need to worry,
> no need to be sad. Shout that out. So tune in, I said tune in.
> Because I'll take your minds off things, oh yes, I will. (*He
> brings the music in louder*). Hear that—some music! Music for
> Len's farewell. Tune in, I said. (*very loud*). TUNE IN. This
> is how we like it. I've got some great times for you, oh yes.
> You know I'll never let you down. That was Competition
> Week. This is Len Brazil. Be seeing you. (*Fade*)

Strawberry Fields, commissioned by the National Theatre
and the first play to be staged by them in their small Cottesloe
Theatre, is similar to *Heroes* but much more directly related to
present-day Britain. Some of Poliakoff's regular themes recur—
for example the criticism of dirt and poor quality in cheap
eating-places. The play includes predictions of civil war and
warnings of the dangers of right-wing extremism. The action
takes place during an exceptionally hot summer, like the
summer of 1976 when Poliakoff was writing it. This period is
seen as the end of an era and as the threshold of something
disturbing and dangerous. A respectable middle-class girl and

a strange male companion who claims to be going blind are driving around the motorways distributing literature against pollution, immigration and Communism. They want to keep Britain 'pure', and in the process they are collecting arms in preparation for violent conflict. They think nothing of shooting a policeman when he is about to search them, and at the end of the play they also shoot a hitch-hiker who has been travelling with them and knows too much about what they have done. They claim that violence is needed to protect the country against violence and defend their killings as no worse than the 'murders' regularly committed on the roads by motorists. *Strawberry Fields* seems like a logical extension of the gloom about Britain shown in Poliakoff's earlier work.

But Poliakoff does not see his plays as pessimistic, though he does see a great deal wrong with our society and is as yet quite uncertain how it can be remedied. Left-wing in his sympathies, he is very different, politically, from writers like David Hare, Howard Brenton and Howard Barker. 'I'm not in any way a Marxist—I hardly would be considering that my father's family fled from the Soviet Union—and I don't think there will be a violent revolution. I think quite a lot of political drama is very remote from anything the audience can identify with. I'm concerned with individuals reacting to the pressures on them— authority, the environment, that sort of thing—rather than with political theories or themes. I'm writing about what's happening now, about people searching for beliefs in what is no longer a religious country, and about how individuals of charisma and power can polarize things. I start with a general atmosphere and feeling, and with one or two central characters, and the plays develop from there. There's an anarchic streak, a high energy level, a frenetic feel. I'm not an anarchist but I'm reflecting the uncertainty of our time. Until about 1968 or 1970 everyone assumed that things were going to get better and better, that there would be inevitable progress towards more freedom, love not war, all that sort of thing. That belief in the future disappeared very, very quickly—it was killed mainly by violence in Northern Ireland and by the economic crisis at home. Now people are casting around to discover where we are going; a lot of students and young people are very right-wing, even joining the National Front. Look at some pop stars saying they're quite happy to be thought fascists! I suppose it's quite possible we may get a right-wing government, and in that case I'll probably find myself moving further to the left.'

'*Strawberry Fields* illustrates the dangers of wishy-washy liberal attitudes—it shows how easily well-meaning people can be defeated by determined, strong-minded fanatics. I'm very conscious of that danger. But my characters always refuse to be trampled on—even the girls in *City Sugar* are not totally destroyed or made into zombies. I think *City Sugar* is my best play yet—it's not just about a disc jockey, it's got a wider resonance.'

Poliakoff first turned seriously to writing plays through chance. A picaresque novel he wrote at the age of 14 had to be dictated because he had broken his thumb. 'It was quicker and easier to dictate dialogue, and I got bored with writing the linking sentences. So then I thought I'd write plays, and I did *Granny*.' Another bit of chance: the Royal Court returned *Granny* with the reader's report still inside saying 'encourage this young boy'. He was duly encouraged. And his 'manic unhappiness' in his first term at Cambridge also stimulated him to keep on writing.

Cambridge stimulated his social conscience too. 'It was a finishing school for people who were going to run the *Sunday Times* or the National Theatre. Oxbridge has a very bad effect on English life. Oxbridge graduates get all the good jobs, because they've learnt how to sell themselves and the confidence to do things. But they tend to be very uncreative'. Poliakoff admits that inverted class snobbery or guilt about his educational advantages permeated his first plays.

After Cambridge, he read plays for Hampstead Theatre Club, which took an option on his *Clever Soldiers*, finished in 1973 but not produced till the following year. He reckons the growth of studio and fringe theatres at that time was another bit of luck. 'My plays would not have got staged so soon, without all those studio and club theatres. I also wanted to write movie scripts at first, but I'm not so keen now—so few of them ever get made'.

Clever Soldiers was seen and admired by Peter Hall and Harold Pinter. 'That's why I'm at the National Theatre. I used to get very affected by what the critics said about my plays, but now I realise that in many ways what influential people in the theatre think is much more important.'

Poliakoff works very intensely, about eight hours a day or even through the night. 'I can only think about a play in spurts but I can write continuously for long periods, stopping only to eat. I work very much better under pressure—the pressure of a deadline and of contacts with actors and the director, so I do lots of rewriting during rehearsals until the very last moment before the first night'. He thinks one reason why playwrights today are so involved in rehearsals is that their plays are complex, trying to deal with a complex world.

'Earlier plays were usually comparatively simple in construction—conventional drawing-room comedies or dramas didn't need complicated direction, nor did verse dramas. Playwrights nowadays tend to want numerous scene changes and a mixture of styles; so they must be in at every stage of rehearsal. So much can go wrong, in casting or in the direction, and the play can easily be wrecked. I'm still looking for a really experienced director, in tune with me, whom I can fully trust, who will help me and improve my plays. One problem with them is that they require terrific energy, which comes more naturally to American actors than British'.

Energy is one of Poliakoff's favourite themes when talking generally. 'It isn't just the energy and the self-discipline to keep on working that one needs—that is comparatively easy. But one is exposed to so many voices, opinions—one needs the discipline and energy to stick to one's own views. Of course I've been influenced by other writers, especially Edward Bond who had a great influence on a play of mine that was never produced. I'm not conscious of a Pinter influence, but Osborne probably—*The Entertainer* may have influenced *City Sugar*. Who hasn't been influenced by Osborne? Brecht too. But in the end one has to be true to oneself. I'm hoping one day to prove that I can write a really good play. I don't think I've done that yet. One must just keep writing the best plays one possibly can.' He worries about whether he can maintain the energy.

'It's the loss of it that causes the early creative deaths of so many playwrights—they go off badly, stop writing, get involved in other things. Having started so young, I naturally wonder how long I'll last.'

Conclusion: New Drama Tomorrow?

Stephen Poliakoff wonders how long he will last as a playwright; most of the playwrights wonder how long Britain will last; and in the present economic climate we must all wonder how long, and in what form, the theatre can last. 'The new British drama' of recent years, with all its wide variety of subjects and styles, has had one thing in common. All the serious dramatists have, in one way or another, been expressing doubt and discontent about the state of the country. Even when not politically left-wing, they have all been radical in approach. They have questioned our assumptions and pushed us forward into new areas of tolerance and permissiveness. They have not put forward ready-made solutions to our problems, and in most cases they have not put forward any solutions at all. They refuse to 'spoon feed' their audiences with a complete recipe for a better life, and they often refuse to bring their plays to any definite conclusion, preferring to leave them open-ended and ambiguous.

There are now signs that the national mood is swinging to the right with a backlash against permissiveness and a wish for a return to more rigid and disciplined rules of behaviour and morality. It could be that this will soon be reflected in the theatre, both by new right-wing writers and by plays written in more orthodox styles. Many theatregoers still want a more logical plot, a more recognizable structure, than most of the new writers at present offer. Many theatregoers actually want to be 'spoon fed'.

Professional critics and theatrefolk were surprised and disappointed by the short west-end runs of three highly-praised plays:—Trevor Griffiths's *Comedians*, David Hare's *Teeth 'n' Smiles* and Stephen Poliakoff's *City Sugar*. There were various reasons for these failures; I believe that the lack of definite form and plot, and the absence of any clear conclusion, were among the most significant. It seems that wit, theatricality and topicality are not enough for the majority of theatregoers, who still demand that plays should also be 'well-made'. Playwrights may increasingly have to come to terms with this demand. If our society resolves some of its problems. and finds some new certainties, it may become easier for them to do so.

On the other hand it is possible that the experimental unorthodoxies of today will become the accepted conventions of tomorrow, in accordance with the usual pattern of progress in the arts. The dramatists of the future will then be seeking new ways of shocking or amazing us. If British society undergoes traumatic changes, or further social, political or economic crises, these will stimulate writers with new ideas and possibly into new dramatic forms.

Of course public subsidies to the theatre are at risk and nobody can tell how many theatres may have to close. The public's ability to pay for seats is likely to be affected by rising unemployment and inflation. However the very economic factors which led young writers to concentrate on the theatre rather than on books or journalism are likely to continue operating, and the idea that it is comparatively easy to find outlets for new ideas in the theatre is well established. There are now a vast number of playwrights or would-be playwrights in Britain. The *New Playwrights Directory* (TQ Publications, 1976) listed 121, while the Theatre Writers Union a trade union for dramatists, had 142 members.

Most of these dramatists are writing for fringe, 'underground' and club theatres, where costs of production are modest, prices of admission are comparatively low, and only a small audience is needed. Economic recession, however severe, is unlikely to destroy this kind of theatre; it may actually encourage it, at the expense of the larger, more conventional theatres with their higher rentals, overheads and production costs. Theatregoers may increasingly turn to the 'fringe', as prices of admission in the 'commercial' theatre come nearer to New York or Paris levels.

At the same time, it seems likely that money will somehow or other be found to continue subsidizing the main non-commercial theatres in London and the regions. It is now generally accepted by politicians, as well as by artists and intellectuals, that the arts are an essential part of a flourishing modern society. More cynically, they may also feel that when people cannot afford very much bread, they have an even greater need of circuses, or an up-to-date equivalent, Moreover British theatre now makes a powerful contribution to the export drive; British plays and players are very successful overseas and the theatre is one of Britain's biggest tourist attractions. Indeed the West End theatre nowadays seems to be largely dependent on foreign tourists for its audiences.

The actual physical existence of so many new theatre buildings up and down the country also acts as a powerful argument for keeping them going. Many of them have become social and cultural centres for their communities, with a wide range of activities far beyond their main function. Like most of the new theatres, the National Theatre was planned in more affluent days, and the people running it may sometimes wish that they were not saddled with three auditoria and so many subsidiary spaces and foyers. But they are there, and must be used, not just for prestige but because it would not be much of an economy to run only half the huge building.

One advantage of the National Theatre complex, and of the way it is being run, is that it provides a well-publicized and attractive home for new drama. If there had been only one auditorium, as originally envisaged by the first dreamers of a National Theatre, it would probably have been exclusively for the classics, British and foreign. It is now generally accepted that the National must also present new plays, though there is considerable argument about what proportion of its resources should be used for that purpose and about how far it should support the untried and experimental. Its smallest auditorium, the Cottesloe, seats just over 400—about the same size as the Royal Court—and should be ideal for many new plays. Some writers fear that their plays will automatically be staged there, rather than in one of the larger auditoria, and this might indeed seem sensible with untried work. But the staging of Howard Brenton's *Weapons of Happiness* at the Lyttelton soon after the National first opened shows that no such cut-and-dried policy is being applied.

There is another danger, that the National will 'steal' many of the plays which would previously have been produced at the Royal Court or elsewhere. By the beginning of 1977 the Royal Court was indeed suffering a financial cricis caused partly by its inability to find successful new plays. It may be that some of the experimental and studio theatres will actually have to close. Sad though this will be, especially in the case of theatres which have built up a tradition and a following, it need not necessarily mean any significant reduction in the quantity of good new drama. New locales often spring up as old ones close, and there is no reason for new and experimental theatres to get too attached to particular buildings.

One of the main preoccupations of the Theatre Writers Union has been its negotiations with the National Theatre about royalties and conditions for playwrights whose work is produced there. The writers feel that whatever may happen in the commercial and privately-run fringe theatres, the National has an obligation to give its writers adequate financial support. Advance fees paid for commissioned plays are very small, and there is no guarantee of any large number of performances. One result of larger fees would probably be a reduction in the number of new plays commissioned and produced. Young playwrights will probably have to continue supplementing their incomes in other ways. There is nothing new or surprising about that. What is new is that there are now more opportunities for playwrights to do this than ever before. They can be 'playwrights in residence', reading manuscripts and advising theatres on repertory, like the German *dramaturgs*, they can meet the constant demand for plays on radio and television, and for film scripts, and they can teach in the recently developed university drama departments.

I am therefore reasonably confident that the stream of interesting new plays is not going to dry up in any economic drought. I am much less confident about what sort of plays these will be. The playwrights of tomorrow may take the revolution in the theatre still further, or they may appear to be counter-revolutionary, consolidating what has been achieved and finding ways of making it more acceptable to a wider public. I do not believe, however, that they will allow the theatre to stagnate.

Bibliography

(Alphabetical list of published plays)

ALAN AYCKBOURN
Absurd Person Singular*, Absent Friends* and *Bedroom Farce* in
   Three Plays by Alan Ayckbourn, Chatto & Windus Ltd. 1977
Confusions, Samuel French Ltd. 1977
Countdown in *Mixed Doubles*, by various authors, Methuen &
   Co. Ltd. 1970
Ernie's Incredible Illucinations* (a children's play), in *Playbill 1*,
   Hutchinson Ltd. 1969
How The Other Half Loves, Evans Brothers Ltd. 1972; Samuel
   French (New York) 1973
Just Between Ourselves, French 1977
Relatively Speaking, Evans 1968; French (New York) 1968
The Norman Conquests*, Chatto & Windus 1975
Time and Time Again, French 1973

HOWARD BARKER
Cheek in *New Short Plays No 3*, Methuen 1972
Claw and *Stripwell*, John Calder (Publishers) Ltd. 1977;
   Stripwell also in *Plays and Players*, Hansom Books, Nov and
   Dec 1975

EDWARD BOND
A–A America!, Eyre Methuen Ltd. 1976
Bingo, Eyre Methuen 1974
Early Morning, Calder & Boyars Ltd. 1968; Hill & Wang
   (New York) 1969
Lear, Methuen 1972; Hill & Wang (New York) 1972
Narrow Road to the Deep North, Methuen 1968
Saved, Methuen 1968; Hill & Wang (New York) 1966
The Fool, Eyre Methuen 1976 (with *We Come to the River*)
The Pope's Wedding, Methuen 1971
The Sea, Eyre Methuen 1973, Hill & Wang (New York)1973
We Come to the River, Eyre Methuen 1976 (with *The Fool*)

HOWARD BRENTON

Christie in Love, Methuen 1970, with *Heads* and *The Education of Skinny Spew*
Lay-By (with other authors), Calder & Boyars 1972
Magnificence, Eyre Methuen 1973
Revenge, Methuen 1970
Saliva Milkshake, TQ Publications 1977
Scott of the Antarctic, in *Plays for Public Places*, Eyre Methuen 1972
The Churchill Play, Eyre Methuen 1974
Weapons of Happiness, Eyre Methuen 1976
Wesley, in *Plays for Public Places*, Eyre Methuen 1972

SIMON GRAY

Butley, Methuen 1971
Dog Days, in *The New Review* Vol 2, No 20.
Dutch Uncle, Faber and Faber Ltd. 1969
Otherwise Engaged*, Eyre Methuen 1975
Spoiled, Methuen 1971
The Idiot (adapt. from Dostoievsky), Methuen 1971
Wise Child, Faber 1968

TREVOR GRIFFITHS

Comedians, Faber 1976
Occupations, Calder & Boyars 1972
Sam Sam, in *Plays and Players*, Hansom Books, April 1972
The Party, Faber 1974

CHRISTOPHER HAMPTON

Don Juan (adapt. from Molière), Faber 1973
Hedda Gabler (adapt. from Ibsen) French (New York) 1972
Savages, Faber 1973
The Doll's House (adapt. from Ibsen), French (New York) 1972
The Philanthropist, Faber 1970, French (New York) 1971
Total Eclipse, Faber 1969, French (New York) 1972
Treats*, Faber 1976
When Did You Last See Your Mother?, Faber 1967, Grove Press (New York) 1967

DAVID HARE

Brassneck (with Howard Brenton), Eyre Methuen 1974
Fanshen, Plays & Players, Hansom Books, Sep & Oct 1975

Knuckle*, Faber 1964
Slag, Faber 1971
Teeth 'n' Smiles, Faber 1976
The Great Exhibition, Faber 1972

PETER NICHOLS
A Day in the Death of Joe Egg*, Faber 1967, Grove Press (New
 York) 1967
Chez Nous*, Faber 1974
Forget-Me-Not-Lane*, Faber 1971
Privates on Parade, Faber 1977
The Freeway, Faber 1975
The National Health, Faber 1970

STEPHEN POLIAKOFF
City Sugar* and *Hitting Town**, Eyre Methuen 1976

PETER SHAFFER
Black Comedy, French 1967
Equus*, André Deutsch 1973
Five Finger Exercise*, Hamish Hamilton, 1958; Harcourt Brace
 (New York) 1958
Shrivings, Deutsch 1974 (*Equus, Five Finger Exercise* and *Shrivings*
 together, Penguin Books Ltd. 1976)
The Private Ear* and *The Public Eye**, Hamish Hamilton 1962,
 Stein & Day (New York) 1964
The Royal Hunt of the Sun*, Hamish Hamilton 1965; Stein &
 Day 1965
The White Liars, French's acting ed. 1967 and new version 1977

TOM STOPPARD
After Magritte, Faber 1971; Grove Press (New York) 1972
Albert's Bridge*, Faber 1969
Dirty Linen and *New-Found-Land*, Inter-Action 1976
Enter A Free Man, Faber 1968; Grove Press (New York) 1972
If You're Glad, I'll be Frank, Faber 1969
Jumpers, Faber 1972
Rosencrantz and Guildenstern Are Dead*, Faber 1967; Grove Press
 1967

Tango, Cape 1968
*The Real Inspector Hound**, Faber 1968; Grove Press 1969
Travesties, Faber 1975

DAVID STOREY
Cromwell, Jonathan Cape Ltd. 1973
*Home**, Cape 1970; Random House (New York) 1971; Penguin 1972
*In Celebration**, Cape 1969, Penguin 1971 (with *The Contractor*)
Life Class, Cape 1975
The Changing Room, Cape 1972, Penguin 1973
The Contractor, Cape 1970; Random House 1971; Penguin 1971 (with *In Celebration*)
*The Farm**, Cape 1973
*The Restoration of Arnold Middleton**, Cape 1967

E. A. WHITEHEAD
Alpha Beta, Faber 1972
Mecca, Faber 1977
Old Flames, Faber 1976
The Foursome, Faber 1972
The Sea Anchor, Faber 1975

*Plays marked with an asterisk are also available in French's acting editions.

Index